MASTERING a New Paradigm in
MANAGEMENT CONSULTING

Marilyn E Harris
With: Gerard F. Becker, Anne Hallcom,
Richard L. Ponschock

Acknowledgments:

Cover Photograph © 1998 – 2005 Charles Winpenny All rights reserved
P. 31: From *Organizational Development* by W. Warner Burke. Copyright © 1994 by W. Warner Burke Published by Addison-Wesley Longman Educational Publishers.
P. 58: From *Working with Emotional Intelligence* by Daniel Goleman. Copyright © 1998 by Doubleday, Inc. Copyright Clearance Center.
P. 72,73,96,190,193,209,210: From *Systems Thinking: Managing Chaos and Complexity* by Jamshid Gharajedaghi. Copyright © 1999 by Jamshid Gharajedaghi. Published by Butterworth-Heinemann.
P. 94: *Harvard Business Review* from "Leading Change: Why Transformation Efforts Fail" by John Kotter, March-April 1995. Copyright © 1995 by the Harvard Business School Publishing Corporation; all rights reserved.
p. 109: From by Thomas Isgar. Copyright © 1993, 1996. Published by Seluera Press.
P. 116,118: From *Enabling Knowledge Creation* by Georg Von Krogh et al. Copyright © 2000. Published by Oxford University Press, NY.
P. 120,125: From *The Knowledge Evolution* by Verna Allee. Copyright © 1997 by Butterworth-Heinemann. Copyright Clearance Center.
P. 136,137,139: From a paper entitled "Presencing: Learning from the Future as It Emerges" by Otto Scharmer. Reprinted by permission of the author.
P. 132 Scharmer, C. Otto (2007) Theory U. Cambridge, MA: SOL (Society for Organizational Learning)
P.218,219: From "Making It Happen: The Implementation Challenge" by David P. Kreutzer and Virginia Wiley as appeared in The Systems Thinker Vol. 7, No. 3, 1996. Copyright © 1996 by Pegasus Press.
P. 252 : Columbus Medical Association, Columbus, OH

For practicing consultants and clients,
past, present and FUTURE --

PART 1
UNDERSTANDING AND MASTERING A NEW PARADIGM

PART 2
UNDERSTANDING THE CHALLENGE OF LEARNING "TO BE"

PART 5
Learning TO LEARN from the FUTURE

Foreword to Second Edition

C. Otto Scharmer suggests that the key to addressing the multiple unfolding crises of our time as well as the future course of human development lies in learning how to access the source of mastery collectively. In Scharmer's (2007) book, *Theory U* – the source identified is the *Social Technology of Presencing*. *Presencing* or *leading from the future as it emerges* <u>is</u> not only possible, but at the heart and center of innovatively moving forward *collectively* creating a new future quite different from the past. What could be more important to management consultants than being able to master the challenge collectively?

To learn from the future requires a new source and process of learning, one that Scharmer describes as Type II, the other learning cycle in contrast to Type I: The Kolb Type Learning Cycle: Learning from the Experiences of the Past. Type I is based in reflecting on the experiences of the past; while Type II is grounded in *sensing and enacting emerging futures*. Type II learning (*Presencing*) is needed to face the challenge of coping with the various waves of disruptive, revolutionary change redefining the context of business. Today's management consultants are leading in a fundamentally new world where they must be innovators and revolutionaries rather than agents of improving the status quo.

In the Type II learning cycle, Scharmer (2000) describes Seeing, Sensing, *Presencing*, and Enacting as the four places to operate from in addressing the contextual challenges of digitalization, globalization, and spiritualization. Leaders and managers need to know how to learn from experience *when the experience that matters most is the not-yet-embodied experience of the future*. What does this mean for management consultants; how can they assist clients in accessing the *not-yet-embodied experience?*

Scharmer (2007) shows moving from a system-centric to a human/life-centric emergence; in reality, moving from the challenges of stability, growth, externalities, and ecosystems of the 18th to the early 21st century respectively, to new power places of planetary acupuncture points, where new cultural, market and democratic infrastructures are innovations, globally supporting human/life-centric transformative change.

The second edition actively learns from the future capitalizing on the work of a team of four co-authors cooperating to unfold and build an emergent new future for individuals, organizations, and society through individual and collective mastery designed for consultants. The message is subtle, but dynamic in the demonstrated success presented by the *co-author collective*.

In the second edition, a collectivity of co-authors: Marilyn Harris, Jerry Becker, Anne Hallcom, and Richard Ponschock energized the new version presenting the learning paradigm: BEING, LEARNING, and DOING as central to enacting a new future. Most exciting is that this new version is a result of a collective *seeing, sensing, Presencing,* and most importantly **enacting**.   The emphasis throughout the revision is on application in the real world. The co-author collective met the inherent application challenge modeling for users in management consulting and beyond: moving through the paradigmatic cycle is positively productive and that it is exciting, energizing, and fun!   Fully applying the new learning paradigm creates human/life-centric innovative designs supporting development of new infrastructures in a global society only now emerging that work.   The challenge is now for individual and collective users to apply the learning paradigm systematically and systemically in their lives to deal with the emerging issues of a seemingly complex and chaotic global existence. The second edition is our gift to you, the 21st century user

Marilyn E Harris
With: Gerard F. Becker, Anne Hallcom,
Richard L. Ponschock
Spring, 2008

PREFACE

The second edition of *Mastering a New Paradigm in Management Consulting* is unique for two reasons: a *collectivity of co–authors* address; transforming the systems of real organizations, and using a *new learning paradigm system of BEING, LEARNING, and DOING*. This book fully considers the learning role of the individual client – now so critical to the success of the client in each engagement, and *basic* to consultant success. No other book considers in depth the importance of the holistic aspect in the consultant-client relationship. No other book offers a comprehensive, implementable perspective as such. In the comprehensive approach of this book, it speaks to everyone for whom the joy of thinking and innovating is still alive and thriving, and whose enthusiasm and energy to entertain exciting but unfamiliar conceptions in implementation is not yet exhausted.

In cooperating to produce the second edition of *Mastering A New Paradigm in Management Consulting* the unique co-author collectivity of Marilyn Harris, Gerard Becker, Anne Hallcom, and Richard Ponschock have not only produced a dramatically stimulating presentation to view, but have more fully explored new ways to learn through using new cases to strengthen conceptually the application section, introducing sustainability of transformative change in the Socio-Economic Equation for Systemic Success, and formatting the presentation with definitive diagrams and sidebars of relevant examples. It is noteworthy that while producing the second edition the four produced an outstanding collective, a team having fun enlightened by the self-same *understanding* and *mastery* of the learning system in the book.

Mastering a New Paradigm in Management Consulting is an extraordinary book developed for extraordinary audiences in the global consulting world in an age of ever accelerating change, increasing uncertainty, and growing complexity. This book is about unleashing human potential. The book is for developing consultants -- those new to consulting and those who may be well seasoned, but who desire to stay abreast developing the collectivity in the wide variety of consulting audiences. It is for both management consultants *and* their clients who are end users of the knowledge and practices presented. The design of this book explicitly recognizes that choice is at the heart of building competency, and in unleashing human potential. In consulting, development is the vehicle-enhancing choice based on understanding the problem, and then designing a solution to build a desired future. Consultants seek to *choose* rather than predict the future. In this book, they learn to use what they already know, how to realize what they do not know, and how to learn what they need to know.

The focus is <u>understanding</u> first, in order to <u>master</u> the critical learning processes -- relevant for clients and consultants alike. The co-authors show that in truly successful consulting, the consultant advises the client's management to influence and to make the change in the <u>system</u> – not in the employees – thus effecting lasting change. Hence, this book addresses gaining understanding first, and then gaining mastery through practice to be successful each time afresh and in each engagement.

<u>This book</u> is extraordinary in its development of an inclusive process framework augmenting intervention and implementation. The framework is a four-phased Consulting Systems Worldview [CSW] incorporating Systems Thinking methodology – both the framework and a methodology are sorely needed to improve consulting practice.

Systems Thinking is about a new mode of seeing, doing, and being in the world; it is a way of thinking through complexities and learning from the future. Systems Thinking is an important mode for advancing consulting, whereas, in the past a tired analytical approach took apart what it sought to understand, and attempted to explain the behavior of the parts taken separately, never aggregating understanding of the parts into an explanation of a purposeful whole. In reality, this is not different from what many firms market as consulting services today. However, in contrast, Systems Thinking uses a different process – it puts the system in the context of the larger environment of which it is a part and studies the role it plays in the larger whole. Systems Thinking responds to two major shifts in our global existence: first, developing a sociocultural view of organizations, recognizing the multi-minded reality of organizational structure, process and function and context; second, it uses *synthesis*, in contrast to analysis, in a holistic approach – now, so needed in our global economy.

<u>This book</u>, in its use of Systems Thinking, does not throw out the 'baby with the bath water,' but uses a new holistic language, a language of consulting systems that allows the users to see through the complexities of our time. This is a language of interaction and design that help both consultants and clients learn a new mode of living by considering various ways of seeing, doing, and being in the world. The language makes possible the design of new methods of inquiry, new

modes of organization, and a way that will allow the rational, emotional, and ethical choices for interdependent yet autonomous social beings.

This book is developed as a non-traditional textbook to be used in practical learning settings, where the classroom may be extended into the field. It is developed to be used in the order presented: Learning to BE, Learning to LEARN, and Learning to DO. However, most adult learners using this book will have had great experiences to build on and may be determined to proceed in other ways – choosing what might meet their immediate need or answer a specific burning question – and that's OK. What is important is to get a 'systemic sense' for "being, learning, and doing" first for oneself and then for the others involved – whether they are co-consultants, clients, students, or others. Try to go through this exercise of figuring out what "being" is in a situation, then what "learning" is relevant, and finally what is "doing." Try to go through this exercise, no matter where you enter the system – for yourself and for the others involved – it will aid you immeasurably in "making sense" in the situation and moving forward positively in the future. Each piece of your experience fits in, continuing to learn the use of the 3 part *learning system* only strengthens the user – whether consultant or client.

Mastering A New Paradigm in Management Consulting is divided into five parts. Part 1 identifies the all encompassing value of *understanding* and *mastering* relevant to the specific context of management consulting. Of key value is the realization that acquiring capability in understanding and mastering are not a one-time proposition. That both understanding and mastering are emergent properties, dependent on spontaneous outcomes of ongoing processes – that must be reproduced continuously! The chapters address two critical perspectives preparing the developing consultant to understand the various waves of disruptive, revolutionary change – essentially to understand how the game of change is itself changing; and learning the meaning of transformative change for consulting. The second perspective broadens the view on how consulting has evolved over more than a century, recognizing that thriving now defines the necessity to *learn* in a new system: Learning to BE, to LEARN, and to DO – individually taken, these define the next three parts of the second edition.

Part 2 describes a much needed cultural education by management consultants – a form of education never formally considered. This section presents an opportunity to develop human assets – individually and collectively, within and beyond cultural boundaries. This type of cultural education results in arts, languages, sports, traditional ceremonies, and other quality-of-life enhancing activities. Those specific to management consulting are: increasing and improving emotional intelligence, unburying ethics and focusing values, developing breakthroughs in creativity and art, using language learning to energize cultural education, defining leisure, recreation and sports, and rekindling the necessary desires to do so. The Learning to BE section is not only valid for management consulting and users of consultants in our global environment, but literally every professional may gain from a better understanding of a culture they seek to participate and lead in, in their desired future. This holds for professions, and would be professionals involved in major cultures and subcultures of the world.

Part 3 focuses the challenge in understanding learning to LEARN and to facilitate the learning of Others. Basically, it takes the learner to a new level of interdependence in learning, freeing each participant to be a *self-educator* as well as a collective educator. This is not only freeing, but significantly raises the bar in learning to reach new heights and to co-create new ways of learning. Consultants learn the value of learning, unlearning, and relearning – learning application of these concepts in practice, developing and unleashing human potential in the consulting engagement. Consultants learn to leverage knowledge in many different ways, better use of time enabling knowledge creation. Enabling knowledge creation is critical in the unlocking of tacit knowledge and in releasing the power of innovation in the organization. In this section, consultants will learn to understand the importance of innovation as the major source of wealth production, sub-optimization is no longer wealth producing. Users will learn why they must constantly innovate to succeed.

In order to learn to innovate, the learner is exposed to *Presencing*, learning from the future as it emerges. Classical methods and concepts of organizational learning are all variations of the same Kolb (1984) based learning cycle: learning based on reflecting on the experiences of the past. However, several currently significant leadership challenges cannot be successfully approached this way because the experience base of the team often is not relevant to the issue at hand. In order to do well in the emerging new business environments, organizations and their leaders have to develop a new cognitive capability:

Presencing is the capacity for sensing, embodying, and enacting emerging futures. New learning for both the consultant and the client is apparent in learning to Presence.

Part 4 develops the use of the framework: The Consulting Systems Worldview in four distinct iterative and interactive phases. The developing consultant has the opportunity to work through each phase, first conceptually in terms of identifying key tasks to be accomplished along with the rationale and emergent issues in consulting. There are two full cases [included in the Appendix] for the developing consultant to work through using the key tasks indicated along with the comments and explanation of what was actually done in the case in the real world.

In Part 4, a chapter is devoted to each phase: I – Entry & Contracting, 2 – Data Collection & Problem Definition, 3 – Problem Solution and Action Planning, and 4 – Implementation & Evaluation. Each is designed to aid the user in Learning to DO.

Part 5 concludes focusing Learning to Learn from the Future. It capitalizes on **Presencing**, learning from the future and is key to our success in the emerging business environments. It recognizes the all critical "Return on Imagination" a new ROI, making it possible for the first time in history *to work backward from our imagination rather than forward from our past*. In learning from the future, we come to realize that the past is not the sole determinant, but only a co-producer of the future. Finally, in accessing learning from the future the learning door is opened still wider and encouragingly invites all to innovate.

Producing this book, the second edition, has changed all of us. It has deepened our passion to cooperate – defined by simultaneously making both the *ends* (output) and *means* (processes) compatible in a situation. This co-author application has created a resolve to continue a lifetime of *leadership learning from the future* facilitating professional development of ourselves and others. It has provided ample opportunity to reflect on our leadership, to focus on our passion, and get energized in acting on our learning. Further, we have had the opportunity to make this second edition happen through our cooperative efforts bringing purpose to light. Through this experience, we have become more trusting, more intentional and strategic about building new networks, and globally extending our strategic goals in transformative leadership, deepening our responses to digitization, globalization, and spiritualization in our world. It has led to a new decisiveness and bold action, building trust and character based on firm values, while supporting the leadership of others. The real value of this writing goes beyond focusing application knowledge and skills to develop a new and necessary resource for every consultant to have in hand – available in hip pocket format as a ready reference. The relevance for all is in *learning TO BE, learning TO LEARN, and learning TO DO* key practices capitalizing on participation as the vehicle for unleashing our human potential. In this writing, we have learned from other learners, clients and co-consultants far more than we have ever taught them; for this book integrates the knowledge gained from our lifetimes of interaction with innovative collectivities in many different communities of practice in the world.

Marilyn E Harris

With: Gerard F. Becker, Anne Hallcom

Richard L. Ponschock

Spring, 2008

Part 1   UNDERSTANDING AND MASTERING A NEW PARADIGM

The Big Rocks

One day an expert on the subject of time management was speaking to a group of business students and, to drive home a point, used an illustration those students will never forget.

As this man stood in front of the group of high-powered over-achievers he said, "Okay, time for a quiz."

Then he pulled out a one-gallon, wide-mouthed clay jar and set it on a table in front of him. Then he produced a dozen fist-sized rocks and carefully placed them, one at a time, into the jar. When the jar was filled to the top and no more rocks would fit inside, he asked, "Is this jar full?"

Everyone in the class said, "Yes." "Really?" he replied. He reached under the table and brought out a bucket of gravel. Then he dumped some gravel in and shook the jar causing the pieces of gravel to work themselves down into the spaces between the big rocks. Then he asked the group once more, "Is the jar full?"

By this time the class was on to him. "Probably not," one of them answered.

He said, "Good!" Then he grabbed a pitcher of water and began to pour it in until the jar was filled to the brim. Then he looked at the class and asked, "What is the point of this illustration?"

One eager beaver raised his hand and said, "The point is, no matter how full your schedule is, if you try really hard, you can always fit some more things into it."

"No," the speaker replied, "that's not the point. The truth this illustration teaches us is:

If you don't put the big rocks in first, you'll never get them in at all."
What are the "big rocks" in your life?
A project that you want to accomplish?
Time with loved ones?
Your faith, your education, your finances?

A cause?

Teaching or mentoring others?

Remember to put these BIG ROCKS in first or you'll never get them in at all. So tonight or in the morning when you are reflecting on this short story, ask yourself this question: What are the 'big rocks' in my life or business?   - Author Unknown

PART 1:
Understanding and Mastering a New Paradigm

Understanding and Mastering a New Paradigm presents an overarching challenge to consultant and client alike to **succeed in the new age of innovation** (Prahalad & Krishnan, 2008). There are three critical aspects of innovation relevant in the 21st Century that make it quite different from the 20th century: value will increasingly be co-created with consumers; no single firm has the knowledge, skills, and resources it needs to co-create value with consumers; and the emerging markets can be a source of innovation. Innovation is the name of the game making the 21st century quite different from the 20th century.

Choosing the right BIG ROCKS to innovate requires both understanding and mastering of a new learning paradigm: **Learning to BE, Learning to LEARN,** and **Learning to DO** (Gharajedaghi, 2006). BEING, LEARNING, and DOING take on new meaning in developing leadership in management consulting as the future emerges.

Unfortunately, in the past, learning in the three-part paradigm has been addressed from the last first, or singly focused in Learning to DO. There is little attention on Learning to BE, identifying relevance in understanding cultural education; or on Learning to LEARN, where mastering formal education routes occurs. Understanding and mastering the three part learning paradigm develops both the management consultant and client alike, now so necessary in co-creating unique value with the consumer.

In the new paradigmatic *learning* system the user is simultaneously introduced to structure, process and function in context while *transformatively* changing the whole. In this new learning centered context several new rocks are identified, while some other rocks are polished and re-cut to meet generative and innovative requirements.

First, consultants must grasp the meaning of *"understanding"* in a way that is actionable; Understanding the evolving management consulting industry and at the same time understanding how to change in a high velocity world. The second part of the challenge is in understanding *"mastering;"* and becoming a skilled performer – applying knowledge in practice. For many, mastering management consulting is quite incomprehensible; it is only filled with chaos and complexity. However, most recently, many are capable of addressing the two-part challenge of understanding <u>and</u> mastering through a *holistic learning* approach – leading from the future as it emerges.

<u>Understanding</u> is to capture the meaning of a message, to grasp the reasonableness of a relationship, and to demonstrate expertness in practice relative to a specific instance. Where knowledge makes one capable of imparting knowledge, understanding comes from internalizing and personalizing knowledge so that its meaning can be shared with others. Further, understanding goes beyond knowing the meaning of a concept; it frees the individual to put into practice the meaning in a wiser fashion. It is the capability to fully answer the "why" question. It is quite different than possessing information or knowledge. Gharajedaghi and Ackoff (1984) say that one can survive without understanding, but not thrive. Without understanding one cannot control causes, only treat effect and suppress symptoms. With understanding, one can design and create the future. Ackoff continues that people in an age of accelerating change, increasing uncertainty, and growing complexity often respond by acquiring more information and knowledge, but not understanding.

We must do more than coexist with information and knowledge; we must interact with others and learn that we can thrive through our generative understanding. In many cases, management consultants may understand first, and then move to facilitate understanding in others, *or* in fact, consultants may first gain understanding from other's learning, and then facilitate wider dissemination for all. Moreover, many create and design futures in management consulting utilizing a holistic approach evident in the new learning paradigm, central to innovative action.

To achieve basic understanding in the beginning has immediate value despite the time consumed. An initial understanding gains even more value over time. Clearly, understanding is the unit to measure, not time. Many linear thinkers believe this is lost time. However, taking time initially to gain understanding develops the interactive capability to move faster, both for the individual and the collective. On this point, research demonstrates that the initial time used to gain understanding is more than made up within the total period of time used. Many times the whole activity is completed in a shorter time than projected, and more successfully. Thus, the guiding principle is "go slow to go fast." It is worthwhile and necessary for management consultants to spend creative energy and time to understand first, while at the same time continually striving to master the interactive relationships involved.

Understanding is the first critical step in mastering. Any developmental effort demands understanding first before action. Understanding frees the individual to make decisions, and to freely follow the decision with appropriate actions. This creative freedom born of understanding is an important energizer in developmental learning, and in mastering. The management consultant must take full advantage of the value of learning understanding, for it is not enough to survive in the 21st century – one must go beyond – to take initiative and responsibility, to design and create a bright new holistic future in *learning* management consulting.

Mastering is to become skilled or proficient; it is to be successful in the performance of a specific set of knowledge and skills. In management consulting, mastering is the art and science of application through practice. Mastering makes it possible to set direction and to lead. Successful practice comes through intervention, human interaction and feedback applied in the context. People are most successful at mastering when they work at the application process, using constructive feedback to redesign and to transform in successful outcomes.

Mastering, like understanding, is an emergent property – it is best understood as a process of becoming. Emergent properties are the spontaneous outcome of ongoing processes – they are not one-time propositions; they must be reproduced continuously. If the processes that generate them end, the phenomena will also cease to exist.

Understanding and mastering are basic huge rocks that must be regenerated and shaped continuously. There are many more rocks, however, that need to be understood and mastered in a fast -developing consulting industry, striving for professional success coupled with understanding where we have been, are, and want to be. In *understanding* and *mastering a new learning paradigm*, the challenge for developing consultants is recognizing how the game of change is changing, and meeting the high need for success by thriving in a high velocity and continually evolving global industry.

The changing game transforming business and industry in a fast growing consulting industry are the subjects of the first two chapters – yielding needed guides defining a contemporary management consultant in the context of a Consulting Systems Worldview. Finally, these introductory chapters of Part I provide a foundation for defining the new learning system and developing new competencies relevant in the 21st century. The new learning system defines three distinct functional areas: Learning to BE a management consultant; Learning to LEARN as a management consultant while facilitating the learning of others; and Learning to DO as a management consultant; the foci of parts 2, 3 and 4 of the book.

Chaos and complexity are managed in the new *Learning* system prescribed in this book, transcending the Consulting Systems Worldview and introducing the management consultant to many new leadership responsibilities to understand and master while transforming. In this learning context several new rocks are identified, making it possible to thrive in each consulting context while leading from the future as it emerges.

Chapter 1   Understanding how the game is changing

US Supreme Court Justice Oliver Wendell Holmes said this about simplicity: "I would not give a fig for the simplicity this side of complexity, but I would give my life for the simplicity on the other side of complexity. To live on the edge is to search out "simplicity on the other side of complexity."

Searching out simplicity on the other side of complexity is the challenging task overwhelming contemporary consultants. Management consulting is a fast moving profession – and more importantly for clients, it is about developing responsible business practice. But, to accomplish this change, the consulting industry must change and must clarify itself. It must move from being a "tale of mystery and imagination" to a recognized profession, ***competent in giving advice to managers so they influence systems change*** in a high-velocity world.

A common misunderstanding regarding how the game is changing for the consultant is reflected in the following story.

A young man pulled up in an SUV next to a shepherd, tending his flock. The young man said, "If I guess how many sheep you have, will you give me one of them?" The shepherd looked out across his flock, quietly grazing, then responded, "Sure."

With that, the young man pulled out his notebook PC and modem, entered NASA's Web site and scanned the field using NASA's global positioning satellite system. He then opened a spreadsheet database, entered the information retrieved from the GPS, and printed a 50-page report from his high-tech mini-printer. After studying the report before him, he turned to the shepherd. "You have 1,112 sheep."

"You're absolutely right," said the shepherd. "You can have your sheep," whereupon the young man loaded one of the animals into his vehicle.

The shepherd spoke next. "Now, if I can guess your profession, will you pay me back in kind?"

"Sure," answered the young man.

"You're a consultant," said the shepherd.

"Why, yes. How did you know?"

"Very simple," explained the shepherd. "First, you came here without being called. Then, you charged me a fee for something I already knew. Finally, you don't understand anything about my business — now, may I have my dog back?"

-Author unknown

WHY consultants need to understand the changing game

To avoid irrelevance, the consultant needs to understand that both change itself and the consulting game are changing. In the case reported, the consultant turned out to be irrelevant because he did not identify the shepherd's problem – if, in fact, the shepherd had a problem warranting consultation. The shepherd didn't need an accurate count of his sheep; he already had that. The consultant could have first secured a meaningful relationship with the shepherd and contracted to advise the shepherd on how to better manage his business. Perhaps the shepherd needed help increasing his share in the wool market, which requires an entirely different kind of knowledge. There is little evidence that the consultant in the story used a new mode of seeing, doing, and being in the world— thinking through chaos and complexity to simplicity. He simply zoomed to simplicity via technology, that is, simplicity on this side of complexity – not beyond complexity – and *failed.*

In the story, the consultant, having already understood the sheep raising *business* and its *nomadic culture,* could have approached the shepherd with a different opening statement. For example, "I'm interested in helping you boost your share of the wool market. Could we talk?" In this way, the consultant would have engaged the client in possible new learning and *choice,* at the same time suggesting that he had relevant knowledge to contribute.

If *relevance* is the issue, the developing consultant needs to communicate to the client about Systems Thinking – for Systems Thinking is a way of working through chaos and complexity. Systems Thinking offers a different mode of seeing, doing, and being in the world that frees the developing consultant to create new futures.

For the developing consultant to remain relevant several key aspects of Systems Thinking are reviewed in detail in this chapter. Each is important for the consultant to develop a firm foundation of phenomena affecting change and the changing consulting game. This book relies heavily on the clarity brought to Systems Thinking by Jamshid Gharajedaghi (2006), a seer on the subject. Seeing how the game is currently changing is important, but not a stopping place – it is important to always be looking ahead to the next change on the horizon. The developing consultant must stay abreast of successive change. Relevance will always be a key issue in consultation.

This chapter is about selecting the big rocks that need to be placed first in your jar. It describes rocks to include that aid "seeing, doing, and being in the world." More importantly, to be relevant it may mean *doing things differently*. In this chapter, doing things differently begins with first seeing systems with new eyes and seeing the importance of Systems Thinking in consulting. Once seeing differently, one can begin to "make-sense" for self and others.

How seeing systems "with new eyes" makes a difference

Seeing with new eyes how the game is changing requires a new way of

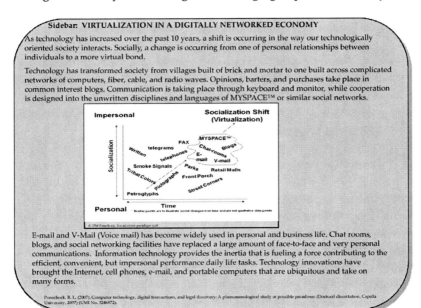

Sidebar: VIRTUALIZATION IN A DIGITALLY NETWORKED ECONOMY

As technology has increased over the past 10 years, a shift is occurring in the way our technologically oriented society interacts. Socially, a change is occurring from one of personal relationships between individuals to a more virtual bond.

Technology has transformed society from villages built of brick and mortar to one built across complicated networks of computers, fiber, cable, and radio waves. Opinions, barters, and purchases take place in common interest blogs. Communication is taking place through keyboard and monitor, while cooperation is designed into the unwritten disciplines and languages of MYSPACE™ or similar social networks.

E-mail and V-Mail (Voice mail) has become widely used in personal and business life. Chat rooms, blogs, and social networking facilities have replaced a large amount of face-to-face and very personal communications. Information technology provides the inertia that is fueling a force contributing to the efficient, convenient, but impersonal performance daily life tasks. Technology innovations have brought the Internet, cell phones, e-mail, and portable computers that are ubiquitous and take on many forms.

Poruchock, R. L. (2007). Computer technology, digital transactions, and legal discovery: A phenomenological study of possible paradoxes (Doctoral dissertation, Capella University, 2007) (UMI No. 3246872).

thinking which is foreign to many of us—foreign because it is based in our past, limited exposure in education. The new way of thinking is *thinking in terms of systems*. A "system" is defined as a regularly interacting or interdependent group of items forming a unified whole. There are many examples around us all the time – in fact, your body represents a system. More accurately stated, your body is a series of interacting, interdependently connected systems that form a unified whole.   However, to fully understand a system requires more transparency.   Ackoff (1997) points out that consultants must change *thought patterns*, not just processes, in making change. It is critical that the *thought pattern* on systems is specific and includes:

"A system is a whole defined by one or more functions, that consists of two or more essential parts that satisfy the following conditions: (1) each of these parts can affect the behavior or properties of the whole; (2) none of these parts has an independent effect on the whole; the way an essential part affects the whole depends on what other parts are doing; and (3) every possible subset of the essential parts can affect the behavior or properties of the whole but none can do so independently of the others." Some important conclusions follow:

- A system is a functioning whole that cannot be divided into independent parts and remain effective
- An essential part of a system is one without which the system cannot perform its defining function(s)
- The defining properties of a system arise out of the *interactions* of its parts. Therefore, when a system is taken apart it loses its essential properties

These appear rather straightforward and clear as written; however, it is difficult for many people, even consultants, to respect this understanding in practice. Take for example, the infamous case of Enron Energy Corporation, where Andersen Consulting persisted in dividing the system into independent parts—focusing only on analytic technique in the accounting practices, and not on the synthesis of the whole system. This action exemplifies the action of many consultants who persist in separating out a part and focusing on that part— rather than considering the whole. A consultant "must understand that evaluation of a part requires determining its effect on the performance of the whole (Ackoff, 1997, p. 17)." It is important to get a full grasp of the meaning of "system" before going on.   If this is not clear to you, go back and work through it again and again until it has meaning for you. This understanding is basic to working with systems, and to get meaning from thinking in terms of systems.

The term *Systems Thinking* is often used to refer to concepts relevant to understanding change in systems terms – and one should not be turned off or slowed in their use of systemic concepts. Rather, one should be concerned with increasing your capability to think and act in systemic terms. In our experience, Systems Thinking is required to manage both chaos and to see through complexity in our time. Seeing how the game is changing identifies what the consultant needs to focus on in order to succeed in today's consulting world. Essentially, the consultant must become familiar with Systems Thinking to thrive.   The important difference is now seeing with new eyes the *whole* in systems. It focuses the importance of the perspective of the whole and stresses that the defining properties are in the interactions. Therefore, to plan change in a system the consultant focuses on the interactions of its parts. It is for that reason that consultants intervene at points of interaction of parts in a system.

How to play the game "successfully"

In beginning to use new eyes, it is often difficult for people to grasp that playing a game successfully changes the game itself. Most people, consultants included, are inclined to want to repeat the same activities that initially led to success in the first place. These people believe that if "x" is successful, more "x" will be even more successful. What they fail to realize, however, are the negative consequences of success – the same old ways will not work when used over and over. "Once success is achieved or a problem is effectively dissolved, the concerns associated with that problem are irreversibly affected" (Gharajedaghi, 2006, p. 7).

For the industry-wise consultant, understanding how the game is changing is the basis of future business, especially so in our high-velocity world where rapid change is a matter of course. Success brings clients a new set of problems, and the consultant must be ready to address these problems and to aid in the design of a new solution. Understanding the role of success is important for the management consultant who wants to work actively on one success after another to create the future.

An example is in Henry Ford's famous statement regarding his popular Model T, "They can have any color as long as it is black." This one statement reflected Ford's lack of learning regarding his company's success and his unwillingness to play the new game.

Ford's inflexibility gave GM's Alfred Sloan the opportunity to dominate the automotive industry. Sloan's idea of a product-based divisional structure turned out to be an effective design for managing growth and diversity. The new game, artfully learned and played by corporate America became the benchmark for the rest of the world to copy (Womack, Jones, & Ross, 1990).

Another example occurred when Ohno, chief engineer at Toyota, studied ways in which his company could replicate certain production systems used in the American automobile system. Ironically, this exercise led Ohno to develop an altogether new design called "lean production" with respect to die changes, allowing Toyota to achieve in three minutes what took American manufacturers three days. Once again, success transformed the game. This time, the differentiating factors were flexibility and control.

At the time, American manufacturers were too overwhelmed and overjoyed by their own success to notice the emergence of the new game. Their inattentiveness provided Japanese manufacturers the opportunity to launch an effective challenge. The insidious manner in which the new game evolved underscores another important principle of systems dynamics, something akin to the story of the frog that boiled to death, sitting happily in water that gradually grew hotter.

Sidebar: The Monkey Club Story: Reaching for Success

There once was a six year old girl who was a little pudgy. One day she came home from school in tears. Her father asked why she was crying, and she proceeded to tell her father that she could not get into the Monkey Club at school, and all of her friends were teasing her. When the father inquired about the Monkey Club, she explained that in gym class you had to climb this really high rope (in actuality it was about five feet from the floor at its highest point). From her perspective this was really high. She went on to explain that once you reached the top you had to reach over to a second rope, let go of the first rope, and proceed to climb back down on the second rope. She was really frightened about letting go of the first rope because she might fall.

Her father explained that sometimes in life you have to overcome your fears in order to succeed. You must do something different. He went on to tell her that they would practice this together in the backyard over the weekend, starting with the rope very low and working up to the five foot height. After they had practiced all weekend, the father took his daughter to school on Monday and told her to remember that he would be with her in her thoughts when she was climbing that rope. He suggested that when she reached the top and was ready to grab the second rope she should look only at that second rope and think of him smiling; because he was so proud of her.

That night she came home overcome with happiness as she hugged her Dad and showed him her Monkey Club certificate! It's amazing what preparation, positive thinking and letting go of the past experience can do toward achieving a new success experience.

Playing the game successfully requires recognition that: *Success marks the beginning of the end.* It is time to begin thinking about creating a new success, not repeating the same case just completed successfully. The developing consultant needs to always start afresh in each context —

treating each context as new and different. This is the basis of playing the game successfully, over and over again.

What is the relevance of a double paradigm shift?

The current global reality of the changing game is probably best understood through understanding a paradigm shift. A paradigm shift occurs when we see the world differently. Columbus' view of a 'round' world was a paradigm shift from a 'flat' worldview that many of the uninformed believed to be true. A shift of paradigm can happen purposefully by an active process of learning and unlearning. However, more commonly a shift of paradigm occurs as a reaction to the frustration produced by events that nullify conventional wisdom. Faced with a series of contradictions that can no longer be ignored or denied, or an increasing number of dilemmas for which prevailing mental models can no longer provide convincing explanations, most people accept that the prevailing paradigm has ceased to be valid and that it has exhausted its potential. Thus begins a painful struggle, the end result of which is a re-conceptualization of critical variables into a new ensemble with a new logic of its own – a new paradigm that affects the whole.

Shifts of paradigm can happen in one of two ways: either from a change in the *nature of reality* or a change in the *method of inquiry*. It is possible for a dual shift involving both dimensions — what we are currently experiencing – which complicates even further how the global game is changing.

Gharajedaghi (2006) best describes the origins of the current dual paradigm shift. He notes that change from one level to another occurs from forces that *convert success to failure*. The sidebar on converting success to failure shows the forces that form a five-level hierarchy as: imitation, inertia, sub-optimization, change of the game, and shift of paradigm. "Each level represents a distinct tendency, but together they form an interactive whole in which the higher level provides the context for the lower levels."

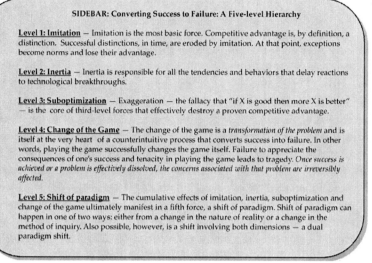

The cumulative effects of imitation, inertia, sub-optimization and change of the game ultimately manifest themselves in the fifth force, a shift of paradigm.

The dual paradigm shift The significance of any paradigm shift cannot be overestimated, but a dual shift is a formidable challenge. It tests the outer limits of human capacity to comprehend, communicate and confront problems. For example, the shift of paradigm from a mechanical to a biological model, despite its huge impact, represented only a shift in organizational models, not a change in the method of inquiry where analytical inquiry remained the same.

We are now facing the challenge of the dual paradigm shift – a shift in the conception of the organization from a biological model to a *socio-cultural model* or a multi-minded system – *and* a shift in the method of inquiry. The shift in the method of inquiry as a means of knowing, is from analytical thinking (dealing with independent sets of variables) to *holistic thinking* (handling interdependent sets of variable). The complementary nature of these two dimensions is at the core of both understanding how the game is changing and identifying the drivers for change.

About the first current paradigm shift The first paradigm shift involves moving from a biological model to a sociocultural model. This new model views the organization as a voluntary association of purposeful members who manifest a choice of both ends and means. Mechanical or biological models cannot explain the behavior of a system whose parts display choice. Therefore, a social system must be understood on its own terms. For both Ackoff and Gharajedaghi, these terms are "purpose" and "information-bonded."

About purpose Ackoff (1972) writes that an entity is purposeful if it can produce 1) the same outcome in different ways in the same environment and 2) different outcomes in the same or different environment. As a purposeful system, an organization is part of a larger, purposeful whole – society. At the same time, its members consist of purposeful individuals. The result is a three-level hierarchy of purposeful systems: society, organization and individuals. Aligning these purposeful parts with each other and that of the whole is the main challenge of the system. Under the sociocultural model, an organization's purpose is to simultaneously serve the purposes of its members and of the environment.

This presents an altogether different view for the consultant rooted in the earlier, biological model of organizations. In the biological model, *growth* is the measure of success, the single most important performance criterion, and profit is the means to achieve it. Under the biological model, the desire for profit can drive change. Compare this to the sociocultural view, which considers the purposes of its members and the environment as the main change drivers. This has meaning for the consultant in terms of how he/she advises the organization. Consider for a moment, the difference in Wall Street directions to CEOs, firms, and stock purchasers if they understood the double paradigm shift. New directions underscoring purposes of a multi-minded organization may develop trust, the new social capital [so important in economic development], and in expanding the human potential in all environments. It is quite clear that Wall Street leadership would no longer be rewarding based solely on growth and profit. Could the lack of understanding on Wall Street leadership actually be a negative driver of change in the stock market, driving the daily stock reports down? Consider what action on this new understanding of the paradigm shift may do toward increasing confidence in our financial consultants and accountants. Covey, Covey and Merrill, in *The Speed of Trust*, contend that trust is an accelerator for substantive and positive change. Conversely, trust can be a decelerator if not properly embraced.

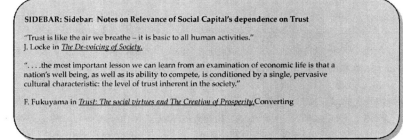

About information-bonded systems Gharajedaghi (1985) writes that elements of a sociocultural system are information-bonded in contrast to the elements of mechanical systems which are energy-bonded. Information-bonded relationships are an agreement based on a common perception. An example compares an energy-bonded system of an automobile and driver to an information-bonded system of a horse and rider:

"An automobile yields to its driver regardless of his expertise and dexterity. If a driver decides to run a car into a solid wall, the car will hit the wall without objection, but riding a horse presents a different perspective. It matters to the horse who the rider is, and a proper ride can only be achieved after a series of information exchanges between the horse and the rider."

Horse and rider form an information-bonded system. That same system is required of the consultant and client – a system in which guidance and control are achieved by a second-degree agreement (agreement based on common perception) proceeded by a psychological contract.

Buckley (1968) saw the sociocultural system as a set of elements linked almost entirely by intercommunications of information. Information-bonded relationships bring an organization of meanings that emerge from a network of interactions among individuals. Information-bonded interacting networks are becoming more common each day in business and industry. However, the consultant may need to focus on both the agreement in an information-bonded network, and on achieving the second-degree psychological contract based on a common perception, which is less common.

About the second current paradigm shift The second paradigm shift is about the change in the nature of inquiry. It is the change from the use of the analytical thinking to Systems Thinking. Analytical thinking and Systems Thinking are quite distinct. Handling independent variables is the essence of analytical thinking. It assumes that the whole is nothing but the sum of its parts. Increasingly we find that our independent variables are no longer independent. As systems become more sophisticated, the reality of interdependency becomes more pronounced. Understanding interdependency requires a way of thinking different from analysis; it requires Systems Thinking.

Analysis is a three-step thought process. First, it takes apart that which it seeks to understand. Then, it attempts to explain the behavior of each part separately. Finally, it tries to aggregate understanding of the parts into an explanation of the whole. Systems Thinking uses a different thought process. It puts the system in the context of the larger environment of which it is a part and studies the role it plays in the larger whole. In contrast to analysis, this process is synthesis.

Ackoff (Wardman, 1994) writes that synthesis is the opposite of analysis. With synthesis, understanding is achieved, while with analysis one gets only knowledge. Ackoff defines synthesis as a three-step process.

- The first step is to determine the larger system within which the system to be examined is a part.
- The second step is to try to understand the larger system as a whole.
- The third step is to disaggregate the understanding of the whole into an understanding of the part by identifying its role or function in the larger system.

Contrasting the two approaches, through analysis, one begins with the parts while through synthesis, one begins with the whole. Unfortunately, by using analysis one never reaches an understanding of the whole; analysis of the parts and then aggregation of the same parts does not yield understanding of the whole. It is important not to throw the baby out with the bath water; clearly there are times when analytic techniques are needed and should be used. However, one may be much farther ahead by starting with synthesis in a holistic approach, and then using analysis as it may be appropriate in some of the problematic parts identified later.

One of the major values of the holistic approach is that many of the modern complexities cannot be simplified into a list of independent variables. It takes considerable search and exploration before even the interdependence can be mapped. Using the perspective of the whole provides the developing management with an immediate and successful resource to grapple with the complex problem, beginning to make progress and clarification right from the beginning. And probably most importantly, synthesis yields new understanding – not achievable through analysis.

Why a new language of interaction and design are needed

Using Systems Thinking effectively requires a new holistic language. Full understanding requires many changes. Understanding, in this case requires that we learn "a holistic language – that is, a language of systems – that will allow us to see through chaos and to understand complexity. A language of interaction and design that will help us learn a new mode of living by considering various new ways of seeing, doing, and being in the world. We can then design new methods of inquiry, new modes of organization, and a way of life that will allow for rational, emotional, and ethical choices for interdependent yet autonomous social beings" (Gharajedaghi, 2006).

A new language of interaction and design is needed because what we have is inadequate and does not capture the essence of the required change. Increased communication is absolutely critical – at all times, but especially during times of change, when uncertainty is heightened over new complexities, and not yet explainable in the current language. Dave Longaberger, president of Longaberger Basket is quoted saying: "I don't care what business you're in, your success will ultimately depend on the relationships you [through your communication] build with people." This is especially true for the developing consultant. Successful businesses are built on communicated trust between customer and company, employer and employee, and employees and their colleagues. Consultants must prove themselves to their clients, day in and day out. Consultants have to earn their trust. And once consultants earn that trust, they have to keep earning it. Trust, once compromised, is difficult to regain. The developing consultant needs to continually work on the development of a new language that communicates the change necessary to the client in a way that he can take action on in the designed solution.

To reach the other side of the paradigm shift requires significant development in terms of learning — this means learning a new holistic language, learning a language of systems, and learning a language of interaction and design. However, emotionally and ethically, there is great resistance to learning in these new areas. This resistance to change stems from our past experience in the formal educational system that has had no place for Systems Thinking. In "Learning as A Way of Being," Vaill (1996) writes that resistance to learning a different way is reinforced by our institutions of higher learning, causing institutional blockage. Breaking down this past resistance and blockage would require many changes in the formal educational systems and institutions of higher learning. Thus, in changing each of us must also battle this resistance of the past and the institutional blockage to using Systems Thinking.

These are huge developmental changes each of us must make and which are absolutely critical for each of us to understand first, before we can attempt to help clients reach a new level of understanding. Then they, too, may thrive interdependently and still be autonomous social beings while the game is continuing to change. The name of the new game may be to "become comfortable being uncomfortable" in change.

Allow time to achieve this new understanding and the use of a new systems language. First, consider *what* the learning task consists of, then *why* it is necessary. Use this adage as your guide: <u>Go SLOW at first, to go FAST later on</u>. One can take time to gain understanding, yet one can continue moving towards the future as study of the new language progresses.

To achieve the necessary understanding use of a new systems language is basic to the consultant's success in practice. It will take time and effort to make the transition, and the change will not come overnight as it involves considerable unlearning and relearning of concepts and experiences.

The consultant will be called upon to "make sense" of chaos and complexity while developing himself, which tends to complicate matters. When this happens, often the consultant tries to "make sense" in the situation – but in fact, it doesn't make sense. Making sense, under these conditions, takes additional understanding and potentially, the development of timing and skill in successfully setting direction – this is the topic of the next section.

How does "making sense" capitalize on change?

The challenge for the developing management consultant is to "make sense" of the new reality presented by the dual paradigm shift communicating and advising management to influence their system to change appropriately. Using a new language and a new methodology in "making sense" to the client is challenging, but necessary. For example, experience has shown that:

In the case of problem dissolving solutions; it may be necessary to enlighten the client on how "problem dissolving" strategies are based in the new reality – where time and cost are very important issues. It may be important to be clear that problem-dissolving strategies are means "to cause the problem to disappear – that is, to cause the problem to pass into solution in such a way, that the problem does not reoccur at a later time. Often this means finding root causes and dealing with them rather than giving symptomatic relief at the time. Finding the cause of the problem may take more time, but in reality it saves time when the problem itself is *dissolved,* and does not reoccur.

Research shows that dissolving problems may take more time initially, but over the period of time set aside for solution, it not only saves time but lowers cost due to higher quality involvement early. In this example, "sense" had to be made of "problem dissolving solutions." In retrospect, this may seem simple. However, in the beginning the tendency is just to move quickly ahead with a keen new term that has meaning to you, the consultant. This example may be likened to many other system change issues, where "sense making" is important.

For example, it is important to remember that many system change issues are not obvious; they are subtle, yet often may be contested; they may be nonlinear metaproblems with long lead times; they may have unintended side effects; and unclear cause-effect structures with consequences that are often irreversible. All of these contribute to problematic, unclear situations for the management consultant to address with clear direction. At the same time, these issues demand change and can provide a real trap for the developing consultant.

Weick (1995) likens these issues singularly or together to an onrushing wall of fire, and he says they are just as tricky to manage. Weick argues that system change issues present a problem for consultants that call for *"sensemaking."* Sensemaking, he says, is similar to the experience a consultant "feels" as he enters a new problematic setting and is asked to provide immediate direction. Sensemaking is about sizing up a situation while you simultaneously discover what you have and what effect must be achieved. "Sensemaking is seldom an occasion for passive diagnosis. Instead, it is usually an attempt to grasp a developing situation in which the observer affects the trajectory of that development." This is a situation many developing consultants frequently find themselves involved in today.

Sensemaking is relevant for consulting because it is important that consultants develop some sense of what they are up against, what their own position is relative to what they sense, and what they need to do – including walking away from the scene. It must be remembered that clients may not want to *make sense*, they may only want to solve the problem quickly and efficiently – never mind effectiveness. However, it is important that consultants work to keep clients in the loop and not walk away from the situation – otherwise they lose the value of the clients' participation and learning, and probably more importantly the client is left to carry-on in the situation once the consultant leaves.

If consultants are to make sense in comparable situations they must first **unbury the limited set of cues in a plausible, pragmatic, momentarily useful guide for actions**. This must be done rather quickly once in the situation, so it is wise to be aware of this unburying task before one enters the consulting engagement. It is important to realize that the **consultant's actions are in themselves partially defining, and act as a guide for others in the immediate future**. However, these actions— though often quite tenuous – are important for the management consultant **to support the client's initial efforts** in order to get positive movement in the situation to reach the new reality.

Sensemaking is often a problem for management consultants in their management of meaning, vision, and relationships. Sensemaking can be a problem because object and subject are hard to separate – as the object is to "put out the fire," and the subject is to "fight the fire."

Misunderstanding the value of initial diagnostic "size-up" or diagnosis in consulting terms is another common problem. Although size-ups may seem short-lived their influence is enduring, because once a hypothesis is formed, people tend to look for evidence that confirms it. This tendency is more likely if people are under pressure to act quickly and if it is hard for them to find time to question their initial beliefs – as is often the case in consulting. Furthermore, initial actions are often publicly chosen and hard to revoke, which means that people are often bound to those first actions and end up searching for reasons that justify the actions taken as rational.

It is not an easy task to "unbury" the limited set of cues that circumscribe the new reality, or to make sense by elaborating those few cues into a "plausible, pragmatic, momentarily useful guide" for actions. The actions made by the client, although quite tenuous, must be supportable by the consultant to get positive movement in the situation to reach a new reality. Reviewing a disaster in problematic sensemaking, serves to clarify and strengthen the basic guides for developing consultants. The Sidebar describing the Mann Gulch Disaster is an extreme example in problematic sensemaking that actually happened.

Sidebar: The Mann Gulch Disaster as Problematic Sensemaking

On the afternoon of August 5, 1949, 15 smokejumpers — trained firefighters who had never worked together as a team — parachuted into Mann Gulch. The crew's leaders originally believed that the blaze was a basic "ten o'clock fire," meaning the crew would have it under control by 10 the next morning. Instead, the fire exploded, forcing the men into a race for their lives.

The fire started the day before when lightning set fire to a small tree. The temperature reached 97 degrees the next day and produced a fire danger rating of 74 out of a possible 100, indicating the potential for the fire to spread uncontrollably. When the fire was spotted by a mountain lookout 30 miles away, the smokejumpers were sent at 2:30 p.m. from Missoula, Montana in a C-47 transport. A ranger posted in the next canyon, Jim Harrison, was already on the scene, trying to fight the fire on his own. Wind conditions that day were turbulent, so smokejumpers and their cargo were dropped from 2,000 feet rather than the usual 1,200.

The parachute connected to their radio failed to open, and the radio smashed as it hit the ground. But the remaining crew and supplies landed safely in Mann Gulch at 4:10 p.m. The smokejumpers then collected their supplies and grabbed a bite to eat. While the crew ate, foreman Wagner Dodge met up with ranger Harrison. They scouted the fire and came back, concerned that the thick forest near where they had landed could become a "death trap." Dodge told the second-in-command, William Hellman, to take the crew across to the north side of the gulch, away from the fire, and to march along its flank toward the river at the bottom of the gulch. While Hellman did this, Dodge and Harrison ate a quick meal. Dodge rejoined the crew at 5:40 p.m. and took his position at the head of the line moving toward the river. He could see flames flapping back and forth on the south slope as he looked to his left.

A general and more stark rendering of the story of Mann Gulch follows. Individuals who are strangers to one another are spread out, unable to communicate, unfamiliar with the terrain, in disagreement about who their leaders are, and they're told to do something they've never done before, or they will die. They don't do it. They die.

Contrast this stark rendering with the situation many managers and employees face when consultants enter to assist them in changing their system. To address the changing game, consultants also face many factors:

- Strangers with diverse experience
- Face-to-face contact for intermittent, short periods
- Unknown leaders
- Temporary systems
- Proposed solutions that make no sense
- An inability to communicate and share experience
- Terrain consisting of unfamiliar troubles (or opportunities)
- Failures and possible fatalities

The context for addressing change in management consulting often bears an uncomfortable resemblance to the context at Mann Gulch. Some of the dysfunction at Mann Gulch may be understood as a failure to organize sensemaking. The capability of sensemaking is an important rock to add to your Big Rock collection. The developing management consultant relies on making sense of the time and events as they are happening and at the same time choosing the learning that is necessary for himself and the client.

Making sense to thrive in management consulting

Applying the skills identified in sensemaking to a consulting engagement is one important use of the capability. However, making sense of the existing conditions in the evolving management consulting industry is paramount to understanding and mastering in the fast developing profession of management consulting. The next chapter provides a foundation for developing a working perspective on the fast evolving consulting industry. The new perspective not only "makes sense," but it makes it possible to set defining direction; a direction – much needed – if the business of management consulting is to thrive in the 21st century.

The question immediately arises: Why is thriving necessary for management consulting in the 21st century?   The dictionary defines thriving as: *to prosper or to flourish; to be successful, especially as the result of economical management.*   Kelly (1998) identifies the new rules for the new economy, making it crystal clear that prospering and flourishing are only possible through innovation – the base of wealth in the 21st century. Thus to thrive, innovation is a necessity, and also the means to prosper.

Basically, thriving is opposite of surviving [defined by Webster as *"living on, in particular, existing beyond a specific negative event"].*   Thriving in the 21st century demands some differences from the 20th century approaches in consulting.   Thriving demands innovation and wealth production as a result.   For management consulting to thrive, the fast developing industry must change, leaving behind a survival mode where slowly evolving from stage to stage has been sufficient.   The challenge is clearly focused in the next chapter, after a careful review to understand the developmental history of management consulting.   The challenge is to innovatively move forward in learning to understand and to master the art and science of management consulting.   This is the challenge to thrive.

Chapter 2   Understanding the challenge to thrive

Marcel Proust once wrote, "The real voyage of discovery consists not in seeking new lands, but in seeing with new eyes." To date, discovering direction and relevancy to thrive remain a significant challenge.

There is little question that seeing with new eyes the *whole* evolutionary experience in the consulting industry will yield a new understanding – challenging the developing management consultant to thrive. Until recently, the evolutionary process in consulting has been one of continuous, gradual change from a lower, simpler form to a higher, more complex form. Now, the industry appears as if transfigured; acting in a high velocity world – but seemingly, questioning next best steps.

To understand the predicament, one must understand the context of a high-velocity world. In such a world efficiency is a function of speed, with nonlinear acceleration and mass-producing drag. In this information-dense environment there are sudden turns and no clear finish line. This is a world in which implementation is key because implementation now drives strategy. Understanding the need to thrive in this high-velocity context begs the question of preparation.

It is widely known that the fast developing management consulting industry is not well grounded – it does not have a strong professional base, nor can it rely on a healthy world-wide practice of the past. A case in point is the Enron Energy debacle, where Andersen Consulting contributed significantly to the energy giant's downfall. Looking forward, development of consultants appears rather bleak. Recent studies show that there are only a few courses in a few institutions – with no programs or curricula in management consulting (Adams & Zanzi, 2001). Chris Argyris (2000) showed "that currently most consultant advice is flawed and not actionable," and further "that 21st century companies will be managed differently than the 20th century companies." It now appears urgent to better understand the past evolutionary perspective in consulting, in order to better develop a new learning perspective specific to management consulting.

How the consulting industry evolved

Interestingly, in retrospect, the business of consulting arose as a direct response to the many transformations in work environments evident at the time of the Industrial Revolution. For the first time, managers called upon an outside source for assistance -- seeking to maximize efficiencies in the factory. For example, as early as 1870, Charles T. Sampson used the experience he gained from reorganizing his shoe factory to consult with the owner of a laundry. Slowly this practice of "giving advice to management" grew. Increasingly, consultants became "management consultants" – meaning that they were giving advice to the manager in the organization. However, in retrospect, the clarification made in "giving advice to the manager" was not well understood, for consultants at the time did not give advice, but often actually "did the work" or "made the change themselves." The lack of clarity around the task of the management consultant remains today. It is important to note, that this text will use the term "management consultant" as meaning "one who gives advice to the management to influence the change in the system." The management consultant does not actually make the change or "do" the changing advised.

In terms of the first occurrence of management consulting, Kubr (1993) notes that only when the process of managing was isolated as a distinct area of human activity and field of learning could management consulting become possible. These conditions were not met until the birth of the "scientific management" movement in the latter part of the 19th century.

In the beginning – scientific management The pioneers were Frederick W. Taylor, Frank and Lillian Gilbreth, Henri Fayol, Henry L. Gantt and Harrington Emerson. They gave major impetus to the development of consulting and the scientific management movement. Initially, by developing approaches that simplified work processes and raised worker and plant productivity. These pioneering efforts gave rise to a very important branch in management consulting – industrial engineering.

Consulting that emerged from the scientific management movement focused mainly on factory and shop-floor productivity and efficiency, rational work organization, time and motion study, eliminating waste, and reducing production costs. Often called "efficiency experts," these consultants were admired for their drive, methodical approach and, perhaps most of all, the spectacular improvements they achieved. However, sometimes their ruthless interventions in the workplace were feared and detested by workers and trade unions. This intervention behavior contributed to an early negative image for some management consultants.

A general management approach The limitations of industrial engineering led to a broadened interest in consulting opportunities, and a general management approach. Elton Mayo's famous Hawthorne experiment in the 1920s gave impetus to research and consulting in human relations. Mary Parker Follett was among the first consultants to specialize in human resource management and motivation. Harold Whitehead, an Englishman and author of Principles of Salesmanship in 1917, fostered interest in more effective selling and marketing.

The work of these and other individuals naturally paved the way for the type of consulting firms known today. One of the first such firms was established in 1914 in Chicago by Edwin Booz under the name Business Research Services. More firms followed in the 1920s, offering a variety of services to diagnose and assist in solving manufacturing and productivity problems, and to operationalize sales and business-expansion opportunities.

Consulting to the financial side of operations developed rapidly during this time -- as many of these pioneering consultants were experienced public accountants, practiced in "doing" rather than "advising." One such pioneer was James O. McKinsey, an early protagonist of the general management and comprehensive diagnostic approach to a business enterprise. He established his own consulting firm in 1925 and is regarded as one of the founders of the consulting profession.

In the 1920s and 1930s, management consulting was gaining ground in the United States, Great Britain, and across industrialized Europe. A few, small, prestigious firms dominated the market, plying their services mostly to the large corporations that could afford their services. Then, assignment requests began rolling in from government, heralding the start of public sector consulting.

Management consulting for governments played an important role during World War II. The United States, in particular, understood that the war was a major management challenge and that mustering the country's best management expertise was essential to winning the war (Kubr,1993). In turn, operations research and other techniques applied for military purposes rapidly found their way into business and public management after the war, adding a new dimension to the services offered by consultants.

Building toward the "Golden Years" of consulting several post-war factors created a favorable environment for rapid growth and opportunity. Chief among these factors were the rapid business expansion and technological change during post-war reconstruction; the emergence of developing economies; and the globalization of the world's industry, commerce, and finance. Most of the major consulting firms of today were established during this "Golden Age" of management consulting. It was during this time that the consulting business attained the power and technical reputation it enjoys today. For example, PA, the UK's largest consulting firm, grew from six consultants in 1943 to 370 by 1963 and to 1,300 consultants in 22 countries by 1984 (Kubr, 1996). The firm boasted 1,700 consultants in 1993. By the end of the 1980s, the number of full-time management consultants in the U.S. had reached 1 million, six times the number that existed in the mid-1960s. While industry growth during this time was impressive by any standard, a significant number of qualitative changes also occurred, including:

- Diversification in consulting services
- Consultants at the forefront of technological innovations
- Increased competition for consulting contracts
- Emergence of the "Big Eight" accounting firms as consultants
- Continued business expansion into global markets
- The advent of internal consulting
- Progress in the methodological process of consulting
- Increased trust in the use of management consultants

It was during the golden years that some professional consulting organizations first began. Some were short lived, fueled mostly by university professors interested in bringing credibility to the field. The International Association of Applied Social Scientists (IAASS) was one of these. Many of the IAASS leaders claimed roots in the National Training Laboratories Institute of Applied Behavioral Scientists (NTLIABS) in Washington, D.C. The Institute of Management Consultants (IMC) was begun as an American branch of the International Institute of Management Consultants. In addition, IMC has done significant work in certification and recertification of qualified management consultants.

Upon full qualification IMC offers the "Certified Management Consultant" – the CMC designation to be used after one's name – advertising that certain qualifications have been met and the holder is certified to consult to management. These are the main efforts in professional development that occurred at the time – interestingly, outside of consulting firms.

Two basic roles emerge By the 1960s, two distinct types of management consultants had evolved, the resource consultant and the process consultant. The resource consultant, also called an expert or content consultant, provides expertise with a given management problem. The services of these consultants range from supplying information to diagnose, assess, design, train, and implement a new technique or management project. More so then – as today – business managers collaborated with resource consultants to get the work done. However, the resource consultants were not expected to deal with the social or behavioral work-place aspects of the change they recommended.

In contrast, in the role of process consultant, the consultant is an agent of change, helping the organization to solve its own problems by making it aware of organizational processes, of their likely consequences, and of the many intervention techniques for stimulating change. Instead of passing on technical knowledge and suggesting solutions, the process consultant passes on his or her approach, methods, and values so that the organization can diagnose and remedy its own problems. Specialization and a thorough understanding of the process approach is a major contribution of organizational development (OD) consultants to management consulting.

Edgar Schein (1987), a major proponent of process consulting, defines it as "a set of activities on the part of the consultant that help the client to perceive, understand, and act upon the process events that occur in the client's environment." He explains that while the resource consultant tries to suggest to the client *what* to change, the process consultant suggests *how* to change and helps the client in the change process deal with human problems as they arise.

During the Golden Years of consulting, most consultants were either resource consultants or process consultants. Today, however, more and more consultants feel comfortable in both roles, regard resource and process consulting as complementary and, in many cases, employ both techniques as part of every consultation. What may be significant about the role of the process consultant is that it signaled the entry of academia and university consultants in business consulting.   The entry of academics demonstrated a different level of expertise in process and change management consulting, introducing academic research-in-practice.

The focus on management of the change process and on the use of theory and research brought Kurt Lewin's (1946) three-step procedure for the management of change to light.   Lewin's first step in the process of change is *unfreezing* the present level of behavior.   The second step, *movement*, is to take action that will change the social system from the original level of behavior or operation to a new level.   The *refreezing* step involves establishing a process that will make the new level of behavior "relatively secure against change."   Later, Schein (1987) pointed out: "These stages overlap and may occur very rapidly, but they are conceptually distinct, and it is important for the helper (OD practitioner – management consultant, in this case) to be aware of what stage he is working in."   Figure 1. Comparison of Four Models of Change, shows other contributor's refinements in the understanding of the change process to be managed.   The three-step model became the basis for the promulgation of *action research,* an approach pulled together by Lewin (1946) who stated that there is "no action without research, and no research without action."   In the practice of action research, research is conducted first and then action is taken as a direct result of what the research data are interpreted to indicate.

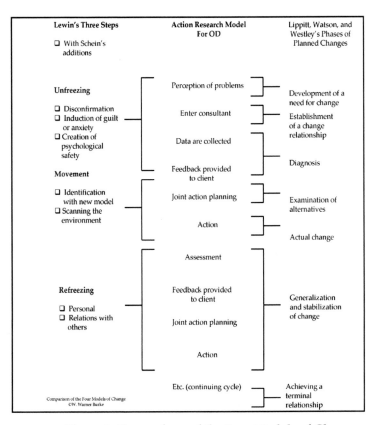

Figure 1. Comparison of the Four Models of Change
© W. Warner Burke

Lewin talked about lasting change (or transformative change) which means initially unlocking or unfreezing the present social system. Often this requires some kind of initial confrontation or a process of reeducation. In perspective, the three steps are simple to state, but not as simple to implement. Implementation remains an ongoing challenge for management consultants today and we suspect forever, due to the numerous aspects that must be considered and worked with in practice to be successful.

Based on the Lewinian concepts of change and the phases of planned change, Warner Burke (1992) identifies seven distinct but overlapping phases -- currently used in OD practice. They are:

- Entry
- Contracting
- Diagnosis
- Feedback
- Planning Change
- Intervention
- Evaluation

These phases are the basis for management consulting interventions in contemporary organizations, demonstrating the continuing influence of OD in the evolving industry.

Consulting bridges training, research and practice The relationships between management training, research, and practice have not been synergistic as in other professions, like medicine. However, so far the consulting industry has been unable to fully integrate training, research, and practice. As such, the consulting industry remains rooted in a traditional dichotomy with consultants eager to produce results for their clients on the one hand and theoretically oriented professor/researchers on the other hand, eager to demonstrate their findings in practice.

There are signs of progress in bridging the gaps. Most consultants now view training (both informal and formal) as a key intervention tool, and they use it extensively. Likewise, similar comments may be made about the relationships between research and practice. Previous generations of consultants liked to stress that they were down-to-earth practitioners who had nothing in common with researchers. This perception, however, stemmed mostly from a lack of theoretical preparation of many, and the lack of knowledge of the practical demands on consultants doing research -- rather than any real conflict.

Fortunately for all concerned, the relationships may be bridged rather rapidly and easily through self-education on the world-wide-web. Consultants learn a lot from researchers, and vice versa. Action research (AR), coined by Lewin, is an example of research that includes both research and consulting: AR simultaneously aims at solving a practical problem and yielding new knowledge about the social system under study. Action research involves changing that which is being investigated, conventional research does not. Action research also seeks to conserve time, a major factor influencing client's decision in buying consultation.

Diversity reflected in consulting-organization types   The diversity of the clients and markets services provided, approaches taken, and personalities involved is reflected in the several types of management consulting organizations listed below:

- Large multi-functional consulting firms
- Management consulting services of major accounting firms
- Small and medium-sized consulting firms
- Sole practitioners
- The "consulting professors"
- Consulting services of management institutions
- Non-traditional suppliers of consulting services
- Internal consultants
- The internal-external consulting team

The growth in the number of internal consultants has been impressive in recent years. Use of these consultants is no passing fad, nor will it replace continued reliance on external consultants. The latter will continue to be preferred in situations where an internal consultant does not meet the criteria of impartiality and confidentiality, or lacks expertise. A growing number of assignments are entrusted to joint teams of external and internal consultants. This is a technically interesting arrangement as it can reduce costs, help external consultants to learn quickly about the client organization, quicken the pace of facilitation, contribute to the training and knowledge base of internal consultant,; and, many times, ensure support for recommended changes from key stakeholders.

In retrospect, what is impressive is that roles flow in two major streams of development that afford the developing management consultant a choice. She may choose to go with a large firm that does its own training in a particular methodology of consulting, or she might choose to go it alone or join a smaller firm, depending on the consulting expertise one brings to the situation. It is clear that there is no agreed on path to becoming a management consultant, or for that matter becoming a *professional* consultant. Neither of the streams grows from a professional development curriculum base.

Pursuing the desirable status of a professional management consultant leads one to David Maister's work. Maister (1997) states that "inside" most firms being a "professional" is based on the number of hours one can bill, or if one can make "partner." Maister himself has devoted a whole book to defining true professionalism as "the courage to care about your people, your clients, and your career." Maister's statement opens wide a gap in the industry that must be addressed in a forthright fashion.

The current landscape The consulting industry's evolution has had a direct impact on the type of management consulting and the corresponding manner of contemporary service delivery. The current market may be described as global where large consulting firms operate through offices or subsidiaries in dozens of countries.

Consulting across national borders is common practice. . Worldwide consulting is big business as dollar figures in the billions attest.   The current market is *competitive* where supply has outgrown demand. Under these conditions, clients can be selective, and service quality and innovation have become important criteria in judging consultants. The current market also is *open and liberal.* Language and cultural barriers aside, entry into foreign markets is relatively easy as there are few legal barriers to develop consulting services. It also is a market with relatively high and rapidly evolving *centralization* and *polarization.*

Consulting is a *professionally challenging market.* Several factors make management consulting less repetitive, routine, or boring than law, accounting and auditing. Demand has not only grown, but also changed in nature. Cultural change of the whole organization, globalization, information and communication technologies, regional economic groupings, the fall of the communist regimes, major paradigm shifts, privatization, and many other developments have not only increased demand for consulting, but have also changed the content and quality of demand. In consulting, the demand side requires continuous creativity and innovation. The supply side provides unlimited opportunities for initiative and intellectually rewarding work.

Today's consultants tackle a variety of business problems – problems as straightforward as researching a new market or as complex as totally rethinking the client's organization (Wetfeet.com, 1999). No matter the engagement, few can scoff at the power consultants wield. They can advise a client to acquire a company worth hundreds of millions of dollars or reduce the size of its workforce by thousands.

The big names in consulting – Accenture [formerly Andersen Consulting], Bain, Booz-Allen, The Boston Consulting Group, Mc Kinsey – and a solid crop of similar firms vie for contracts from the Fortune 500 club. All do comparable work, yet each firm has a slightly different focus or way of going about its business. The phrase "management consulting" is often used interchangeably with "strategy consulting," providing advice about strategic and core operational issues. In many cases, however, "strategic" is used to mean a specific consulting endeavor, such as technology, human resources, corporate communications, health care, financial services, real estate, e-commerce, or other specialized fields.

Consultants report that there is much to like and dislike about their role. Consultants generally like the variety of assignments, working for different clients in different industries, and intellectually challenging themselves to tackle complex business problems. The money and perks are good, too. These likes are balanced, however, with complaints of 60-hour work weeks, frequent crunch times and deadlines, extended travel, and limited time or energy for life outside work.

Consolidations and growth are rapidly changing the landscape of consulting today. Wetfeet.com (1999) identifies six categories to group today's consulting firms as seen in the sidebar. Consulting Firms Grouped by Type.

Although each consulting firm has its own specialties and product lines, there are several trends emerging that characterize opportunities for industry growth. Most evident among these is e-business consulting.

Because it is fundamentally changing the way companies do business, the Internet is also altering the consulting landscape. As a company's success increasingly depends on how it positions itself on the Web, many of the cornerstone frameworks and strategies of consulting are in danger of becoming less relevant, even obsolete. For example, eyeing its new e-competitors, KPMG radically transformed its consulting practice into an e-business strategy and implementation shop. This means tomorrow's consultants will require a somewhat different skillset than those of today.

Sidebar: CONSULTING FIRMS GROUPED BY TYPE

The Elite Management Consulting Firms
The bulk of these firms provide top executive officers in Fortune 500 companies with strategic or operational advice. In return, they charge high fees and carry the most prestige. Consultants in these firms are well paid, work long days and have attitudes that match the prestige their firms have achieved. Representative firms: A.D. Little, Andersen Consulting Strategic Services, A. T. Kearney, Bain & Co., BCG, Booz-Allen & Hamilton, Boston Consulting Group, L.E.K./ Alcar, Marakon, Mercer Management Consulting, McKinsey & Co., Monitor Company

The Big Five-Affiliated Consulting Firms
These firms may sound like they're filled with bean counters, but names can be deceiving. The five consulting practices affiliated with the Big Five of the accounting world are actually legitimate -- and rapidly growing – consulting practices that annually appear on the top 10 list of the largest consulting firms. The Big Five provide a range of strategic advice, information systems support and specialized consulting services to many of the same corporations served by the elite consulting firms. Most boast strong information technology capabilities on projects requiring heavy systems implementation work. They tend to be larger and more complex than the elite strategy firms. The Big Five keep their competitive eyes trained on each other rather than on other firms in the field. The Big Five: Arthur Andersen, Deloitte Consulting, Ernst & Young, KPMG and Price-Waterhouse Coopers. Andersen Consulting -- now name changed to Accenture also falls into this category. The number and the firms keep changing, thus the 'Big Five' is nominal only.

Boutique Strategy Firms
A significant number of firms specialize in a particular industry, process or type of consulting. These firms offer excellent career opportunities in a particular industry or type of consulting. Representative firms: CSC Healthcare (a division of Computer Sciences Corporation that specializes in health care consulting), Cornerstone Research (litigation support), Gartner Group (high-technology research), ICF International (public policy consulting), Kurt Salmon Associates (health care consulting), Pittiglio Rabin Todd McGrath (high-technology operations consulting), Navigant/SDG (decision consulting), Swander Pace & Co. (food, beverage and consumer products), Oliver Wyman (financial services)

Increasingly, companies are turning to consulting firms for recruiting and other HR services. Combined with changing workflows caused by technological integration of the workplace, globalization, and an increased need for responsive service, HR consulting has become a major growth segment.

To manage growth while maintaining staff and service quality, many consulting firms have placed renewed emphasis on retaining seasoned staff, focusing a "better lifestyles" trend in management consulting. In particular, The Big Five have come a long way toward making their work environments more enjoyable and helping employees balance work/family commitments. Many offer such perks as business casual attire, free flights to visit significant others, and concierge services such as dog walking (reported by Wetfeet.com, 1999). Improving work/life conditions for staff affect firm retention levels and service quality, making it a worthwhile investment.

Sidebar: CONSULTING FIRMS GROUPED BY TYPE (Continued)

Technology and Systems Consulting Firms

For individuals with a strong inclination toward technology and computer systems design and application, these firms provide excellent consulting opportunities. These firms typically take on large projects to design, implement and manage client information and computer systems. In contrast to strategy consulting, which involves work that can often be done at a home office, technology consulting takes place at the client's work site. A typical project might involve creating a new inventory–tracking system for a national retailer, a project that would require analyzing the client's informational needs, acquiring new hardware and writing source code to run the new system. Most such projects involve teams of consultants working together. Representative firms: American Management Systems, Andersen Consulting (as well as the Big Five consulting firms), Baan, Cambridge Technology Partners, Cap Gemini, Computer Sciences Corporation (CSC), EDS, IBM, PeopleSoft, SAP, Symmetrix,

E-Business Consulting Firms

Strategic Internet services, Internet professionals services, transactive content integrators. . . .these are just a few of the names used to describe consulting firms dedicated to helping companies do business on the Internet. Most such firms got their start making Web pages or CD-ROMs for clients. Today, these firms provide a range of services covering all aspects of e-commerce, whether it's providing high-level strategic consulting, creating content and software for online transactions, developing marketing plans, or analyzing Internet Infrastructures and network management. Unlike traditional consulting firms that may work on a single project for several years, e-business consulting firms focus on getting a client on the Web quickly and then continually fine-tuning the site. With e-consultants in high demand, this area should be extremely competitive. Representative firms: Agency.com, BroadVision, Cambridge Technology Partners, iXL, Proxicom, Razorfish, Sapient, Scient, T3 Media, USWeb/CRS, Viant

In technology sectors, it has become increasingly common for capital-constrained companies to offer consulting firms' equity in exchange for advice, demonstrating a trend called "equity consulting." This works for a couple of reasons. If the consulting firm offers useful advice that propels the company forward – helps it issue an IPO or get to the front of an industry – the consulting firm can earn more than it might otherwise have made from fees. The consulting firm also can gain valuable experience in a relatively new sector of the economy, which it can then sell to other businesses, establishing itself as a specialist.

Sidebar: CONSULTING FIRMS GROUPED BY TYPE (Continued)

Human Resources Consulting

Several consulting firms specialize in providing human resources advice. This can include everything from designing an employee-evaluation and compensation system to conducting organizational effectiveness training. Because this work is so important, HR consulting firms often work with relatively senior employees of client organizations. Representative firms: Andersen Consulting (Change Management Group), A. Foster Higgins, Alexander Consulting Group, Buck Consultants, the Hay Group, Hewitt Associates, KPMG, William M. Mercer Co.,The Wyatt Group PricewaterhouseCoopers, Towers Perrin,

Excerpted from Wetfeet .com, The Insiders Guide, 1999.

- The prodigious rate of expansion. Since 1990, revenue growth among consulting firms has averaged 10% or more annually. Among industry leaders, annual growth has exceeded 20%. These figures could be higher were it not for a shortage of quality recruits
- Firms have been busy colonizing the fast growing economies of Asia. Andersen Consulting alone added 4,000 new consultants to its Asian operations in the early nineties
- The earliest definition of management consulting – "advice giving to managers who must influence the system to change" – is not being heeded by specialized IT and business outsourcing firms that offer bright ideas without understanding the definition of management consultancy
- Consultancy's runaway success is remarkable for three reasons. First, it is so new. Second, unlike other professions, it generally lacks professional standards. Finally, companies do not have to employ consultants in the same way as employees within the enterprise

Ernst & Young and Andersen Consulting are leaders in a trend called "knowledge management." Each is familiar with the new technologies and information management tools. Each also excels in packaging and sharing the knowledge gained from the information collected. As a result, knowledge management offers a means by which client companies can work more effectively. The key to this area of consulting lies in creating meaningful "knowledge packages" that provide clients new understanding to enhance work outputs. Knowledge management is growing as a field and is fast becoming a priority trend for all consultants to make sense of.

Any attempt to draw conclusions about the evolution of the industry and the meaning it may have for the future would be futile without including an outsider's view.   The next section briefly describes the findings of a longitudinal effort to study the industry and provide guidance.

A view questioning consultants' business image An article appearing in the *Economist* summarizes the outsider's view of management consultants as advice givers. But the article's damaging conclusion — that "the management consulting business is a tale of mystery and imagination" – draws attention to how consultants are perceived in business circles today.

Mystery and imagination? This conclusion may have merit based on the following: In attempting to explain why management consulting firms have done so well, the *Economist* article reports that consultants are often the only ones willing to respond to "complexity" and "uncertainty." It has become both fashionable and necessary to respond quickly. For example, in projects requiring re-engineering and downsizing, which require consultants to change core processes, there is often little time or expertise to respect a holistic approach.

Much of consultancy's rapid development has to do with size – for the global imperative among most firms is "Grow, grow, grow!" Yet this imperative fails to consider core competency development, which is central to improving the consultant's image. It also fails to demystify the question of whether consultants are part of a full-fledged profession.

In retrospect, the evolutionary approach describing management consulting does not represent a unitary phenomenon, nor a successful perspective that might be utilized in the future. In contrast, the evolutionary perspective described here has produced a very problematic situation. It has produced a significant set of problems in search of a creative solution. Recognizing the importance of change in this context values the words of The Florida Speaker's Advisory Committee on the Future: "Strangely enough, in the midst of change, the present course may often be the most risky one. It may only serve to perpetuate irrelevancy." Pursuing the past evolutionary approach may only perpetuate irrelevancy for the consulting industry and its major proponents – consultants and clients alike. Pursuit of an evolutionary perspective must be abandoned. A new perspective focusing professional development to develop new, relevant competencies is needed.

A new perspective in management consulting Developing management consultants need a new perspective based in systemic learning; briefly defining the problem now evident, and then designing a solution that develops a new perspective is in order. The problem defined may be seen in fast moving, management consulting entities and unrelated masses, simultaneously moving on multi-directed courses, and embracing a dramatically changing environment without the necessary structure, function and process to guide development in the engagements undertaken. An innovatively designed solution for individuals and the consulting collectivity is required. It must be driven by a new generation of self-educators. It must be revolutionary in design, and "ideal seeking" to cultivate the unknown, learning from the future – as well as, the past. A new perspective describing an ideal-seeking learning system is clearly a worthwhile challenge in order to understand and to master management consulting.

Meeting the challenge of a new perspective to thrive

The new perspective gained by seeing the evolutionary process with new eyes not only helps one design a learning solution, it moves beyond to create a learning system. For the developing professional management consultant and the collectivity, the new perspective highlights the significance of learning now as well as in the future. The new perspective helps to fashion a learning system not only aids understanding and mastering, but perpetuates the search for the ideal in management consulting – ensuring that the developing management consultant is always in the process of *becoming*.

Designing a new learning system The learning system formulated has three distinct, iterative, and interactive parts to meet the developmental needs of both consultants and clients. They are: **LEARNING to BE** a management consultant; **LEARNING to LEARN** as a management consultant and to facilitate the learning of others; and **LEARNING to DO** as a management consultant. The learning system encompasses the next three parts of the book.

The initial identification of the three focal areas in the learning system was developed and used by Jamshid Gharajedaghi (2006) in his developmental work in Systems Thinking with the Oneida Nation. Focusing learning in these three areas is key to both his work in Systems Thinking practice and the structure of this book in its elaboration for the management consultant. This book has an applied focus that goes beyond the mere "how to" formulas that seldom work; the focus also seeks to strengthen the consultant's understanding — which directly effects his competency development and his performance in house and in the field.

LEARNING to BE is unique now, never existing in previous developmental approaches. LEARNING to BE is cultural education, where the culture of management consulting is identified and fostered. LEARNING to BE a management consultant does not focus on the knowledge required "to become," but in stark contrast focuses on creating the "desire necessary to become" a management consultant. LEARNING to BE is an emergent property – it is an ongoing and lifelong task. Essentially, this is new learning – learning to embrace desire in the fast developing culture of management consulting, and learning to develop the desire to move successfully with the newly forming profession.   LEARNING to BE remains a continuing challenge for consultants new to the field as well as the very seasoned – in reality, the management consultant is always in a "state of becoming."

LEARNING to LEARN is equivalent to formal education, but differing from our past formal education experience by redefining the goal of formal education as *self-education.* Becoming a self-educator frees the management consultant to consistently facilitate his own learning as well as that of others. Basically, the task is one of creating self-educators capable of learning, unlearning, and relearning accordingly in a non-linear fashion. Finally, learning from the future is critical to meet the challenges of today. Russell Ackoff says "the future is not completely contained in the past; much of it is to be written." Systems Thinking regards the future as co-producer along with the influence of the past and present. LEARNING to DO is professional education. In this part, **structure** and **function** are added to the consulting **process** by developing the application technology. The application technology identifies key strategies of intervention as applied in a four phased consulting systems framework – the consulting Systems Worldview (CSW). In Part IV two actual cases are worked through using the CSW for practice of the developing management consultant.

Requirements for system implementation The structure of the learning system provides considerable new learning for the developing management consultant as well as the seasoned consultants. Closer examination of this system demonstrates many new aspects to guide the consultant in development. Still, new guides to development are needed to bridge the distance.

New guides to development needed

Understanding and development of the necessary and sufficient structure, process, and function for the developing management consultant to thrive is a worthwhile challenge. Unfortunately, there is no magic or mystification that will do the work of understanding and development to thrive in the current environment.   Defining a new learning system perspective requires new guides to understand idealized design, new role definition, and a transformative process framework.

About idealized design in a new learning system Idealized design is a process for operationalizing the most exciting vision of the future that the designers can produce. It is the design of the next generation of the system to replace the existing order.   Idealizing does not design a nonfunctional dream system. The ideal learning system is designed to be self-sustaining in the current environment. The design has sufficient sources of variety to learn and adapt to possible environments. The beauty of an idealized learning system is that it is not a one-time proposition. Successive approximations in each use make up the process by which the transformation in learning is accomplished.

About a new role definition required Defining the contemporary role of management in the new environment is important. The boundaries of responsible work have been significantly enlarged as management consulting has evolved to a more complex form in a high-velocity world. It is still "advice giving to managers who then must influence the system to change," but many aspects of the advice giving are knowingly qualified. For example, in assisting in the change process, it has become critical to "transform" the organization. In another instance it is important to aid in "leading change" rather than simply facing change. A new definition of the management consultant is offered as a guide in transition: an advisory service to transform organizations, contracted for and provided by specially trained and qualified persons [Management Consultants] assisting in an objective and independent manner; working interdependently within the client system to participatively define the problem [system of problems] and to participatively design a solution that it solves the systemic problem in an evaluated implementation; by enveloping competencies that demonstrate new understanding and success, innovative results and meaning for the whole organization in leading systemic change.

About the Consulting Systems Worldview [CSW] framework The management consultant operates most successfully in a systemic fashion, using a four-phased transformation process as shown in Figure 2. The Consulting Systems Worldview (CSW). The structure of the Consulting Systems Worldview is the containing framework used by the consultant to   work   systematically   through   the   transformation   process   in organizations.   The CSW provides direction and boundaries for the management consultant in his interaction with the client system.

The transformation process in the Consulting Systems Worldview (CSW) has four defined phases approached systematically.   They are: A) Entry & Contracting, B) Data Collection & Problem Definition, C) Problem Solution & Action Planning, and D) Implementation & Evaluation. Intervention in the four phases of the CSW defines the management consultant's core competency, developed to successfully move through the transformation in every system addressed.   The fourth part of the book provides in depth knowledge and skill development, intervening in the four transformative phases using two unique, applied cases with different methodologies.

Transformation Process

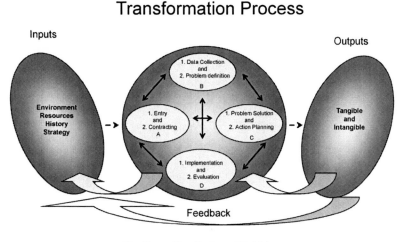

The Consulting Systems Worldview
© Marilyn E Harris, 1996

Figure 2.   The Consulting Systems Worldview (CSW)

Both the role of the management consultant (in terms of definition) and the Consulting Systems Worldview (CSW) will be presented in detail as each part develops.   Taken together, the management consultant's role definition and the new worldview form a foundation for a closer examination of how the consulting industry may develop and what may be required for it to thrive.

In reality, the learning foci introduce the management consultant to additional responsibilities to help meet the challenge inherent in mastering. For example, increasing the consultant's leveraging capability increases effectiveness in the assignment, and increases the consultant's capability to successfully develop client capability to lead change in the organization. This book opens wide the learning door for a century or more, identifying key rocks to understand and to master, and for developing management consultants creating ideal-seeking learning systems in each context to thrive now and in the future.

PART 2:
UNDERSTANDING the challenge of learning "TO BE"

To be, or not to be, that is the question: From Hamlet *Act 3, scene 1, line 55*
William Shakespeare [1620]

Could it be that the first line of Hamlet's speech -- undoubtedly the best known line in English literature – indicates the importance of "being" for the developing management consultant?   A careful reading of the first two chapters shows no easy road for the contemporary consultant to choose, and to follow in Learning to BE.   Many important rocks have been identified to place in the jar; but none that speak directly to "being." The challenge in Learning to BE is new.

PART 2   UNDERSTANDING
the challenge
of Learning
"TO BE"

Learning to BE is cultural education and development.   Ordinarily, neither cultural education, nor its development have been addressed in traditional educational settings.   In the past, formal delivery of cultural education was not necessary.   Cultural education was informally delivered by family members or special groups in localized settings – and only on a very individual basis.

However, in the late 20th century it became evident that local cultures had not developed sufficiently to become integrated global communities. Later, it became clear that this same lack was apparent in communities of professionals, businesses, and industry. Essentially, cultural education had been overlooked, for it was not necessary.   Later, it was recognized that these same groups and communities did not respect differences, nor were they capable of managing the conflicts created by these differences in their cultural settings and beyond.

The real challenge of Learning to BE is in the development of *human assets*, individually and collectively, within and beyond cultural boundaries. Cultural education is about reinvigorating the *ability* and the *desire* of the members to satisfy these needs -- both individually and collectively.   It is not easy to talk about reinvigorating the ability to desire. For the most part we are raised to believe that if we desire we have a right to attain. This is not so! It is important to learn how to develop the desire to BE -- to BE a management consultant in the 21st century. To BE is to develop the ability to desire first, separately, and then move into knowledge application.

Cultural development involves desires. This part of the book focuses on the cultural development of the management consultant and the importance of developing "a desire to do" before focusing on "ability" required in professional development. Desire appears to be the essential ingredient for an achieving society – and therefore critical for both the consultant and the client in Learning to BE. The additional task for the consultant-in-learning then becomes how I educate the client in developing "a desire to do?"

Chapter 3 focuses on Learning to BE, covering the whole spectrum of learning experiences that result in development in cultural education relating to management consulting. This type of cultural education results in both individual and collective development in arts, languages, sports, traditional ceremonies, and other quality-of-life enhancing activities. Specific topics to deepen the cultural learning are: increasing and improving emotional intelligence, unburying ethics and focusing values, developing breakthrough in creativity and art, using language learning to energize cultural education, defining leisure, recreation and sports, and rekindling the necessary desires to do so.

The challenge of managing chaos and complexity in the 21st century points to management consultants' need to learn differently. Specifically, the needs are spelled out in learning to BE **successful**, and in learning **leveraging** to lead transformative change – the foci of chapters 4 and 5.

In Learning to BE successful, the necessity of developing an attitude of success is explored through first understanding it in the context of failure. For example, one sees that when successful, it is actually a signal of failure. Thus, success is interpreted accordingly. Commonly, people interpret success as indicating direction for the future. In fact, in many cases "if an action result is good [successful], why not double or triple it?" The means of developing an attitude is discussed and the importance of conscious attitude change is stressed for the developing consultant. An attitude of success is necessary in rekindling Learning to BE.

Learning to lead transformative change is learning leveraging. Leveraging is likened to using a trim tab on a ship. A trim tab is a small mechanism on the rudder of ship, used to more efficiently and effectively turn a huge ship in the water. This analogy for the consultant leads to a comprehensive examination of leveraging to change systems rather than people. Leveraging uses a comprehensive framework to intervene – developing key metacompetencies to aid intervention and to reach success. The management consultant is challenged to lead change for transformative results.

As a result, the management consultant examines many new approaches to learning to BE in Part 2, adding many more big rocks and exploring relevant alternatives to his jar. Learning to more fully BE prepares the developing consultant for the next parts – Learning to LEARN, Learning to DO, and Learning from the FUTURE. This section sets a development pattern for the management consultant-in-learning, to think and act for himself first, and then consider the meaning and the value for the client in the current engagement and beyond.

Chapter 3   Learning to "BE"

Learning to BE defines a new area of study for the management consultant. Learning to BE is cultural education. Cultural education is developed both individually and collectively in management consulting. In the cultural education component, learning <u>how</u> to BE is focused in order *to create understanding and a full recognition of the need to BE* – a value for the individual consultant as well as the fast developing industry of consulting professionals. The focus and understanding of Learning to BE, as an integral part of the management consultant's developmental approach, is new.

Learning to BE is considered primary in the career development of the management consultant. In Learning to BE, the individual learner develops a reservoir of strength, vitality, energy, and initiative – a reservoir that will require refilling many times over a lifetime. Learning to BE is cultural education – now sorely missing in the developmental experience of management consultants.

It is important to develop the cultural education component of the developing management consultant for several reasons. First, to strengthen the character, the values, and the ethics of the developing person   and consulting collective.   In so doing, individually and collectively, management consulting becomes a stronger, healthier culture and can legitimately confront the current image of "of mystery and imagination," – in demonstrating a stronger healthier cultural foundation. The second, equally important if not primary, is in having the energy and vitality to manage both chaos and complexity so apparent in the world.

Learning to BE is a transforming experience. The individual gains intangible capability, energy, initiative, and vitality to lead in a fast moving world. Capability, energy, initiative, and vitality are needed to manage change for oneself, and to work cooperatively in the workplace.

The third reason is abilities remain latent unless they are energized by relevant desires. The many stresses of the fast paced competitive world (where management consultants must consistently intervene) require a constant intangible strength gained from energizing desire in Learning to BE. Chaos and complexity consistently drain desire, making re-energizing necessary.

Defining a new area

In learning to Be the cultural education covers the whole spectrum of learning experiences that result in both individual and collective development in arts, languages, sports, traditional ceremonies, and other quality-of-life enhancing activities that involve leisure time. Gharajedaghi (2006) says Learning to BE is essentially a character building activity. It is about values, worldviews, and identities.

"It involves desires as opposed to abilities; the capacity rather than the content; the direction rather than the speed; the whys rather than the hows; the feeling rather than the thinking; the meaning rather than the action; the process of becoming rather than the state of having. It is about doing the right thing rather than doing it right. Learning to BE involves aesthetics. Aesthetics, contrary to common belief, is not a luxury."

Gharajedaghi (2006, p. 205)

Ackoff (1997) explains aesthetics (art) from the apparently contradictory perspectives of Plato and Aristotle's different conceptions – as the two inseparable aspects of *ideal-pursuit,* most necessary in Learning to BE. Plato wrote in THE REPUBLIC that art was a potentially dangerous stimulant that threatens the stability of a society. Aristotle saw it as cathartic, a palliative for dissatisfaction, hence a producer of stability and contentment. He saw art as something from which one extracts satisfaction here and now, as recreation.

These contradictory views of art are actually complementary; they are two inseparable aspects of ideal-pursuit – which is actually what Learning to BE is all about, *"for art inspires, it produces an unwillingness to settle for what we have and a desire for something better."* Learning to BE helps the learner to experience being inspired, and to experience inspiration of others. Inspiration is important in pursuing the ideal, and in realizing the energy it takes in attainment of the ideal – an ideal, that in reality is quite impossible to attain.   Further, it helps with the understanding that although one may never reach the ideal, one may still be inspired to try.   Understanding the need for inspiration and consistently reaching out to attain the ideal makes inspiration and stretching to reach the unattainable ideal acceptable. Inspiration is an important desire in itself, and it has tremendous value to the individual and to the collectivity in management consulting – for both the client and the consultant.

Art is the product and the producer of creative activity and change. Art is essential for continuous improvement. Art is so necessary in our contemporary competitive settings. Art entertains, recreates, yielding fun from what we do regardless of why we do it. Ackoff (1997) says of art, that it is the satisfaction derived from "going there" in contrast to the satisfaction derived from "getting there." Recreation provides "the pause that refreshes." It recreates creators. We would not be able to maintain the continuous pursuits of ideals without rewards along the way.

The cultural education of Learning to BE inspires, and develops desire for something better. Cultural development involves acquiring the feeling or sense of and the experience of desire. It is noted that desires are the essential ingredient for the creation of an achieving society.

Recognizing the meaning of and understanding the use of "desires" is the critical aspect to learn in the Learning to BE component for management consultants. Creating desire and learning to create desire takes time. Creating desire is difficult to acquire in many instances, because there is little time and effort focused on developing the desire to BE. Many persons in the fast developing industry simply say: "I want to be a consultant!" And in many cases, "*abbra cadabbra*," like magic, they are named one! Simply by saying the words, no actual effort or energy is expended in developing the necessary desire to BE. At this time, many appear to become, in fact, without first becoming.

Why management consultants need first to Learn to BE

To avoid short circuiting the learning process, it appears that one must go seriously about character building activities first. Directly addressing learning, in this case, requires a conscious effort and time to develop the "desire" to BE. Although conscious and intentional, it may not be the same "how to" process for each individual. The process may be exploratory and defined individually for each participant in the learning process. It takes time to intentionally design the learning experience, based in one's own initiative. It must be done when the individual is ready – not on someone else's timeline. Sometimes, one must experience a sense of question and "iffy-ness," -- actually wondering as one proceeds, if this is the right road. The self-questioning involved is a part of the ownership process creating desire.

Educational experiences for management consultants in Learning to BE focus on developing "desire" in contrast to developing ability. Developing desire is not a classroom activity, similar to teaching math or science. First of all, the desire to be developed is internal to the learner, not external being transferred to the internal. For the individual learner to increase his capacity to desire, the opportunity to observe exciting, vivid experiences with deep feeling in the life space of an active model, is basic, but not sufficient. Learning, in this case, requires deep change in retooling of ingrained habits of thought, feeling, and behavior.

Further, developing desire requires the opportunity to practice a new habit, and to develop the neural circuitry in the brain. It's not like sitting in a classroom. For example, take the case of learning a new language which requires much trial and error, much change of the neural circuitry in the brain over a period of time. To be able to speak in another language is ability, and the process of getting there is developed through "desiring." Desiring is a separate, but closely related process. It is the desiring that gets one to the ability. "Desiring" is a closely related process that is usually not recognized. This "unknowing" may be due to the focus on practicing the new ability. It is "desiring" that is the critical component in learning, and thus in acquisition of the ability. In reality, once desiring is operationalized, learning becomes possible and then fun. The process of acquiring the ability is actually hastened.

Reflect for a moment on some of your learning experiences that have been fun – is it not because of your attaining or near attainment of a new ability that is desired. One often sees this "fun of learning" in young children who yet cannot name desiring, but who are most actively desiring the attainment of a specific ability – and enjoying it. For an adult to unbury "desiring" is an important step in Learning to BE.

The learning required in 'desiring' It is important to think and act on the character building in Learning to BE as a separate learning activity. This is difficult for many, for it may soon appear as an ability to learn. It is not. In character building the management consultant has four factors to consider:

- Understanding how *learning* occurs
- Understanding that *learning* is an emergent property
- Understanding that for the best results *learning* must be a conscious and an intentional activity

- Understanding that *learning* in Learning to BE is both an individual and collective experience

For most people, management consultants included, actively responding to these factors individually and simultaneously is a huge challenge. It often requires some thinking and experience of first respecting the idea of Learning to BE to be able to meet the challenge. Often in the consultant learning context the need to Learn to BE is not apparent. There is no value attached to desiring. In many cases, the arrogance of "I am" or "I know" short-circuits any learning. Some reflection on these factors may be helpful.

First, recall that *learning results from being surprised: detecting a mismatch between what was expected to happen and what actually did happen. One has learned only when understanding of the mismatch occurs, and that mismatch can be avoided in the future.* Thus, learning can be said to occur only when the new behavior observed is different from the earlier response. However, the difference is not guaranteed to be in a positive direction. Positive or improved behavior in a situation takes additional structuring in the learning experience to develop movement in a positive direction. Thus, when learning occurs from a mismatch, in the Learning to BE context, the management consultants must gain capability in recognizing the mismatch in the use of time and realizing the focus that desiring brings. The challenge is in enjoying or having fun desiring something. It is like suspending "time" in space. This is very much of an unplanned event, which makes it difficult to experience in many situations. Essentially, the intangibility contributes to its difficulty in experiencing it. Trying to be alert to something that one does not know or value at the time, makes it difficult to experience learning through a mismatch.

Learning to BE is an emergent property – meaning that the desire-generating processes in learning must be continuously reproduced online and in real time. As we have seen, the property of learning BEing cannot be stored or saved for future use. Learning BEing results from developing the capacity to desire. Therefore the continual use of desiring is critical, otherwise the learning being phenomena will cease to exist.

Intentionality experienced in a conscious effort at learning appears to make learning 'desiring' possible, and clearly more visibly known to the learner. For when one is attending intentionally, there is more of a chance that one may notice the subtle differences that are apparent.

Understand that learning necessarily comes first for the individual and yet quite simultaneously for the management consulting collectivity – for cultural learning does not happen in a vacuum or only through individual work. It is not natural for individuals or for collectivities to think about the need for cultural education, and to consciously make the effort to be involved and to learn. Learning occurs when the individual brings thoughts and meaning to the verbal level, articulating the concept publicly. Psychologists tell us that verbalizing the thinking is a reinforcing process that involves several systems and makes "learning" as such possible. This process of expression in learning desire is just as important for the individual as for the collectivity involved in cultural education.

At this point, realizing that there is much more to learning how to BE than simply addressing a new form of learning in the traditional rote sense is a major first step. The recognition of a new type of learning to BE gives credence to cultural education for management consultants. To learn 'desiring', one must be able to manage the interactions involved in the areas of feeling or emotional competence, aesthetics and the arts, language and languages, generativity, ethics and values, creativity and recreation. These are the key components involved in developing the capacity to desire in Learning to BE.

Consultants must first Learn to BE to develop the stamina necessary to manage complexity in the consulting assignment. To successfully manage complexity the consultant must be culturally sensitive to his own needs and to the developmental requirements of the client population. For many, this two-step management process is new and not surprisingly, a real challenge. Coping with the all-encompassing magnitude of this challenge is at the base of understanding why management consultants must first Learn to BE. Managing both chaos and complexity in the client system takes a tremendous amount of energy. The toll is even higher when the consultant has not learned to BE and is 'desiring' to be an outstanding management consultant. The issues appear non-understandable and therefore non-addressable. Usually, then these issues are avoided in the consulting assignment.

Reviewing for a moment the complexities caused by the dual paradigm shift [using a newly required sociocultural organization model and a new synergic systemic process of inquiry] focuses the complexity of change in the world. Both of these shifts require diametrically opposed outcomes than those required in the 20th century. To address these successfully, certainly the consultant must be together in his own Being, before attempting to assist the client developing new understanding to make the necessary change.

Proceeding systematically, first it is important to develop consulting capability in Learning to BE. That is, in desiring to BE a management consultant, while at the same time proceeding on a collective theme in strengthening the management consulting culture. The latter is challenging, for it is a culture that does not exist as a unitary culture. To strengthen the management consulting culture, consultants must begin to value their culture, not their jobs as consultants. The culture will be strengthened as individual consultants strengthen themselves in Learning to BE, in this way strengthening both the product and the producer.

Management consultants must clarify their need of "desiring" in their own practice, recognizing the value contributed to "Being an outstanding consultant", likewise, knowing the difference between desire and ability respecting the contribution of each in development. The constant task is to re-energize both self and clients in revitalizing the complex situations. Reviving ethics and values as a means of measuring success in the results is basic. Recreation provides a freshened spirit and the drive to continue in difficult circumstances. Developing desire to Be focuses energy in character building, assisting the collective learning to Be.

Learning to BE is . . .

Learning to BE is developing competence in creating "desire and the ability to desire" to relate in a specific culture. The term "ability to desire" means "owning" it. It is creating a psychological identity with the culture by creating desire for it. For example, in consulting the desire and the ability to desire may be developed in several ways. Initially, desire may be developed by shadowing consultants to identify that which exists. One may investigate other's existent desire:

- By attending meetings with consultants
- In conversation, clarifying the role of the consultants
- In experiencing, albeit second hand, the excitement and sheer joy
- of the consultants when they identify the transformative outcomes that will produce an order of magnitude improvement in the client situation

- By spending leisure time with consultants by learning to understand what their life is like when they are alone and separate from the client
- By experiencing the sense of dilemma in diagnosis which consultants often face
- By observing how consultants sort out the words to use in "advice giving"
- By experiencing what it is really like when the consultant is with the client
- By grasping the meaning of ethical dilemmas
- By identifying with the stresses of consulting, and
- By recognizing the value of limitations and boundaries

Investigation leads to understanding the need for developing the capacity to desire in Learning to BE. More active development in creating desire comes through managing interactions in a variety of settings. The settings identified earlier are: emotional intelligence, creativity and aesthetics, ethics and values, languages, and leisure and recreation. These areas are described below, opening some new doors for the developing management consultant to explore in Learning to BE.

Increasing and improving emotional intelligence   Recently several authors (Rueven Bar-on, John D. Meyer, Peter Salovey, and Daniel Goleman) have done considerable work in the area of emotional intelligence, defining emotional competence as an important factor in the business success equation, Goleman (1998) describes the generation of desire as motivation.   He has developed an Emotional Competence Framework as shown in Figure 3, defining emotional competence in two broad areas: personal and social competence. In his defining framework, motivation (desire) is made up of the personal competencies of achievement drive, commitment, initiative, and optimism.

Daniel Goldman (1998) says the rules of work are changing. He says "we are being judged by a new yardstick. This new measuring device is emotional intelligence and essentially it is how well we handle ourselves and each other." In Goleman's research he points out that close to 90% of leadership is emotional intelligence (Goleman, 1998, p.34). Until recently many thought that leadership was about 80% technical knowledge. These findings certainly support management consultants developing their emotional intelligence as a means of creating desire to BE.

Increasing generativity   Generativity is about generating good things (and people). Giving birth to a child is perhaps the most fundamental form of generativity. People can give birth to many different kinds of things – starting from a new company, to making music, to consulting, and coming up with a new solution to a problem. Generativity is also about caring for those things (and people) that are generated, with an eye toward promoting the next generation. In generativity, one comes to accept that people will not live forever, and therefore seeks to leave a positive legacy for the future, in that way leaving a part of oneself behind. According to the noted psychoanalyst Erik Erikson, who gave us the term "identity crisis" – people begin to focus their lives on generativity as they move in their thirties, forties, and fifties. In the middle-adult years, Erikson wrote, a person may come to realize, "I am what survives me."

A growing body of psychological research shows that being highly generative is a sign of psychological health and maturity. People who score high on measures of generativity tend to report higher levels of happiness and well being in life, compared to people who score low. High generativity is also associated with low levels of depression and anxiety.

While generativity may be good for the developing and seasoned management consultant alike, it is good for the 'society of management consultants' as well. The two faces of generativity are power and love, forces that often conflict in people's lives. Our narcissistic need to develop and expand the self may conflict with our more altruistic need to care for and help others. In generativity, however, we have both. What we generate becomes a legacy of the self, and we care for that legacy selflessly. The fullest expressions of generativity blend power and love. Many consultants when interviewed talk of a highly generative career. Many life stories reflect the theme of personal redemption.

Highly generative adults, consultants in this case, tend to tell stories with what psychologists call "redemption sequence," where a bad scene or event gives way to a positive outcome, which redeems the initial bad event. The diagnosis or problem definition is often seen as the bad scene and the positive outcome is in the implemented problem solution. Adults inclined toward generativity tend to see their own lives and world in redemptive terms. Bad things may happen. Suffering and pain are inevitable. For example, the psychological pain associated with change is important and inevitable in changing. But good things will often result, if one keeps faith and hope alive. Erik Erikson argued that to be generative, people must have a basic "belief in the species." People must have faith that despite suffering and setback, despite evil, human life can be good, for generations to come. This belief sustains the most difficult generative efforts. Holding out hope for ultimate redemption gives us faith that our legacies will be good, and that things may work out in the long run.

Psychological health depends on how we see the future and what we do to bring about the kind of future we wish to see. Generativity takes people beyond the short-term gains we often seek in daily life and orients us to the long run. "I am what survives me." It is important to imagine what is pictured as the good that will outlive you. Perhaps the consultant sees the client flourishing as a result of her interventions. Perhaps the management consultant sees successful organizations structured in some new ways. Perhaps you see a world at peace.

The most generative people are constantly imagining bright futures. For example, they envision a better world for themselves, their families, and their society. When one imagines the future that way, it sensitizes you to the sacredness of life on earth. The most generative people among us cherish life as if it were a beautiful infant.

The Emotional Competence Framework
PERSONAL COMPETENCE

These competencies determine how we manage ourselves

SELF AWARENESS: Knowing one's internal states, preferences, resources, and intuitions
    Emotional Awareness: Recognizing one's emotions and their effects
    Accurate self assessment: Knowing one's self-worth and capabilities
    Self Confidence: A strong sense of one's self worth and capabilities

SELF REGULATION: Managing one's internal states, impulses, and resources
    self- control: Keeping disruptive emotions and impulses in check
    Trustworthiness: Maintaining standards of honesty and integrity
    Conscientiousness: Taking responsibility for personal performance
    Adaptability: Flexibility in handling change
    Innovation: Being comfortable with novel ideas, approaches and information

MOTIVATION: Emotional tendencies that guide or facilitate reaching goals
    Achievement Drive: Striving to improve or meet a standard of excellence
    Commitment: Aligning with the goals of the group or organization
    Initiative: Readiness to act on opportunities
    Optimism: Persistence in pursuing goals despite obstacles and setbacks
SOCIAL COMPETENCE

These competencies determine how we handle relationships

EMPATHY: Awareness of others' feelings, needs and concerns
    Understanding Others: Sensing others' development needs and bolstering their abilities
    Developing Others: Sensing others' development needs and bolstering their abilities
    Service Orientation Anticipating, recognizing, and meeting customers' needs
    Leveraging Diversity: Cultivating opportunities through different kinds of people
    Political Awareness: Reading a group's emotional currents and power relationships

SOCIAL SKILLS: Adeptness at inducing desirable responses in others
    Influence: Wielding effective tactics for persuasion
    Communication: Listening openly and sending convincing messages
    Conflict Management: Negotiating and resolving disagreements
    Leadership: Inspiring and guiding individuals and groups
    Change Catalyst: Initiating and managing change
    Building Bonds: Nurturing instrumental relationships
    Collaboration and Cooperation: Working with others towards shared goals
    Team Capabilities: Creating group synergy in pursuing collective goals

Figure 3. The Emotional Competence Framework
© Daniel Goleman 1998

An African proverb says, "The world was not left to us by our parents. It was lent to us by our children." What survives me are the world's children, for those whose sake I act today. It is as if the most generative people among us most readily envision the future's children, as if they see the baby watching them. Innocent and dependent on our own efforts to care, the future looks to each of us with hope. When consultants can act in a generative manner, transferring the generative capability to employees and to leaders alike, in the organizations in which they intervene, there is much hope for the future – with all of its chaos and complexity to manage.

Unburying ethics and focusing values Generally, ethics and values are communal creations within a culture. They are conceptions or principles of good and bad that emerge in the process of relationship. Management consultants in the past have been encouraged to develop a set of ethical principles or a code of conduct to practice and live by. This has always been touted as "desirable" means of approaching the base of successful practice.

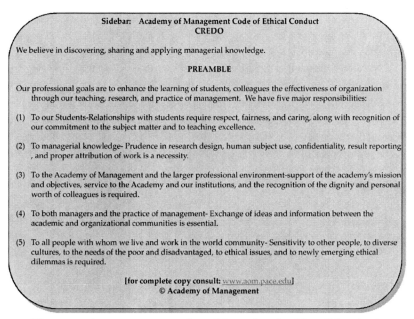

Sidebar: Academy of Management Code of Ethical Conduct
CREDO

We believe in discovering, sharing and applying managerial knowledge.

PREAMBLE

Our professional goals are to enhance the learning of students, colleagues the effectiveness of organization through our teaching, research, and practice of management. We have five major responsibilities:

(1) To our Students-Relationships with students require respect, fairness, and caring, along with recognition of our commitment to the subject matter and to teaching excellence.

(2) To managerial knowledge- Prudence in research design, human subject use, confidentiality, result reporting, and proper attribution of work is a necessity.

(3) To the Academy of Management and the larger professional environment-support of the academy's mission and objectives, service to the Academy and our institutions, and the recognition of the dignity and personal worth of colleagues is required.

(4) To both managers and the practice of management- Exchange of ideas and information between the academic and organizational communities is essential.

(5) To all people with whom we live and work in the world community- Sensitivity to other people, to diverse cultures, to the needs of the poor and disadvantaged, to ethical issues, and to newly emerging ethical dilemmas is required.

[for complete copy consult: www.aom.pace.edu]
© Academy of Management

However, in many cases when this code of ethics did exist it was foreign or never consciously raised with the organization contracting the consultant. In reality, the code when it existed, was always extrinsic to the organization. In the case of moral principle and pragmatic sanction of an ethical code, perhaps the problem is that of extrinsic origin – that is, efforts toward the good originate outside the organization itself, and never become a focus in the consultant-client relationship. Globalization has increased complexity significantly, with an enormous intensification of ethical conflict.

For example, as organizations expand into foreign locales, so do they import alien constructions of what is real and good. From their standpoint, their actions seem reasonable, even commendable, local traditions seem parochial, backward, or even reprehensible (surely in need of change). From the local standpoint, however, the ways of life favored by the globalizing organization often seem invasive, insensitive to local customs and community, and even deeply immoral. There is an important sense in which much of the invective directed against the multinational corporation is derived from just this condition – with the corporation and the management consultant evaluated by standards that are largely alien or are differently construed from within as opposed to outside. The problem is not that of ruthless and colonizing organizations seeking world dominion; "ruthlessness" and colonization are the epithets of the outsider. Rather, the problem is that of competing constructions of the good. And without means of solving these conflicts, we face the problem of deterioration in relations, legal warfare, and even bloodshed.

From the present standpoint, we find that problems of ethical conduct are essentially not problems of malignant intention. Rather ethical problems result primarily from the clashing of cultural standards of action. For the management consultant it is clear that whenever an organization coalesces and expands, so does its mission destabilize and violate accepted standards of the good. As a world of globalization without limit continues, what resources are available to the management consultant to proceed?

First, the management consultant must realize that the modern organization has several shortcomings clearly defined as new challenges and adjustments, each of which undermines its viability (Gergen, 1994). For example, the new challenges and adjustments are noted as the: dispersion of intelligibilities, disruption in chains of authority, erosion of rationality, reduction in centralized knowledge, and the undermining of authority – all quite familiar to the management consultant. These shortcomings are the seeds of ethical conflict and render the organization dysfunctional.

For the consultant, Gergen (1994) points out that this means that he does not try to fix these dysfunctions in the traditional way, but considers a new conception of relational processes. Relational processes are developed from interactions between key actors that develop interpersonal relationships. The new conception is evident in the processes of interdependence and relational coordination to achieve the dual ends of organizational sustenance and ethical well being. The relational process is a basis for ethical vision and is intrinsically ethical.

It is essential for the practicing management consultant to shift from the conception of ethical principles from which practices are derived to forms of ethically generative practice. That is, practices providing for conjoint valuing and the synergistic blending of realities. This is a relational process by which management consultants join with client practitioners to develop a range of potentials – concepts, visions, metaphors, stories -- that may encourage the development of ethically generative practices on the site of the consultation (see example in the sidebar). The key management experiences are relational in character and emphasize dialogic process, multiple logics, and permeable boundaries within organizational spheres and between the organization and its external context. Consider the set of practices in the sidebar case that possess ethically generative potential.

> **Sidebar: A Company doing Research on Genetic Engineering showing the Use of Ethically Generative Practice**
>
> The company was placed under sharp critical attack for its research on genetic engineering. An information campaign, mounted to inform the public of the positive effects of such research, did nothing to dissuade an increasingly vocal organization of dissenters. The company then shifted to a relational orientation, in which they proposed to the opposition that they work cooperatively to create a public exhibition informing the public of their diverse views on these complex and emotionally charged issues. After much active discussion, the various participants agreed on a set of informative exhibits that were subsequently displayed at a city cultural center. The exhibition was praised for its balance and open design. Company representatives felt that there had also been an informative exchange of opinions with the opposition; both sides had developed more differentiated and appreciative views, and the public had been exposed to the multiple issues involved.
>
> *Excerpted from Gergen (1999)*

For the management consultant to develop ethically generative practice, she must go beyond self and collective developing the interdependent relational processes of the client organization. This point is raised to clarify that sometimes one must go beyond the defined context to learn from the larger context. The rule to apply is constant recognition of the goal at hand, considering the appropriate context for development to occur.

Some may say that the management consultant cannot develop ethical generative practice without first considering a personal code of ethics. Certainly, one must recognize that an understanding of ethics and values of the individual impinges on any collective approach, and that by the time one is considering being a management consultant, one has been exposed to the basics involved in a code of ethics. However, the basic issue in both cases, is that personal and ethically generative practice is not exposure, but is articulation for practice in the context.

In conclusion, unburying ethics and focusing values means developing interdependent relationships within the organization calling attention to the new forms of coordinated activity. In this sense, both the individual and the collective are dealt with simultaneously. There are no single individuals making autonomous decisions, but forming relationships out of which action decisions become intelligible. An individual, then, is the common locus for a multiplicity of relationships. The capacity for ethically generative practice is dependent on participation in the processes of relational coordination.

Developing breakthrough creativity and art   The value for the management consultant of developing breakthrough creativity and experiencing the art of it is in the process of breaking through to a new reality. The value is in both being capable of being present during the "going there" as well as recognizing the "getting there." Jerome Bruner, a distinguished psychologist, describes the hallmark of a creative experience is the ability to generate "effective surprise."

Effective surprise "need not be rare or infrequent or bizarre and is often none of these things." Instead, it has " the quality of obviousness" about it, "producing a shock of recognition following which there is no longer astonishment."   In other words, the best breakthroughs evoke a delightful sense of inevitability. You see them and say, "Aha, of course!" The surprise is that, in retrospect, it shouldn't have been that much of a surprise. How else could the problem have been solved?

Creating is not a one time experience, it is a lifelong journey. The journey according to Jung, is "a lifetime's task which is never completed, a journey upon which one sets out hopefully toward a destination at which one never arrives." The challenge is Learning to BE is to get started, to take the first step, for it is never too early – or too late to be what you might have been.

J. Robert Oppenheimer talks of this experience as discovery. He says "discovery follows discovery; each raising and answering questions, each ending a long search, and each providing the new instruments for a new search. In that light it is developmental and one does not stay in the same place all the time.

Then for the management consultant in Learning to BE the business of generating effective surprise, that is, producing a shock of recognition following which there is no longer astonishment is an ongoing experience that creates an inward sense of excitement and pleasure with self. Often this creative energy as it is called, this experiencing of Being, powers one or the collective in other areas without further direction to do so. Creating breakthrough in understanding often brings the example to show others, providing entry to a specific operational task. Lynne Levesque's book (2001) on breakthrough creativity is a guide to the developing management consultant.

Using language to energize cultural education In Learning to BE the cultural education component can be significantly energized by developing language. In developing language, either the base language or a new language is for the purpose of enhancing the quality of life in the culture. However, the major value in either case is the flexibility within the brain that is caused through development of the language arts. For example, flexibility within the brain is demonstrated when moving from one language to another, the brain moves to another area to access the second language. This movement actually energizes the brain and the Being with the action involved. There is also a stretching activity enlarging the language capability and it tends to have carry-over in enhancing the quality of life in the culture. Increasing interpretative ability when moving from one language to another enhances cultural aspects.

A holistic language is a language of systems, which allows us to understand complexity (Gharajedaghi, 2006). He describes a language of interaction and design that will help us learn a new mode of living by considering various ways of seeing, doing, and being in the world. It is possible then to design new methods of inquiry, new modes of organization, and a way of life that will allow the rational, emotional and ethical choices for interdependent yet autonomous social beings. This new language is being created as we experience new modes of living – recall some of the things named and in use from NASA experience in outer space. Learning a language energizes cultural education in many ways.

Increasing leisure, recreation, and sports Each area contributes significantly to acquiring desire, from different perspectives. Leisure allows one the time to reflect and to value, making desire to BE a need that can be met. Recreation re-creates the creative experience. Essentially to create again, so as one might experience again the joy and therefore the desire gained in the activity. Recreation takes many forms, and one of them is sports. In participating in the action, the movement of any sport, there is release of tension and anxiety.–tension and anxiety that may be preventing you from fully participating and gaining the experience so as to better desire. This is a type of inspiration, producing an unwillingness to settle for the experience itself, but producing a desire for something better. It is much as art, but has a physical component developing desire.

Participation in leisure, recreation, and sports in the U.S. is greatly aided by avid marketing of travel agents, the many different sports – both amateur and professional – wide visibility on television and radio, and the general hype about involvement in group activities – business and social. However, passive participation as a spectator does not have the same payoff to the individual. The developing management consultant needs to look for and develop means to keep work and play in balance by "planning their play [leisure, recreation and sports] before their work." Increasing leisure, recreation, and sports to keep your life in balance is a critical part of Learning to BE. Most often, the
developing consultant believes that she can get by without leisure, recreation, or sports right now – these are definitely to be planned for in the future!

"To BE, or not to BE, that is the question." Shakespeare wrote Hamlet's immortal speech in the play, containing this first line quoted here, about 1620. It is quite obvious that "being" was an issue even then and it has continued to be high on the list over the years. This soliloquy may be applied to the developing management consultant phrase by phrase – as a reexamination of the relevant aspects of "being or not being' a consultant in the 21st century. For it is in the consideration of "not being' that the real value of "being" becomes known. Shakespeare had a real knack for focusing the crux of the issue being considered. That is one reason his plays have lived so long and done so well at the box office. Can developing professionals, as well as those highly seasoned, not gain from an examination of self being a management consultant – or not being a management consultant from time to time. Is this not a way to become generative around ethics in the workplace? Others may join in and help to answer the question afresh, possibly several times in each engagement or major task. In that way, a centered "being" remains as a positioning tool, moving the management consultant ahead to a point of action regardless of the choice. One may take Hamlet's soliloquy as a means of keeping current and re-evaluating your role in the fast developing profession regularly.

How to rekindle the necessary 'desire to BE'

"The vitality of a culture is in its potency to act as a vehicle for the realization of the societies' shared dreams (Gharajedaghi, 2006)." In management consulting this is developing the capability to desire an outstanding culture with shared dreams and the potency to act. A potent culture can rekindle the necessary desires. Ultimately, cultural vitality is measured by success in getting the traditional symbols and images to support the emerging needs of a progressive society. Management consulting as a culture is on the verge of becoming a progressive society. The challenge is to rekindle the necessary desires in Learning to BE.

Respect for the management consulting culture or any culture, for that matter, does not imply regression nor should progress mean a break with the past. Old values themselves were born in response to new needs. In the context of the developing management consultant, innovation is getting these powerful engines reconnected to the emerging needs that are replacing the ones that may have outlived the reason for which they were born. In summary, rekindling is innovatingly getting the powerful engines of desire reconnected to the emerging needs and generating a stronger, healthier management consulting culture for the individual and for others to join.

In summary, many means to rekindle have been described here. It is now relevant to practice, to try out, and to hone your own approach to Learning to BE, for as stated earlier this is an emergent property that will take regeneration regularly to keep it alive and functioning as a resource to the consultant. It is surprising what a resource Learning to BE can become for individuals and collectivities as they develop the many different aspects in cultural education working through the learning system.

Chapter 4   Learning to BE successful

I am done with great things and big plans, great institutions and big successes. I am for those tiny, invisible loving human forces that work from individual to individual, creeping through the crannies of the world like so many rootlets, or like the capillary oozing of water, yet which, if given time, will rend the hardest monuments of human pride.

- William James

Standard social and business practices are built on certain assumptions – shared understandings that have evolved from older beliefs and conditions. While circumstances may have changed since the start of these practices, their continued use tends to reconfirm the old beliefs and attitudes. For this reason our daily practices feel right and true to us, regardless of whether they have evolved to keep up with the pace of change. In just such a way a business culture arises and perpetuates itself, perhaps long after its usefulness has passed.

This book offers attitudes and practices that are transformational. These may feel illogical or counterintuitive to our normal understanding of how things operate. Their purpose is to initiate a new approach, based on uncommon assumptions about the nature of the world. The history of transformational phenomena – the internet, for example, or paradigm shifts in science, or the spread of a new religion – suggests that transformation happens less by arguing cogently for something new than by generating active, ongoing practices that shift a culture's experience of the basis for reality. So the practices presented here are not about making incremental changes that lead to new ways of doing things based on old beliefs. They are not about self-improvement. Instead, the practices are geared toward causing a total shift of posture, perceptions, attitude, beliefs, and thought processes. They are about transforming your entire world, beginning with developing an attitude of success.

Developing an attitude of success in the management consultant

To learn to BE successful is to learn how to meet the challenge of repeated success in different contexts by creating a new "universe of possibility" (Zander & Zander, 2000). To learn to BE successful is to understand success in the consulting context. Webster defines attitude as "a mental position with regard to a fact or a state". Research defines attitude as "a psychological tendency that is expressed by evaluating a particular entity with some degree of favor or disfavor" (Eagly & Chaiken, 1993). Psychological tendency is explained as an internal state of a person (not directly observable) that produces an evaluative response (overtly or covertly in a cognitive, affective, or behavioral fashion) to a particular entity. The evaluative response forms the attitude. Figure 4. The Attitude Formation Process organizes people's experience, both inferred and observable, according to the processes involved in attitude development.

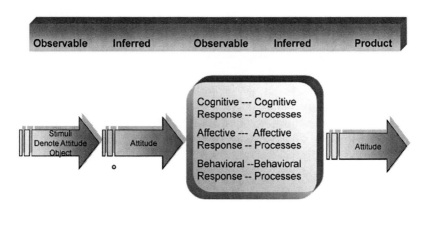

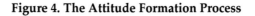

The Attitude Formation Process
© M. E. Harris (adapted 1999)

Figure 4. The Attitude Formation Process

Attitudes are shaped by these functions:

- Adjustment function presumes that attitudes enable people to maximize rewards in their environment and to minimize punishments. Attitudes satisfy this function by means of a presumed tendency for people to form favorable attitudes toward stimuli associated with satisfaction of needs and unfavorable attitudes toward stimuli associated with punishment

- Ego-defensive function enables people to protect themselves from unpleasant realities
- Value-expressive function allows people to express their personal values and self-concept

The key is learning to desire an attitude of success. In developing an attitude of success, two factors are valuable.   First, recognizing that *"learning to desire an attitude of success"* is necessary. Secondly, identifying "success" as the objective before starting to work. Repeating these two steps each time may develop the desire, and an attitude of success in each context of work. However, practice without intention to learn does not guarantee the outcome. The developing consultant must be intentional, must truly desire, and truly objectify success very specifically in each context anew. This opens a vast universe of possibility – in concept and practice. It does, in fact, destroy the opportunity to default and to repeat the old ways of reaching success from the past, just as recycling a prior business plan in a new environment would be ineffective. Developing the desire to BE successful in each context programs the consultant's interventions toward success. Of course, being successful can never be fully programmed, nor guaranteed.

The challenge is to develop a passionate desire for an attitude of success. Developing passion energizes action in the context. Energized action enables the consultant to move through transformative change in the consulting engagement.

Your attitude is the sum total of your beliefs, assumptions, expectations, and values, and therefore influences the way you define and interpret your experiences. Because attitude involves beliefs, assumptions, expectations, and values, it determines the meaning or significance you attach to events and the response to them. Attitude is everything. Attitude is the way one responds to life each day – all day. Our lives encircle all that we are mentally, emotionally, physically, and financially – all 360 degrees contribute to attitude. This is why it is so critical to cultivate a desire to develop an attitude of success.

David Maister (1997) finds that an attitude of success is the defining difference between a professional and technician. In his experience a "professional" possesses an attitude of success, while a "technician" does not. Maister points to the importance of attitude as an energizer, energizing "passion," which defines the difference and the quality of the end product.   With this preliminary introduction to developing an attitude of success, a more robust understanding of success in the context of failure is addressed in the next section.

Understanding Success in the context of failure

Recall the earlier dialogue on the conversion of success to failure. The dialogue pointed out that the forces that convert success to failure form a five-level hierarchy (Level 1: Imitation, Level 2: Inertia, Level 3: Sub-optimization, Level 4: Change of the Game, Level 5: Shift of paradigm). Each level represents a distinct tendency, but together they form an interactive whole whereby higher levels provide the context for lower levels. At each level success plays a critical but different role in causing failure. It is important to note that once the problem is dissolved, or effectively solved, the concerns associated with the problem earlier are irreversibly affected. The problem no longer exists.

It is far better to develop a basic understanding of the hierarchy of forces that cause the conversion of success to failure, than to repeatedly experience failure. It is also important to realize that success happens in the context of failure. Success marks the beginning of the end. Success means it is time to think about creating a new success, and not repeating the same approach completed earlier.

Understanding that there is a hierarchy of forces that cause the conversion of success to failure, and that it is not the devil that is overturning success, is helpful. This knowledge also provides the foundation for focusing on defining success in each situation. The focus should be identify and develop a desire for an *attitude* of success, and not success in and of itself. Yet, being able to define successful results in each situation, in a concrete and specific fashion, is a real accomplishment. Successful results feed and cultivate the desire for an attitude of success in the developing consultant *and* in the client.

Yet, it is still difficult to understand that acquiring desire to have an attitude of success contributes definitively to being successful. Consider for a moment how differently Hamlet's soliloquy may have been spoken had he acquired the desire to be successful, before he began. One clearly sees how the attitude is colored by the *desire* to be successful, or by the lack of desire in the case of Hamlet.

Recognizing the failure quotient in success

Success heralds the beginning of failure from the perspective that *continued* success is contingent upon an ability to always work forward without dependence on old models. It is known that working forward entails a healthy exploration of options, and some of those options will inevitably fail. There is no exception to the rule: *Significant success requires failure.* Failure is one of the most dreaded words in the English language. Although most people hate to be labeled a failure and love to be labeled a success, it is only through apparent failure that most of the greatest successes are achieved. Usually "failure" or "success" are almost entirely in the eye of the beholder. For the developing consultant this may mean a change of perspective, recognizing that failure is an integral part of success, and that the power of failure needs to be leveraged rather than discarded. In this context, failure takes on a more definitive and positive role in achieving success.

Charles Manz (2002) suggests that this new perspective includes seeing challenges as disguised opportunities, differences as gifts, and mistakes as learning opportunities. When the larger whole is addressed, one can be said to fail successfully. Each developing consultant needs to develop a vision of the larger whole – a vision for transforming failure into Learning to BE successful.

In redefining failure and success, some lessons may be taken from these words from "If" by Rudyard Kipling:

> **If you can dream --**
> **and not make dreams your master;**
> **If you can think –**
> **and not make thought your aim;**
> **If you can meet with**
> **Triumph and Disaster**
> **And treat those two impostors**
> **Just the same . . . .**

Redefining failure and success is the underlying concept of these phrases. Failure is not something to be feared. It contains a positive challenge for successful living. Today's failures contain the seeds of tomorrow's successes. The first step in mastering the art of failing successfully is to see both failure and success in a whole new light. The developing consultant needs to see failure as integral to success, as a part of the success quotient. At the same time, each success signals the need for a new cycle of discovery and innovative thinking to fuel solutions that keep pace with a changing system; think of failure and success as an ongoing cycle that continues on for perpetuity in a healthy, developing system. Such a systemic approach to the failure and success cycle results in more substantive and sustainable successes.

How success works in a systemic fashion

Getting to an operational definition of success requires a holistic process of inquiry and design. Most concepts are easier to grasp when one has an image to reference. To think about a complex phenomenon such as success, one may use a model of something simpler and more familiar as an enabling light. The systems approach deals iteratively with structure, function, and process, and is the "enabling" light in defining success in the system.

Structure defines components and their relationships, synonymous with input, means, and cause. Function defines the outcome, or results produced, synonymous with outputs, ends, and effect. Process explicitly defines the sequence of activities and the know-how required to produce outcomes. Structure, function, and process, along with the containing environment, form the interdependent set of variables that define the whole and are critical in defining success.

This notion of the whole can be applied to any context to generate a context-specific set of assumptions for the starting point of the inquiry. These assumptions can then be verified and enriched by successive elaboration of structure, function, and process in a given environment to produce a desired approximation of the whole. Figure 5. Holistic Process of Inquiry and Design is a graphic model of the defining process in describing success.

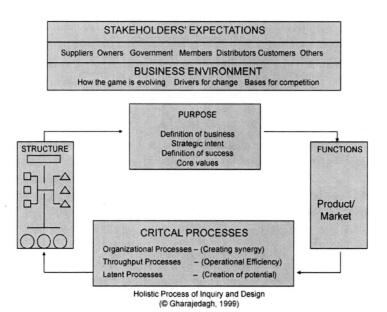

Holistic Process of Inquiry and Design
(© Gharajedagh, 1999)

Figure 5. Holistic Process of Inquiry and Design
Adapted from © Gharajedaghi (2006)

The set of structure, process, function, and the containing environment are complementary. They coexist and interact continuously. Therefore, to handle success holistically requires understanding each variable in relation to the others in the implied equation *and* at the same time. This demands iterative inquiry; that is, going over the process several times. At least three iterations may produce useable results.

Gharajedaghi (2006) provides an excellent example with a holistic view of the heart's function – understanding its function, structure, and process. Starting with the function, it may be simply noted that the output of the system is blood circulation. Therefore the function must be that of a pump. The structure of this pump consists of four muscular chambers and a set of valves, arteries, and veins. And the process, which must explain how the structure produces the function, simply uses alternative cycles of contractions and expansions of the chambers to push the blood through arteries, then pulling it back into the chambers through suction.

Now we need to pause and relate our understanding of function, structure, and process together to appreciate why the heart does what it does. By placing the heart in the context of the larger system of which *it* is a part, we might conclude that the heart is at the core of a circulatory system. The purpose of the circulating system is to exchange matter and energy between the body and its environment.

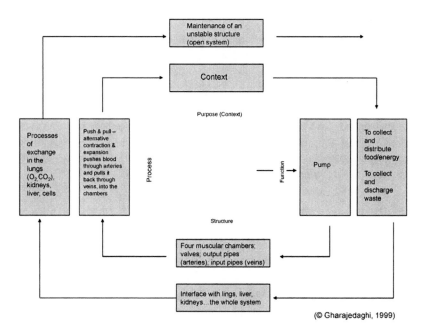

(© Gharajedaghi, 1999)

Figure 6. Understanding the Heart
Adapted from © Gharajedaghi (2006)

Figure 6. Understanding the Heart demonstrates the iterative process that can be used to generate additional information and a better understanding of the heart, which in turn defines success in that context.

A limited definition of success from this first iteration may be as simple as "success is in advancing the maintenance of an unstable structure (the heart) in a constantly operating open system." This definition could certainly be enhanced and specified more fully through additional iterations and knowledge generation.

In attempting to understand the role of success, it may be seen as both the product *and* the producer of the activity and change. Sometimes it is considered the driver in change, trying to achieve competitive advantage. The attitude of success is so important to have and to continually use in our competitive settings. An attitude of success is the satisfaction derived from "going there" in contrast to the satisfaction derived from "reaching success" or getting there. Having an attitude of success may be inspiring to the consultant herself/himself, as well as to colleagues and more importantly to the client.

Knowing the business of success in consulting

Paying attention to the business aspects of success calls for additional work relative to desiring an attitude of success in management consulting. One must make practices transformative in consulting, recognize that time is money, constantly generate the processes involved in desiring an attitude of success, and ultimately own the desire and the attitude of success in Learning to BE. This is a tall order, but necessary to improve the business aspects of consulting.

Making practices transformational In developing an attitude of success in management consulting, the transformational practices described here may "feel" illogical or counterintuitive to our normal understanding of how things operate. The purpose is to initiate a new approach to current conditions, based on uncommon assumptions about the nature of the world. The transformative practices that are relevant here are: 1) identifying a catch phrase that will get you on track and using an attitude of success,, and 2) practicing it in advance, prior to being in the situation. The practices must be learned in advance, for there may be no time to consider use of a new practice in the midst of a situation.

Although these practices appear simple, they are not easy. The practices in developing an attitude of success will take a good deal of time to master. In addition, everything you think, feel and see around you will argue against them. For example, to actually practice an attitude of success will take dedication, a leap of faith, and yes, practicing hard and long to get the attitude into your repertoire for ready use. Rosamund Zander (2000) uses an 'Out of the Boat' metaphor to describe the learning experience involved in transformative practice in the sidebar.

Sidebar: 'Out of the Boat' Metaphor

"A dozen summers ago, I signed up for my first white-water rafting trip, on Maine's Kennebec River. Traveling overland in a rickety bus to reach the launch point, I paid close attention to the guide standing in the aisle, as she undertook our education about this popular sport.

"If you fall out of the boat," she said, "it is very important that you pull your feet up so that you don't get a foot caught in the rocks below. Think *toes to nose*," she stressed, and gave us a precarious demonstration, bracing herself and hoisting one foot toward her nose, *"then look for the boat and reach for the oar or the rope."*

Our guide chattered on as we bumped our way toward the river. Most of us had been on the road since 4 a.m. and were feeling sleepy and mesmerized by the vibrations of the bus. *"Toes to nose,"* I heard again, And then, *"look for the boat."*

By the time we arrived at the river's edge, I had heard the two phrases so many times I felt slightly crazed. We put on our wet suits, gathered our equipment, and stood in a circle for our final instructions. "If you fall out of the boat what do you say to yourself?" *"Toes to nose* and *look for the boat,"* we chimed.

Someone here is mentally challenged, I thought, as we climbed into the boat and started downstream. Surging into the only class 5 rapids of the journey, I vanished into a wall of water that rose up at the stern of the raft, as into a black hole. Roiling about underwater, there was no up and down, neither water nor air nor land. There had never been a boat. There was no anywhere, there was nothing at all.

Toes to nose . . . the words emerged from a void. I pulled together into a ball. Air. Sounds. *Look for the boat.* . . did that come from my head or was someone calling? The boat appeared, and an oar. *Reach for the oar.* . . I did, and found myself in a world inside the boat, on the water, traveling down the Kennebec in a spew of foam."

Excerpted from Rosamund Zander in The Art of Possibility, pp.5-6.

In talking about the metaphor "out of the boat" (see sidebar) Rosamund Zander [2000] describes the experience as signifying more than being off track – she says it means you don't know where the track is anymore. She says that "Out of the boat" could refer to something as simple as losing all memory of ever having been on an exercise program, or it could refer to floundering in the wake of a management shake-up. When you are out of the boat, you cannot think your way back in; you have no point of reference. You must call on something that has been established in advance, a catch phrase, like "toes to nose."

This metaphor can be applied to develop an attitude of success in each new consultation where the consultant may be "out of the boat." To begin the recovery one must use a catchphrase identified in advance to actively move into attitude development. For example, one might intervene with a catch phrase like "There are many alternatives available for action," or "recent research shows." Similar catch phrases have the same value as "toes to nose" in the metaphor. The consultant must have developed a catch phrase in advance that will stop the action and get her back on track, exuding an attitude of success. The catch phrase need not be said out loud, but it may be simply said loudly inside oneself. Further, it must be practiced several times, even rehearsed, before going into each situation, particularly those early in the engagement. The catch phrase must be available as a reflex.

It is clear that in most consulting engagements in turbulent times, the consultant finds herself/himself out of the boat – and most likely in very deep water. It is important to recognize the value of the use of a catchphrase to get one back on track. One may even have to invent and practice a catchphrase to get back in the consulting boat. In developing an attitude of success, the catch phrase must be *identified* and *practiced,* prior to being in the situation. Just as in the case of the rapids experience in the sidebar, the catch phrases would not have been available to use if not identified and practiced several times before. Fortunately, in this case, the identification and practice happened just previous to the experience. In many consulting situations, one is not that fortunate; developing an attitude of success must be done quite a while in advance of the intervention in order to be successful. A bonus from early work on developing the catch phrase for an attitude of success is that an attitude of success can be used in all of life, not just in consulting.

Eliciting transformative change from practices takes time. The change does not happen without considerable conscious effort. For the developing consultant as well as the client "time is money." Ordinarily, time is not put in the consulting contract for making practices transformative. For example, many consultants and clients are still using standard operating practices of the past, and are not aware that their "out of the boat" experiences are related to a lack of desire to BE successful. They have not considered that many of the standard operating practices must be changed to fit that desire to BE successful. In addition, consultants have not considered the time it takes in advance, and just how they should prepare themselves to BE successful. This is a very subtle point, but increasingly important in preparation for actually Being successful. The advance preparation does take time and does cost both the client and the consultant the time required. Whether it is actually itemized as a cost in the contract or not, making practices transformative remain vital to success.

Generating processes in desiring to BE successful Attitudes are emergent properties. Recall the attributes of an emergent property from the earlier description. The generating processes must be continuously reproduced online and in real time. The property of an attitude of success cannot be stored or saved for future use – which is critical to recognize. The property of desiring an attitude of success cannot be automatically transferred to a new situation. It must be realized that what is important about both desiring and the actual attitude formation is that it must first be generated anew each time. Further, that the generating processes to maintain it must be continuously reproduced in real time in each consulting engagement. When the latter statement is fully realized the management consultant is energized and excited. This new energy and excitement produces innovation in the current situation – developing competency in transformational practice. The desire for an attitude of success is nurtured through experiencing success – consciously and intentionally.

Owning the desire to BE successful It appears that changing one's attitude or adopting an attitude of success in each context is not only necessary, but required if one is to master Learning to BE. The task of developing an attitude of success may be only fine tuning your present attitude by specifying success, which may be seen as a small but important change; or, one may be in the position of making a major change to even consider an attitude of success as a component. Learning to desire an attitude of success is learning to realize that possessing the desire for an attitude of success may open a whole new universe of possibility. The basic learning identified adds up to "ownership" of the desire and attitude.

For the developing consultant to succeed, ownership must be public. It must be shared with colleagues in collectivities, in communities of practice, and with clients. Otherwise, the desire and the attitude stand the risk of solely existing internally and not being observable or externally owned. Making ownership public functionally reinforces the need for desiring an attitude of BEing successful.

Making ownership of the desire and attitude public is integral to making practices transformative. The developing consultant is actually developing the "catch phrase" and the action behaviors in the situation. The first step may be to bring to consciousness the thoughts and ideas raised here and then become intentional in the application in one's own life. It may appear as a small and insignificant step – *it is not*. Becoming intentionally conscious increases competence by an order of magnitude in the real world of consulting.

Learning to BE successful opens a new universe

Developing an attitude of BEing successful is the visible output from learning to *desire* such an attitude. It is the constant desiring of the attitude that keeps one alert and open to alternatives and opportunities. It is learning to desire the attitude that opens up a whole new universe of possibility in Being successful. Having *access* to this whole new universe of possibility is what is critical. It isn't knowing what's in the universe in advance – it is just knowing that you have access. Having access frees the developing consultant to consistently generate new ideas, means, models, and modes to BE successful. Focusing on learning to desire the attitude provides the time to access new varieties available in real time. Since learning to desire is new, it is often overlooked as an important first step. The tendency is to go directly to attitude formation, overlooking learning to desire in Learning to BE. However, it is important in learning to desire to understand what the eventual output will be – to aid mastering becoming.

There is no question that possessing an attitude of success in the 21st century is a necessity. It is not commonly known that the road to possession and ownership is through desiring Learning to BE successful. Many times, developing consultants do not take into account the energy expended to BE successful – or perceived as such. Energy and being energized in one's approach is very important to counteract the drag that chaos and complexity place in the environment. As a consultant, one must stay energized for self-development, and to energize others to make change.   It is difficult to understand that desiring energizes the developing consultant. Energizing is likened to inspiration gained from a dream or a well articulated goal.   An energized approach is self-actualizing and necessary in BEing successful.

Evidence of a generative approach in desiring to BE successful is a sign of maturity in the developing management consultant.   The generative approach tends to bring forth the whole person – making the resources of the whole person available to the consultant herself/himself and the client alike. A broad base of knowledge and experience are necessary for perpetual success in management consulting. Desiring an attitude of success contributes significantly in Learning to BE successful in the world.

Chapter 5   Learning Leveraging to Lead Transformative Change

Buckminster Fuller's Trim Tab Metaphor "A trim tab is a small "rudder on the rudder" of a ship. It is only a fraction of the size of the rudder. Its function is to make it easier to turn the ship. The larger the ship, the more important is the trim tab because a large volume of water flowing around the rudder can make it difficult to turn."

The trim tab is a very small device that has an enormous effect on a huge ship. The trim tab, acting on the rudder, does the same for the rudder, as the rudder does in turning the ship. When the trim tab is turned to one side or the other, it compresses the water around the rudder and creates a small pressure differential that "sucks the rudder" in the desired direction. To turn the ship to the left, one turns the trim tab to the right – essentially opposite of the way the ship is to be turned. The leverage of the trim tab doubly capitalizes on the hydro-dynamics at work in turning the ship – for example, in the trim tab's positioning on the main rudder to increase its effect, and in the main rudder's action to increase turning power.

In the same way, leveraging is a "very small device" that management consultants may develop to lead transformative change. Leveraging becomes a new source of competitive advantage for consultants. Leveraging is empowering and actually duplicates power for the consultant. Just as Archimedes stated centuries ago -- "with a lever long enough. . . . single-handed I can move the world."

The Buckminster Fuller metaphor describes two points that are relevant for the management consultant. One is effectiveness and the other is obscurity. The latter relates to the obscure aspect of the trim tab. The trim tab is below the water line and to be effective it must function in anon obvious way. Analogously, the consultant leads transformative change, using Systems Thinking principles in a non obvious way – moving through complexity and chaos. The metaphor focuses the importance of effectiveness and highlights the time saved by operational effectiveness. The non obvious aspect adds a level of difficulty to desiring to leverage for it is more difficult when only the effects are visible. Often to recognize the leveraging action, one must infer it and try to figure out what it was that caused the observable outcome.

Why Leveraging is Important

Answering the "why" question creates understanding of a concept and makes it possible to act on the knowledge. Webster defines leveraging as "acting to gain greater professional, economic, and political influence and effectiveness, in all that one does."   In management consulting, leveraging is the capability to influence others in different positions to positively affect a quality output, product, or outcome.   Usually, leveraged activities are accomplished in a shorter time period than otherwise, the result of simultaneously working cooperatively, influencing at multiple levels in the system.

Leveraging consultant capability must be done very carefully. One must spend some time consciously identifying the capability in the specific context, acknowledging "how to best use it" in the consulting engagement.   In other words, one must learn operational leveraging through first Learning to BE in a specific context. One must, in every case, learn to energize and reinvigorate the desire to leverage one's capability in management consulting contexts, before actually leveraging successfully.

Conserving both client and consultant time and energy The overt experience of leveraging to gain influence and greater effectiveness is very subtle. In many cases it is hard to observe because the action is "below the water line." As in Buckminster Fuller's metaphor, the non obvious aspect contributes to the difficulty in observing. In addition, knowing in advance that one "must turn left to go right!" aids observation. To the unknowing observer, seeing the left turn is seen as an unexplainable curve ball.   "Influence" is not easily seen. Influence is intangible. The intangibility contributes to the difficulty in learning from observation. To become aware of the non obvious, observable events, like outputs, must be noted and then working backwards attempts to construct what leads up to the output. That is, identifying the influence in the situation that directed action.

It is important for the management consultant to realize the value of leveraging in their work. Leveraging is strategizing influence in the system. The outcome is greater effectiveness on the task. Many times the total task is successfully accomplished in less time. In particular, less time of the consultant is required. The developing consultant soon realizes that time is money -- that time is chargeable to the contract whether it is spent preparing to intervene or in the actual implementation with the client.   Time is a valuable factor to be carefully leveraged in each assignment.

Maintaining focus on systems change – not people Another obscure or non-obvious point is in leveraging change in systems rather than people. Many times the system to be changed is not clearly visible in concrete terms, nor has the system been considered as a "whole" as the focus for change. Generally, the focus has been on the "people causing the problem" in a specific part of the organization. The emphasis on the people problem not only gives a faulty perspective for the consultant to address change; but it is nearly impossible to consider leveraging leadership for transformative change from this vantage point. The problem is a systems problem and will not be dissolved by "fixing" people in the system.

For example, a case in point is a department head being held responsible for reaching goals that involve not only other departments, but major divisions of the firm. Furthermore, the department head has no direct access to other department or division heads. In this situation it is difficult for the department head to correct the problem – even with sophisticated communication skills aided by the hi-tech of e-mail, fax, and so on.   In this situation, the department lacks the leverage or influence to be successful.   This is a system problem, not a people problem. The department head is the recipient of the systemic flaw. This flaw blocks successful action, slowing communication and increasing unmanageable conflicts.

For the management consultant, leveraging the systemic problem begins with synthesis of the whole and where the system under consideration fits into a larger system. In this respect, the system at hand is simultaneously a system *and* a part of a containing system. Once this understanding is achieved, the appropriate changes are creatively designed in the structure, processes, and function of the existing system alleviating the dysfunction.   Leveraging is influencing the use of a systemic perspective to get transformative change in the system, which changes the "functioning of people" in the situation. Interestingly, by addressing the systemic problem, the "assumed people problem" is dissolved.

The bottom line is the department head, in this case, fares much better in a systemic change in contrast to a "people change." When the cost of a systemic intervention versus. a people change intervention is calculated, one sees the overwhelming positive effect of the systemic change in dollars saved and increased potential. This is due to the leveraged resources of both client and consultant. Changing systems is relatively new to many change agents and consultants. Usually, they believe their success has been in changing people, not systems. It is difficult to change their way of thinking without a greater exposure to knowledge and experience with Systems Thinking. Initially, it is important to influence for greater understanding of systems change rather than people changes. People are actually very adaptable, and if they "desire" to be a part of the system and have an opportunity to understand the system as a whole – almost immediately they begin to adapt to fit the system of their own volition. It is important to note that adaptation at a personal level is an individual choice. Further, people participate in the systemic change demonstrating interdependence. The systemic approach makes a tangible difference in the output, affecting the quality and quantity of sustainable change undertaken.

Essentially, leveraging is a means of achieving success in consulting by "doing more with less." That is, using resources (including self) more effectively and using new resources better to gain greater influence in every situation to lead transformative change. Transformative change is deep change that changes the basic characteristics of the system in such a way that the system may not return to its prior state. Management consultants must become *systems wise* in leading transformative change.

Leveraging is not magic Leveraging is strategy at work. Understanding and using leveraging takes the "magic" out of consulting. When one can see below the waterline to observe the trim tab in action, much of the apparent magic in turning a large vessel is explainable in observing the hydrodynamics affected by the trim tab. The analogy is true for consulting. It recognizes that leveraging is an integral part of the consultant's approach to transformative change. Further, it recognizes that there is not an unknown, uncontrollable or magical force at work,. Leveraging is intentional influencing to gain greater professional, economic, and political effectiveness in consulting.

Recognizing the strategy involved in leveraging makes clear that this is not a happenstance or magical action. To fully understand the strategy one must consider the reality that we are in the third generation of

Systems Thinking (design) identifying a triple challenge in strategizing change. The triple challenge of *interdependency, self-organization,* and *choice* specify focus in leveraging. There is already good evidence of interdependency, self-organization, and choice among organization members. Thus, the task of strategizing is to consider various means of sophistication and dissemination of the use in the system of interdependency, self-organization, and choice. In some cases, this may simply be legitimizing the use of these capabilities for all involved, while in others more extensive work in understanding is required.

Now, social organizations are purposeful and capable of self-organizing. They can, in fact, create order out of chaos, and they can be organized by design or by default. The latter – default – is where the beliefs, assumptions, and expectations that underlie the system go unexamined, whereas in systems design, the beliefs, assumptions, and expectations are made explicit, and are constantly examined and monitored. Leveraging is key in examining the beliefs, assumptions, and expectations of the system -- and avoiding the possibility of default – which only reproduces the problem all over again and maintains status quo. Using leveraging in the design process is important. Leveraging to fully examine the beliefs, assumptions, and expectations of the system is at the core of designing change. Leveraging in the design process takes the magic out of the consulting by making explicit the mental models involved. In so doing, leveraging prevents the return to the existing order and promotes continued work on the same problem.

Learning leveraging is central to possessing an attitude of success and to being successful in consulting. Developing leveraging as a skill makes a strategic difference in the consulting approach. Leveraging, like the trim tab, is always available for consultant use. The action results are visible evidence of leveraging, comparable to the turning accomplished by the trim tab. In organizations, leveraging is evidenced by new direction leading to transformative results.

What makes leveraging visible?

Leveraging becomes visible through active intervention – the overarching capability for consultants to develop and practice effectively, both systemically and systematically. "Intervention" represents the action taken as a result of leveraging. *Intervention capability* is the management consultant's *marketable competency*, and supports the consultant's reputation for effectiveness in the industry.

The consultant that is comfortable intervening is skilled in stopping the action and acting coherently to redirect the process, helping the client take the appropriate steps to move expeditiously in a new direction to reach the goal.   At the same time, the consultant holds several frameworks in his head, accessing them as needed to support the client's new direction and action. On occasion the consultant may model an action as an example, but should not assume the role or responsibility of the client in a regular fashion.

Developing the intervention capability   Successful intervention, time after time, is what one is striving for, and is exactly what makes one marketable as a management consultant. "Intervention" in a basic sense, means *to stop action in order to help* (Argyris, 1970).   Argyris, in defining intervention, identifies three primary tasks, which are the responsibility of the intervener in each situation. The three primary tasks are:

- Identifying valid and useful information
- Assisting the client to make a free and informed decision, based on valid information
- Aiding the client to develop commitment in implementation of the decision(s)

It is important to note that to accomplish these three tasks, it may take the intervener several interventions.   One may look at an intervention as being several related mini-interventions to accomplish the primary tasks in the situation. A management consultant may implement many interventions to be successful in any one consulting endeavor. However, each intervention succeeds based on how carefully the primary tasks of intervention have been respected by the consultant in each intervention.

Argyris points out that once a consultant intervenes with the client, the management consultant automatically places himself outside of the client system, and is no longer a member of that system. The act of intervention separates the consultant from the system, even in the case of internal consultants. It clearly places the consultant in a position to *help*, freed of any earlier bonds and constrictions evident in the organizational role. However, the client may not be aware of this and may continue to call on the consultant in terms of a previous role – complicating action in the current setting.

A framework for intervention - a Socio-Economic Equation for SUCCESS

The Consulting Systems Worldview (CSW) is a prescriptive framework guiding the management consultant in four distinct phases of organizational transformation: contracting, data collection, action planning, and implementation. In each of these phases there are critical components that must be recognized and addressed to ensure systemic and transformative change. Gharajedaghi states that true transformation occurs when a desired state is achieved with no readily available means to revert to the prior state. Individual change at several levels must be undertaken to transform an organization and make meaningful change. The Socio-Economic Equation focuses on change at several levels with individuals, leaders, and business in the organization to gain successful results in innovation – doing things differently.

Harris and Wang (2001) presented an early form of the Socio-Economic Equation focusing the importance of leadership *unleashing human potential* cubed and then multiplied by the *business approach* squared to provide *Innovative Results* raised to the Nth degree. Out of this early work with the CSW and the S-E Equation developed the Socio-Economic Equation for Success, now focusing innovation as directly related to Success.

Based on the Socio-Economic Equation for Success (Figure 6), human potential is unleashed in the context of a cooperative co-creative and purposeful environment, and is maximized through **Presencing** to gain sustainability. When human potential becomes unleashed in a cooperative and purposeful environment, leadership and new learning emerge enabling co-creation of unique value for the consumer to sustain transformative change. This maximization yields exponential contributions to the emergent SUCCESS when complexity is managed.

Complexity is managed through societal development. "Development of an organization is a purposeful transformation toward higher levels of integration and differentiation at the same time. It is a collective learning process by which a social system increases its ability and desire to serve both its members and its environment (Gharajedaghi, 2006, p. 92)." It is in this developmental process that complexity is managed.

$$S \text{ (Systemic Success)} = \sum \left[\frac{[\, C, P, L(hp)^3\,] \times [\, NL, C^{uv3}\,] \times [T\Delta\, S^i]}{M^{cx}} \right]$$

Legend:

C	COOPERATION
P	PURPOSEFULNESS
$L(hp)^3$	Leadership UNLEASHING human potential
NL	NEW Learning from the Future, PRESENCING
C^{uv3}	CO-CREATE UNIQUE VALUE
T	Understanding and using Transformative Change
S^i	Sustainability institutionalized
M^{cx}	Management of complexity

Source: Harris, Marilyn E & Guilan Wang. (2001). *Mastering the Challenge of Transformative Change: Developing New Leadership for New Learning*. A paper presented at the Midwest Academy of Management, April 3-6, St. Louis, MO.

Figure 7: Socio Economic Equation for Success

An intervention in a system requires an all encompassing framework in terms of developing understanding for application *within* the system. This competency is global, encompassing the total activity of the management consultant with the client.   Figure 8. The Consulting Systems Worldview (CSW) represents such a framework for understanding the macro task of intervention, in a system, to lead transformative change. The framework provides a guide for the management consultant from the first steps in entry to completion of the intervention in final evaluation and reporting. The CSW framework describes a new worldview of the consulting system. The CSW was first introduced in Part 1, Chapter 2, and is revisited in detail using two cases in Part 4, where a chapter is devoted to each phase.

The Consulting Systems Worldview capitalizes on a four-phased transformative process where each phase is considered a macro intervention. Each phase has two components – for example, in Phase 2: Data Collection and Problem Definition, the two components are: 1) data collection and 2) problem definition. Intervening in the phase itself is considered a macro intervention, with each component or critical task termed a micro intervention. Appendix 2 contains a complete chart of the macro interventions with the required micro interventions noted for each phase. In summary, the CSW graphic provides the whole framework of the systemic consulting process as a macro intervention, supported by the micro interventions, to accomplish the organization's transformation.

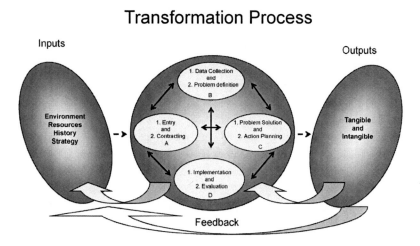

Transformation Process

The Consulting Systems Worldview
© Marilyn E Harris, 1996

Figure 8: The Consulting Systems Worldview (CSW)

Why transformative change is necessary?

Many change agents do not recognize the difference between a transformative effort and a *re*formative effort [see sidebar]. It is important to realize that in transformative efforts "regardless of what they may be called – total quality management, reengineering, right sizing, restructuring, cultural change or turnaround – the basic goal has been to make *fundamental changes* in how business is conducted in order to help cope with a new, more challenging market environment" (Kotter,1995). These factors tend to raise the intervention bar for the management consultant and increase the need for leveraging.

Sidebar: Transforming versus Reforming

Transform, according to Webster's New Collegiate Dictionary, is to change in composition or structure. Further, it is to change the basic characteristics of the situation in a positive way -- but sufficiently changing them, so that actors and leaders in the organization cannot go back to the old way of doing things. Transforming changes the basic characteristics of the organization. Transforming usually requires a significant innovation in the structure, function, and processes of the organization to succeed and it takes a number of years to be institutionalized.

Reform, in contrast, according to the dictionary definition and
common practice, is to form again, to take form again – to amend or improve form, removing faults. Essentially, reform focuses on fixing up the existing form, where transform changes the composition and structure – not adding on to the old, non-functional structure. Transformative interventions are very involve personnel at every level creating new structure, function and processes to meet the goals of change. Generally, transformative efforts tend to be more successful than reformative change, because the former is a holistic approach. Reform efforts usually go on for years ineffectively, because the efforts tend to "fix up" or patch parts of the organization, not considering the whole system in need of change. Transformational efforts are preferred because they are geared at system level changes that force the organization to consider innovative solutions instead of reworked approaches.

Identifying the critical processes in transformation Gharajedaghi and Ackoff (1984) say that transformation has three dimensions of change – purposeful, integrative, and differentiating. A purposeful system is one that can produce not only the same outcomes in different ways in the same environment, but different outcomes in both the same and different environments. A purposeful system can change ends under constant conditions.   This ability to change ends under constant conditions exemplifies free will. Such systems not only learn and adapt, they can also create. Human beings are examples of such systems.

Integration and differentiation are two sides of the same coin. Alone, they self-destruct, together they synergize.   "Society's need for integration is as legitimate as an individual's need for differentiation" (Gharajedaghi, 2006). Differentiation represents an artistic orientation – looking for differences among things that are apparently similar – and moves toward creation of a new structure. Integration is a scientific orientation that is just the opposite – looking for similarities among things that are apparently different – and moves toward the maintenance of structure. Figure 9. Critical Processes in Social System Development helps illustrate the three transformative dimensions.   These three dimensions (purposeful, integrative, and differentiating) form the basis of measuring success in transformative macro interventions.

Often, the purposeful and differentiating aspects are easier to attain. However the integrative aspect is difficult since historically much more effort has been utilized in differentiating. The processes involved in the tendency toward integration are depicted in Figure 7. as: stability, security, collectivity, order, and uniformity. These processes are more difficult to accomplish in a complex environment.

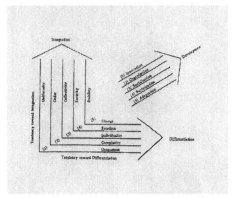

**Figure 9: Critical Processes in Social System Development
Adapted from © Gharajedaghi (2006)**

From a global perspective we are in the third generation of systems design and the need for interdependency, self-organization, and choice – but these aspects are not widely used. In addition, there has been little specific work on the integrative processes institutionally and organizationally. Often, understanding the differences involved opens the door to an opportunity to intervene more effectively.

Metacompetencies expand transformative power Intervention becomes an even more powerful tool through the development of metacompetencies. A metacompetency is so powerful that it affects a person's ability to acquire other competencies. One analogy is in reading; once a person has the ability to read, all sorts of learning communicated through the written word becomes accessible to that person.

Meta in this context refers to competencies situated closely to the marketable competency of intervention, but juxtaposed to expand the transformative power of intervention. A metacompetency can be likened to the trim tab on the rudder of a ship, leveraging the transformative power of the intervention.

The metacompetencies relevant to the prime marketable intervention competency in management consulting are: identity, adaptability, conceptualizing, empowerment, participation, conflict management, action research, and assessment.   These eight metacompetencies are interactive and interdependent, synergizing development of the encompassing intervention competency.   Figure 10. Overview of Metacompetencies in Use provides a perspective showing the eight metacompetencies and shows the relationship to the systems dimensions as well as to the CSW phase.   Metacompetencies actually leverage transformation in consulting. The consultant achieves transformation by using the metacompetency to incisively focus the intervention.

For example: using the empowerment metacompetency in intervention, the consultant incisively focuses "duplicating power in the situation" in contrast to just working at sharing power.   This is a quantitatively different intervention, one which *doubles power* instead of sharing or splitting the present power pie. The use of empowerment in this case is what defines development of a leveraged intervention by juxtaposing the metacompetency. It adds to the dissemination of power in a significant fashion. In using the metacompetency, the consultant models for the client – in this way, the client may easily learn the use of the metacompetencies for use interdependently in the transformative change situation.

In summary, metacompetencies power up the management consultant's intervention capability and are most necessary. Metacompetencies are transferable from one situation to another, increasing the value as the user continues to develop.

Sidebar: Adaptability as a Metacompetency

A metacompetency in adaptability would include behaviors that would demonstrate flexibility, exploration, openness to new and diverse people and ideas, dialogue skills, eagerness to accept new challenges in unexplored territory, and comfort with turbulent change. There are many existing opportunities to heighten adaptability, for example diversity training or an assignment in a new country.

Metacompetencies are key in leveraging learning and development for both the consultant and the client.   The conscious use of the metacompetencies add value for the management consultant and increase intervention capability throughout the consulting engagement.

System Dimensions   METCOMPETENCIES   Phase relationships/Chapter

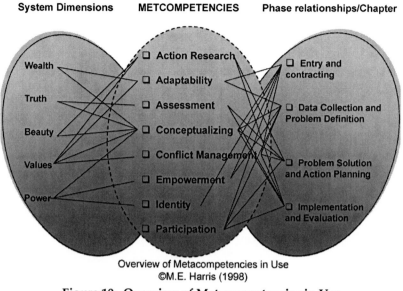

Overview of Metacompetencies in Use
©M.E. Harris (1998)

Figure 10: Overview of Metacompetencies in Use

Leveraging is critical in leading transformative change

Leveraging leading transformative change is at first an overwhelming challenge for both the management consultant and the client.   The challenge is both qualitative and quantitative, based in one's understanding and practice of leadership. Leveraging in leading transformative change is influencing through leadership.   Leading transformative change in today's fast paced world is about the management consultant's understanding and practice, fully utilizing leadership and change capability.

For Ackoff, leadership is always transforming.   He sees the management consultant as one who can produce a mobilizing vision of a transformed system.   Equally important, the leader must be able to inspire, align, and organize an effective pursuit of that vision, maintaining the vision even when sacrifices are required. Kotter (1990) addresses leadership as coping with change by providing direction, by aligning resources to fit the needs of the direction, and by inspiring and providing motivational forces to achieve the direction. For management consultants *"leadership is managing upward; it is about influencing what one cannot control and appreciating what one cannot influence*" (Gharajedaghi, 2006).

The key in the latter situation – where one is trying to influence what one cannot control and to appreciate what one cannot influence – is in learning, quite possibly new learning for the management consultant, the client at all levels, and other stakeholders. Often, it is only to bring the focus on relevant learning to the foreground. In doing, it unleashes tremendous power sources, empowering all involved with almost bottomless resources. The learning may take many forms and involve many different populations to meet the requirements of a mobilizing vision of a transformed system. .

There is an additional challenge in leveraging to lead transformative change that is important – in the interdependence of the variables *leveraging and leading* transformative change. Increasingly we are find that our independent variables are no longer independent, and that the neat and simple construct that served us so beautifully in the past is no longer effective in itself.   As systems become more and more sophisticated the reality of interdependence becomes more and more pronounced.   Interdependency refers to the relationship that exists between individuals, or between people and material things.   For example, the latter may be between a person and a computer producing output – this is an interdependent relationship between a person and a material thing.

Understanding interdependency requires a different way of thinking from analysis; it requires Systems Thinking. Analytical thinking and Systems Thinking are quite distinctly different. Analysis is a three-step thought process. First, it takes apart that which it seeks to understand. Then it attempts to explain the behavior of the parts taken separately. Finally, it tries to aggregate understanding of the parts into an explanation of the whole. This task is rarely accomplished because it is literally impossible to explain the whole coming from a perspective of the separate parts and without consideration of interdependency.

Systems Thinking uses a different process; it puts the system in the context of the larger environment of which it is a part and studies the role it plays in the larger whole.   This process is synthesis.   As noted, synthesis is exactly opposite of analysis. The first step of synthesis is to determine the *larger* system that contains the system to be explained. The second step is to try to understand the larger system as a whole. The third step is to disaggregate the understanding of the whole into an understanding of the part by identifying its role or function in the containing system.   In using synthesis the management consultant usually saves time, but more importantly has a more relevant conclusion in current contexts because he has understanding in contrast to only "knowledge."

Consultant leadership is necessary at first The task of leading transformative change is not only complex, requiring management of many chaotic situations, but is overwhelming to those lacking strong background experience and a healthy perspective on leading change. Most often, there are too many factors to oversee to lead transformative change. The consultant must take leadership at first, using a framework similar to that of Kotter's, to guide transformative change. Even in the beginning the consultant should work as closely as possible with the client leader, making it as joint as possible – to aid in the early transfer of leadership to the client. The client must take responsibility for leading the transformative change if it is really going to work as designed, but needs healthy assistance from the consultant, and almost always in the beginning.

Kotter (1995) shed light from his business consulting experience by identifying the realities that block transformations (in leading change) and why these efforts frequently fail.   Figure 11.   Eight Steps to Transforming Your Organization clearly defines a positive sequence for leading transformative change. [An interesting aside is that Kotter was asked by the Harvard Business Review press to write the book from the article spelling out the eight steps in detail. The press had received more requests for reprints of his original article than any other publication from the press' opening date to the present.]

Eight Steps to Transforming Your Organization	
1	**Establishing a Sense of Urgency** •Examining markets and competitive realities •Identifying and discussing crises, potential crises, or major opportunities
2	**Forming a Powerful Guiding Coalition** • Assembling a group with enough power to lead the change effort •Encouraging the group to work together as a team
3	**Creating a Vision** •Creating a Vision to help direct the change effort •Developing Strategies for achieving that vision
4	**Communicating the Vision** • Using every vehicle possible to communicate the new vision and strategies •Teaching new behaviors by the example of the guiding coalition
5	**Empowering others to Act on the Vision** •Getting rid of obstacles to Change •Changing systems or structures that seriously undermine the vision •Encouraging risk taking and non-traditional ideas, activities, and actions
6	**Planning for and Creating short-term Wins** • Planning for Visible performance Improvements • Creating those improvements •Recognizing and rewarding employees involved in the improvements
7	**Consolidating Improvements and Producing Still more Change** •Using increased credibility to change systems, structures, and policies that don't fit the vision •Hiring, promoting, and developing employees who can implement the vision •Reinvigorating the process with new projects, themes, and change agents
8	**Institutionalizing New Approaches** •Articulating the connections between new behaviors and corporate success •Developing the means to ensure leadership development and succession

**Figure 11: Eight Steps to Transforming Your Organization
[excerpted from Kotter (1995), p.61]**

Kotter has considered the many factors involved from beginning to end and organized them into a sequential framework that can provide much guidance to the developing consultant. The developing consultant is encouraged to carefully study Kotter's book to deepen his experience and understanding in practice. Kotter provides many guidelines in his writing. For example, he says that communication may be increased by 10 x 10 x 10 in order to improve it; the consultant can conclude that most of the time we under communicate – and that we need to increase our modeling of more communication significantly.

Transferring the baton While Kotter's eight steps to transforming an organization provide an excellent framework for the management consultant in designing to lead transformative change, it is also an outstanding framework for transferring the leadership baton more formally. It is very easy to pinpoint the organization's current position in the framework and important leadership factors for consideration. However, the consultant's public leadership role in leading transformative change must be short lived if existent at all.   The consultant's role in leading transformative change should be that of the effective yet obscure trim rudder. At the earliest moment possible the organization itself must provide the leadership to transform, supported by the consultant's transparent and upward support with interventions and influence. Leadership is about influencing what one cannot control and appreciating what one can not influence. The consultant's business is to get the leadership within the organization to lead transformative change – so that it may be fully owned by the organization.

In conclusion, learning to leverage in order to lead transformative change is a key concept for the contemporary management consultant. It is critical that the consultant realize the importance of leadership and utilize all of his leveraging capability; this will instill leadership to drive transformative change in the client organization by forming a powerful guiding coalition. Developing leveraging skill enables the consultant to work from a big picture view of the organization, then to influence appropriately for optimum implementation during the engagement and beyond. Learning how to LEARN and how to facilitate the learning of others is the task of the third part of the book – which will be very helpful in undertaking the transformation of the organization.

PART 3:
UNDERSTANDING the Challenge of Learning "TO LEARN"

*These days, unless you devote an enormous amount of time
anticipating the future, learning, you won't have any future.*
— Ron Chernow

Ron Chernow, a business biographer and historian, points out many
parallels and differences between what's going on today and what went
on 100 years ago. He looks at the explosion of new industries and

PART 3   UNDERSTANDING the Challenge of Learning "TO LEARN"

technologies at regulators
dealing with the antitrust
challenge posed by the rise
of giant corporations and at
people coming to terms with
the philanthropic
distribution of their colossal
fortunes. One difference he
points out is that John D.
Rockefeller, Sr., slept much
more soundly at night than
Bill Gates does today. Today we see the learning needed and evidence of
new learning in every walk of life. A great deal of money is being spent
on developing new learning from research. For example, Bill Gates
spends $2.5 billion dollars per year on research and development. All of
this learning only raises the bar higher for the developing consultant.
Therefore, understanding the challenge of Learning to LEARN is even
more important.

Part 3 clarifies how learning to learn is different now contrasted to
100 years ago– and how learning is continuing to change. It points to an
information-age driven revolution in self-education. In learning cultures
of self-educators the learner is in the driver's seat directing learning. The
revolution in self-education is well under way. For example, many
institutions of higher learning have begun to recognize the power of
distance learning – there are numerous degrees available online. As more
learners get comfortable with access to web technology, and utilize the
search capabilities, the self-education revolution will become deeper and
wider, encompassing the farthest corners of the globe.

The challenge of understanding and mastering Learning to LEARN is
monumental in and of itself, for it encompasses learning, unlearning, and
relearning which require knowledge and skill development of the

individual as well as the collectivity of relevant learners – consultants and clients alike. Getting a grasp on the meaning first and then working toward mastery spells out continuous lifelong learning, and as learners continue to move through several careers in a lifetime, the learning task only increases regularly and dramatically. Understanding the basic task of Learning to LEARN requires gaining new meaning for *learning* itself – that is, that learning results from being surprised: detecting a mismatch between what was expected to happen and what actually did happen. If one understands *why* the mismatch occurred and is able to *avoid* a mismatch in the future, one has learned. Once activating this understanding, the learner is freed to deal with the rapid pace of change, uncertainty, and complexity – all of which make contemporary life much less stressful and enjoyable. Chapter 6 furthers boundary spanning in defining unlearning and relearning as a part of the learning task, and in learning to become a self-educator.

Chapter 7 focuses learning to *leverage* knowledge through many different forms and frameworks. Undoubtedly, most important in learning to leverage knowledge is first enabling knowledge creation. Enabling knowledge creation is critical because it unlocks the mystery of tacit knowledge and releases the power of innovation in an organization. What is important to recognize in consulting is that if knowledge creation is not enabled, the bottom line will suffer. Management consultants often recognize this need and learn to enhance knowledge creation through demonstrating their care for others in *indwelling.* In indwelling, one demonstrates commitment to an idea, to an experience, to a concept, or to a fellow human being at a personal level, and at the same time, at an organizational level. In this chapter, many frameworks are presented to aid both the client and the consultant in leveraging knowledge to maximum advantage within the organizational context.

In conclusion to part 3, Chapter 8 describes the principles of radical innovation and why it is important for the management consultant to work at institutionalizing innovation as a capability in every context. Innovation is at the base of being successful in the 21st century. In order to do well in the emerging new business environments, organizations and their leaders have to develop new cognitive capability -- the capability for sensing and seizing emerging business opportunities (Arthur, 1996). Organizations and their leaders can develop this capability by engaging in a different kind of learning cycle, one that allows them to *learn from the future* as it emerges, rather than reflecting on past experiences. The chapter discusses this new capability called *Presencing* and how the developing management consultant might capitalize on the new capacity for seeing, sensing, embodying, and enacting emerging futures – supporting institutionalizing innovation.

Part 3 opens wide the whole business of Learning to LEARN, in defining the components of learning, in focusing the use of knowledge in leveraging options, and in the stretching capability through learning how to innovate in a collectivity -- learning from the future. Learning to LEARN broadens the challenge in understanding and mastering now, but masterfully sets the stage for learning in the future, today.

Chapter 6: Learning to "LEARN"

Want to build a business that can outlive its first good idea? Create a culture that values learning. Want to build a career that allows you to grow into new responsibilities? Maintain your hunger to learn – and join an organization where you'll be given the chance to learn continuously.
- Robert Reich

Learning to LEARN is at the core of the developing consultant. Robert Reich said of learning that in a knowledge based (global) economy, the new coin of the realm is learning. The challenge for the management consultant in Learning to Learn goes beyond their own learning to facilitating the learning of others – facilitating the client in becoming a self-educator. The challenge is not only to understand the learning process and the transfer of learning, but to identify the knowledge required in new learning, how to package it best for self and others' learning, and then how best to market it to the learner in context. Learning to LEARN is equally important to Learning to BE and Learning to DO (developed later, in the fourth part), and does not take precedence in development. However, in practice, focusing on all three structures (BE, LEARN and DO) for simultaneous work is integral to the necessary challenge in learning.

Marketing the learning or getting the attention of the learner at the right time is the new currency of business. According to Thomas Davenport and John Beck (2001), who coined "attention economy" in their book, the most significant problem in today's business world is not competition, lack of skilled employees, or an uncertain economy, but an attention deficit in our world of information overload.

Learning how to LEARN for the management consultant is essentially creating one's self as a self-educator, capable of learning, unlearning, relearning, and learning from the future (a new type of learning introduced by Scharmer (2000) in contrast to learning only from past experience) – and then facilitating the same for the client. The goal of Learning to Learn is to reach a level of understanding that allows the individual to be free to design and create the future. Actually the revolution in self-education is well underway, constantly spurred on by e-commerce. However, most formal education institutions have not made the dramatic shift in pedagogy, nor do they seek to have the student understand. Thus the job of the management consultant is made more difficult by the existing educational institutions and their approach to learning.

Gharajedaghi (2006, p. 75) notes that "learning results from being surprised, detecting a mismatch: between what was expected to happen and what actually did happen. Further, if one understands why the mismatch occurred (diagnosis) and is able to do things on the way that avoid a mismatch in the future (prescription), one has learned." The definition describes why there are so many "surprises" reported around the globe in a variety of contexts – there is much new learning going on. The challenge for the management consultant is how to harness the new learning, and how to get the appropriate people's attention to take advantage of the surprise. Taking advantage of the surprise in an exciting way begins the learner on the road to self-education: Learning to LEARN anew, over and over in each context.

The traditional view of Learning to LEARN is that of formal education. The learning task is comprised essentially of learning, unlearning, relearning, and learning from the future – both within and beyond the conventional frame-works covering the whole spectrum from preschool to postgraduate studies and beyond – from birth to death. Further, Gharajedaghi notes that, *"the real responsibility of the education system is to convert the learners to self-educators"* (emphasis added). Today's business environment demands self-education both individually and collectively in order to exist. Unfortunately most management consultants first learned in educational systems that did not believe or understand the need for converting learners to self-educators. These educational systems, created in the past, did not realize the learning demands that would be placed on all constituents by global transformative change. For example, the current learning required to be interdependent, self-organizing, and to make choices (third generation Systems Thinking) is not directly addressed in most of our school systems. Management Consultants need to strengthen self education in the individual as well as the organization to aid Learning to LEARN throughout the engagement.

Today, education is essentially a licensing activity, and does not take seriously the conversion task to self-education. In other words, the output of formal education is only a very few self-educators prepared to thrive in a fast changing world. However, formal education continues to approve its limiting activity and communicates through a certificate, degree, diploma, or license that the individual has successfully completed an educational activity -- not necessarily learning to be a self-educator, nor going out in the world to continue learning. Interestedly, Fast Company (October, 2000) notes that education is the only company that "fires" its best performers at graduation.

Thus, conversion to self-education has not been accomplished, nor has there been clarity about the specifics of learning, unlearning, relearning, and -- learning from the future . In most cases, this leaves the management consultant ill-prepared for taking responsibility and leadership in the basic Learning to LEARN task with self and others.

Learning to LEARN is becoming a self-educator

Understanding and acting on the basic Learning to Learn task _is_ becoming a self-educator. Understanding in contemporary contexts is taking initiative in _learning, unlearning, relearning,_ and learning from the future -- utilizing every opportunity to maximize the development of new competencies in general living, and in specific areas of significance to the individual. The basic Learning to LEARN task is inclusive of learning, unlearning, and relearning, and gains direction with the overt goal of becoming a self-educator. Making the goal overtly places the learner in a position of choice about what is to be learned and learned in the service to what end. Thus ownership and use of the learning are less of an issue in practice – for the learner is choosing with a goal in mind. The conversion to a self-educator is an internal one, made by the learner - becoming needs to be a conscious choice on the part of the learner. It is critical that the learner be made aware of the opportunity and the need to self-educate. Often, for learning to occur one must only be made aware that the responsibility for learning and self -education is with the learner – it is not inherent in the educational system. To educate one self is not the challenge today as it was in yesteryear. Currently there is significant electronic capability available to bridge time and space in acquisition of learning. However, becoming requires the desire to BE a self-educator, and then the initiative to search out the necessary new learning, unlearning, and relearning to accomplish the specific learning goals. Becoming a self-educator may not be easy, but is easily addressed once the challenge of learning, unlearning, relearning, and learning from the future are more fully understood. The progression to learning from the future denotes openness to Systems Thinking and co-creating unique value as collective opportunities emerge. All four aspects of learning are essential in the global economy and age of innovation (Prahalad & Krishnan, 2007).

Learning is generally defined quite simply as gaining knowledge, understanding of, or a skill through study, instruction, or experience which results in a behavioral change of the learner. In contrast, the description of learning here (learning results from being surprised and detecting a mismatch) adds value for the novice to better understand learning. Being surprised capitalizes on a common experience of many people in their current context. But most importantly, the surprise is a signal to the learner that something different is apparent.

A surprise acts as a signal and makes it easier for the individual to relate to and identify the experience. Surprise in itself has a way of getting the learner's attention and then it is only necessary to focus what "to do differently" to avoid the mismatch experience in the future. The latter definition of learning is easily applied and the individual can more readily identify "mismatches," signaling the opportunity to learn. In addition, the learner has a new way of looking at these surprises – in contrast to the past, when a mismatch was often seen as something "wrong." In this case, it signals something potentially "good" and is often the basis of a new, creative learning for the present and near future.

"Unlearning" is somewhat different, and perhaps even more difficult. The need to unlearn occurs when the learner identifies that something is not working. Once identified, the learner literally "pulls out" of his knowledge bank or memory that which is to be unlearned. This often is accomplished with an internal conversation telling oneself that this "chunk" of data is no longer useful and it may be removed. The difficult part may be in the "attitude" that was associated with the piece to be unlearned. Usually with new learning there is an attitude of "excitement" associated with the learning. If this attitudinal aspect is preventing necessary unlearning, it must be removed as well. In a sense, it is undoing the *effect of* in addition to the fact, which in some cases may be very extensive. However, unlearning may be seen as removing what has become a mismatch internally. It is like sending the unneeded knowledge to the recycle bin or trash. It is very important to actively get rid of unusable knowledge, skill, or understanding including the attitude associated with it, creating more space for new learning. At the same time, actively working at unlearning saves time and prevents confusion in sorting out the new, relevant learning from the old (unusable learning). This is a rather simple procedure to actively unlearn – simply bring to the verbal level the command to delete, drop, send to trash, or pull out the "learning" that is no longer usable. It is important to reinforce visually by discarding it and going on. Cleaning up your new mental files becomes increasingly important as we see knowledge doubling faster and faster – in shorter periods of time.

Unlearning may be seen as consciously removing what was actively in mind-memory as a learned piece of knowledge acquired in the past. The original bit of knowledge no longer fits. Furthermore, it may cause the learner considerable loss of time in applying the new learning as he reexamines fit and use over and over again. Most of us have not learned to unlearn in a systematic way, or even consider such "mind cleaning" or reorganizing the contents of different files to meet changing requirements. Peter Vaill (1996) clearly identifies that the root cause of the problem with unlearning is in public education's lack of attention to the matter of "unlearning." Formal education has simply continued to "add-on," rather than remove or change anything.

What is important is that the management consultant is the one who must understand first to do "unlearning," and then to do "new learning" in order to actively deal with the situation, often common and confounding for the client. It is difficult to realize that something learned earlier that was apparently helpful does not have meaning now, and furthermore that it could be blocking new learning or relearning. We live in an age of information overload exacerbating the issue with unlearning. With current pressures to compress time, many pieces of information get an individual's attention and get codified into learning before unlearning is even examined. Obviously, this complicates the unlearning experience, for no removal or reorganization is going on.

"Relearning" covers learning again something that was only partially learned earlier, or filling in what has faded from memory over time. Often, relearning may be necessary because in the initial learning experience the learner did not have enough information to be able to generalize the learning to other situations.   In the case of a novel situation, it may call for new learning or relearning. Most relearning is done quite casually, never considering what might have been done differently or more effectively when first considered. Because the individual has accumulated new life experiences and business situations, the relearning is inherently changed by virtue of an ever evolving paradigm. In the casual approach to relearning neither efficiency nor effectiveness have been considered in most instances, whether formalized or not. What is suggested here is that relearning may be more effective, and efficient for that matter, when a healthy structure for learning has been established beforehand.

Understanding learning, unlearning, and relearning in an active ongoing mode provides the skill necessary for successful self-education, and makes conversion a real possibility. However, the step into ongoing self-education needs to be a conscious one, because becoming a self-educator places much more responsibility on the person – responsibility for making choices on how, what, and when learning, unlearning, and relearning may occur.

Realizing the conscious step as an approach to self-education legitimizes learning, unlearning, and relearning any place and at any time, not only in the formal halls of an educational institution. This is important as it frees the learner to learn in a variety of ways and places, possibly uncommon or not available in the past. This also allows the learner to integrate both knowledge and information messages,, decreasing some of the information overload that exists in the context.

By taking responsibility publicly for his/her own self-education through learning, unlearning, and relearning modes, the management consultant is not only freed from reusing the same context, but is free to facilitate the learning, unlearning, and relearning of others in situations that are highly interdependent and quite common.   When the management consultant takes this responsibility for himself/herself, it is a great leap, freeing the consultant to bridge the responsibility for facilitating the learning of the client. As early as possible, the consultant should facilitate the client to take responsibility publicly for their own self-education, thus freeing the consultant to facilitate others' learning. The client may also learn to facilitate the learning for others, following the same pattern as described.

"New Learning" extends beyond the iterative gains from relearning. Where relearning entails the process of learning something similar again with a new paradigmatic view, learning from the future or *Presencing* (the term coined by Scharmer, 2000) is fresh and current. *Presencing* can take place at the individual level and at a collective level. When an individual experiences learning from the future she/he steps away from prior experience or models, cultivating a self-awareness that relies on observation with an open mind and an open heart, or co-sensing

(Scharmer, 2007). When groups of people begin to observe and listen with open minds and hearts, a collective awareness and open will unleash even more potential for learning and innovation. As these groups open themselves to new possibilities and become aware of the creative power in the moments of their interaction, they sense the fertile ground for new learning and can allow new learning to emerge. Purposefulness or collective will is energized and becomes operational. While new learning at an individual level unleashes human potential one person at a time, the same type of emergence at the group level is not only multiplied, but exponential. The outcome of collective awareness, emergent thinking, and presenced opportunity yields a co-created value that by its very nature represents new learning because it could not have existed or emerged with the prior paradigm. When a management consultant can facilitate learning from the future or *Presencing* for a client, the client's new paradigm can fuel a multi-minded and collective approach to emergent learning and ongoing cycles of transformative change. While relearning utilizes some prior knowledge or experience and applies it in a different way, *Presencing* is the output of new thinking by individuals brought together in a specific circumstance to generate unique opportunities. Similarly, individuals in a different circumstance with open minds, open hearts, and open wills generate a systems outcome that is yet again unique.

Developing a learning process tool: C – C 2 Step

In learning, unlearning, relearning, and *Presencing* what is important is that the management consultant takes responsibility for his/her own learning first, and then that of the client . It is important that taking responsibility for the client learning is short lived, and that very early in each new relationship the responsibility be actively transferred to the client. Without client learning there is little progress. The recommended model for the developing consultant is shown in Figure 12. The Consultant – Client Two Step Learning Process Tool [C-C 2-Step]. The first step in the model is diagnosis. The management consultant first identifies their learning needs in all three areas, then moves to identify the client's learning needs in relation to Learning to BE, Learning to LEARN, and Learning to DO. The consultant is in the best position to shape the learning intervention and to tune in to the appropriate level of the client's experience to increase overall success potential. Open communication and understanding on "learning requirements in the situation" are achieved in the consultant-client relationship using the C-C 2-step learning tool. Respecting the use of the C-C 2 step learning tool is a basic to healthy relationship, the latter so necessary in the 21st century.

The management consultant needs to practice diagnosis of his/her own learning in relation to the consulting context as an ongoing task – and likewise for the client – constantly helping the client to learn in the best way at the time. The learning described assists in "becoming." It is not new, but it is now seen as a conscious task for both the consultant and the client. New learning, unlearning, or relearning when self-directed increases the flexibility of the learner. The sooner the consultant helps the client to see their role as "becoming" through developing "learning as a way of being," the easier the larger task of change. The outcome for the client is in_moving significantly down the road of interdependence toward achieving success in the engagement through experiencing shared responsibility for development. Repeated use of the C-C 2-step rapidly moves toward identifying self-education as an important mode for both the management consultant and the client.

Rewarding converted self-educators Interestingly, many businesses and industries have moved to a form of self-education, driven first by a need to survive, and then by the need to thrive -- continually coping with global change in their workplaces. The management consultant may capitalize on this conversion to self-education by publicly complimenting the client individually and collectively as appropriate – essentially making self-education a rewarded, conscious choice of the individual in the work place. They may point out the savings in time and training compared with other institutions. This self-education component needs to be rewarded and verbally reinforced to continue its use and development in the workplace, aiding overall transformative change.

When the conversion to self-educator is not obvious, it is the responsibility of the management consultant to first provide the opportunity for the client to experience on their own, and then conceptualize, complement, and find further uses for the self-educating component to continue. This is a very important conversion to self-education for both the consultant and the client. There is no excuse for not making the conversion happen as soon as possible in the work place, for this now is the client's educational context.

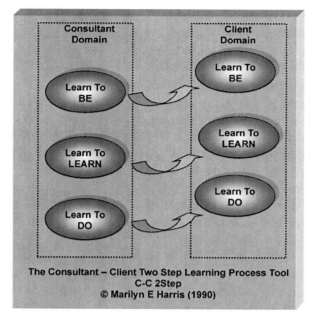

The Consultant – Client Two Step Learning Process Tool
C-C 2Step
© Marilyn E Harris (1990)

Figure 12: The Consultant – Client Two Step Learning Process Tool (C-C 2-Step)

Actively moving in the self-educator role opens many doors, but most importantly offers joint participation and interdependent approaches to work between consultant – consultant, consultant - client, client – client, and in non-human resources such as computers to network with consultants, clients, and others. Participation makes relationship possible and offers the opportunity for building relationships in many areas. The approach in self-education takes much of the authority of knowledge or position out of the situation and provides opportunities to work as peers, which in return facilitates wider resource use and application in practice.

<u>**Information-bonded relationships are key**</u> Currently, the key to building relationships is through the type of bonding that occurs – and information-bonded systems are most successful. In contrast to mechanical systems that are "energy-bonded", information-bonded relationships are an agreement based on a common perception. In revisiting the earlier reference, Gharajedaghi (1985) compares an energy-bonded system of an automobile and a driver to an information-bonded system of a horse and its rider. In this instance, horse and rider form an

information-bonded system, just as consultant and client do in a consulting engagement. In an information-bonded system, guidance and control are achieved by a second-degree agreement – an agreement based on a common perception which is preceded by a psychological contract. The "common perception" may be interpreted as having the same "goal" in mind, but having publicly stated it and agreed to it – different than the horse and rider. The psychological contract is often formally made in the first phase of the consulting systems worldview approach -- "Entry and Contracting."   However, this psychological contract must be publicly renewed or developed afresh on the spot when first establishing a new relationship, even in the same context.

The public aspect of verbalizing it aloud between consultant and client is very important for three specific reasons. One, it is public at that point – and may be questioned or clarified if necessary, but most importantly it is not a secret that may be unclear to those participating in developing the new relationship. The second reason is that it focuses a very important aspect in establishing an information-bonded relationship – the psychological contract. The psychological contract is a necessity if the relationship is to develop.   Many consultants overlook making a psychological contract, for they believe it is covered in the legal document or written agreement stating the terms of engagement which may have been arranged by entirely different people. A psychological contract is usually between persons, but it is not unheard of between a person and a material object, such as a computer system or network (Kelly, 1996). The agreement is psychological – which covers the related thoughts, feelings, and behavior of the parties to the contract. Such a contract is usually spoken and not written, but often confirmed with a handshake or a "pat-on-the-back" in the case of the horse. The third reason is redundancy. Even when the contract is public, there are usually so many issues on the table that it is easy to forget the psychological contract – thus, redundancy is important in reinforcement and in strengthening the point in memory.

Information-bonded relationships in team building Isgar (1993) focuses on information-bonded relationships in his book on teambuilding, The Ten Minute Team, 10 Steps to Building High Performing Teams. Using the ten steps or factors outlined in Figure 13. regularly, and one at a time, each ten minute team dialogue, focuses the team on the "information" that is necessary for bonding. In a sense, as the team members' dialogue together on these ten factors, they make psychological contracts relative to their ongoing team tasks. Of particular note are two factors in the diagram where Isgar focuses on "Team Focus on External Relationships" and "Relationships with Critical Others."

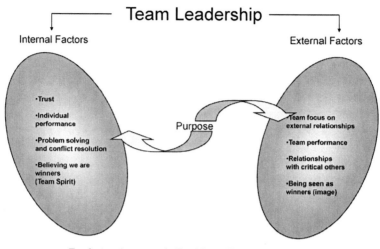

Ten factors important in Ten Minute Team Development
Adapted from © Thomas Isgar, 1989

Figure 13: Ten factors Important in Ten Minute Team Development

Isgar specifically describes developing "relationships with critical others" as Step 3. This step identifies the importance of developing a relationship with critical others outside of the team. Isgar further identifies accomplishments of the team in these relationships as:

- Clarifying the other person's performance expectations of the team
- Getting current feedback about your team's performance
- Maintaining a positive relationship with a critical person in the organization
- Strengthening the team by having one of the subordinates be the primary link between the team and the other manager
- Helping other managers improve her/his own team's performance, which helps everyone

While Isgar's Step 4 is Team Focus on External Relationships, it is described as the step where the team develops a list of critical others, regularly looks for additions, changes, deletions to the list, and identifies recent events which may change the team's credibility. In each case, an individual is identified to work with the critical others. The team, as well as the manager, provides advice and strategic help to that individual. Critical others may include the manager, special resources to the team such as those who have relevant and new knowledge not existent in the team, and even go beyond to include spouses of team members or others important to the team's high performance. These relationships usually are with members of the organization outside of the team who may be important information resources to the team and actually affect performance. Although Isgar's structure is not formalized as a second-degree agreement, he points out the importance of psychological contracts among team members contributing to high performing teams. While relationships are important, they must not be over stressed or under achieved.

Getting the attention of the learner is basic

When developing the understanding required to activate the Learning to LEARN principles, getting the learner's attention does not appear as a significant issue for most management consultants. In the past, for example, in public school settings "attention" was expected whenever the teacher spoke. Actually, this was not the case – many times the teacher never checked to see if she had the attention of the student learners. Often, the teacher continued only with the expectation – not the attention of the learner. However, nowadays, getting the attention of the learner – even oneself, as an individual wanting to learn – is not guaranteed. There are so many stimuli begging for attention in most settings, it is difficult to focus on any one factor, no matter how important it may be. However, it is difficult to learn something new without paying attention to it. It is clear that in consulting engagements getting the client's attention at the right time is a problem for the developing management consultant. The problem is one of balance and correcting imbalance.

Focusing balance in attention Attention is an intangible commodity, difficult to get a hold of and address relative to its focus and use. Davenport and Beck (2001) recognized the need for getting focused attention in the business world -- in fact realized that "attention deficit" is the most significant problem in today's business world. Addressing this problem, they have created AttentionScape, a tool with a patent pending, to advance the state of self-reported attention measurement. The tool assesses how people and organizations allocate their attention. AttentionScape helps diagnose attention distribution problems, determines how attention is being directed, analyzes attention given from persons involved, and evaluates complete tasks that require detailed attention levels. Essentially, Davenport and Beck's AttentionScape measures six different types of attention: captive or voluntary, aversion-based or attraction-based, and front-of-the mind or back-of-the mind -- and in different combinations. AttentionScape measures the level and type of attention and explains how to understand and interpret the measurements. AttentionScape is more rigorous, and much less detailed and tedious than other methods.   The major advantage is that Davenport and Beck have provided consultants with a tool to get "hands-on" experience with an intangible factor, like attention, and have provided some means to make a difference in individual and group responses.

Often employees pay captive and voluntary attention, or front of the mind and attraction-based attention to a task that the boss has given them, and does not use other attention types which may be more appropriate or may correct an inherent attention imbalance.   The AttentionScape tool may be used to create a more balanced use of attention in specific situations, and more importantly, to make new learning possible.   Skilled management consultants know how to use a tool like AttentionScape in their practice.   Further, Davenport and Beck find that skilled consultants know how to produce high levels of all six types of attention – sometimes simultaneously, separately, without recognizing that they are producing these results or even understanding how the results are occurring.

Correcting attention imbalances There are several strategies available for correcting attention imbalances.   Davenport and Beck (2001) have developed strategies for each of the six types of attention noted.   For example, as related to Back-of-Mind attention, a procurement manager who had developed and perfected the system for "paper based" buying did not see the Internet coming and doesn't know how to adapt to it now. In correcting this attention imbalance, one may make the habitual parts of the task more conscious by mixing up the routine and pausing to think about what you really are doing.   You may teach the task to someone who knows nothing about it.   Davenport and Beck suggest using the mantra: "Once more with feeling." The use of this strategy subtly points out that correcting attention imbalance is not punishing, but rewarding in refocusing the methodology that has taken a back seat in a positive way. The mantra has a way of reinforcing a positive aspect in attention getting and making it casual, but serious.   The developing management consultant will find correcting attention imbalances has value in relearning, thus enhancing the output and the bottom line.

The developing management consultant is encouraged to explore and to use different instrumentation to aid focused balance in attention for self and for clients in further developing the overall Learning to Learn task. Since the way attention is used both individually and in a group is so critical, the developing management consultant is encouraged to increase the use of the Learning to LEARN attention-getting and attention-maintaining techniques. In conclusion, the management consultant may recognize the value of Learning to LEARN in terms of the new implications in basic understanding and mastering required in the 21st century. It is clear that capitalizing on the learning processes in learning, relearning, unlearning, and learning from the future, consistently moving toward self-education, is a necessity. However, it is a huge undertaking in contemporary contexts. The management consultant must encourage and enable all he/she contacts to Learn to LEARN in the context – in new ways. The new approach leading to self-education is freeing to the consultant once accomplished. The consultant, and the client, are free to make choices, work interdependently, and to self-organize for action, making it possible to see through chaos as well as manage complexity with more ease. Learning to LEARN richly enhances one's practice in management consulting – it enhances the life of both the consultant and the client, developing the new responsibility so apparent to self-educate.

Chapter 7   Learning to Leverage Knowledge

For your people to be innovative and motivated, you need to consider human needs. If you feel good and appreciated, you are much more open to many things than if you always need to defend yourself.

— Andreas Rihs, CEO, Phonak

Learning to leverage knowledge begins with the understanding that people in human networks are the leveraging agents in organizations and society. Knowledge cannot be separated from the human networks and communities that create, use, and transform it.   For developing management consultants learning to leverage knowledge is a two-step process. First, people in the organization must be freed up to create, use, and transform knowledge.   In all types of knowledge work people require conversations, experimentation, and experiences shared with other people who do what they do (Allee, 2003). Andreas Rihs, Phonak CEO, believes these shared conversations, experiments, and experiences are 'human needs' of people in the workplace, and that they must be considered if people are to be innovative and motivated. Second, but more importantly, people must be recognized for their necessary contribution in leveraging knowledge. People must know that they are important in creating, using, and transforming knowledge – basically in producing social capital. Social capital consists of the active connections among people – the trust, mutual understanding and shared values and behaviors that bind the members of human networks and communities, and make cooperative action possible. Social capital depends on trust. The focus for consultants is based on how people know or are recognized for leveraging knowledge in social capital in the workplace.

Basically Allee (2003) developed a strategic perspective for describing the role of social capital, defined as "intangibles" in the economy. The premise for thinking of intangibles as assets is that knowledge, relationships, and ideas are more important for success today than are the physical assets. In short, intangibles are a nonphysical claim to future benefits and may be classified as: *external structure* (alliances and relationships outside the organization), *human competence* (individual and collective capabilities), and *internal structure* (systems and work processes that leverage competitiveness). The real value that can be realized from new knowledge creation is in the increase of tangible assets. These value gains that show up in ROI figures are for the short term. Ideally, a knowledge endeavor would show both an immediate ROI and longer-term benefits that build capability for future value creation. Intangibles are at the heart of all human activity, and evident as patterns in non-linear exchanges and transactions between people.

Making intangible cognitive and emotive exchanges visible evokes three important attributes of intangibles. Intangibles may be considered as assets, negotiable goods, and deliverables – all important in value creation and prosperity.   Research has shown a strong connection between emotional intelligence and profitability. Emotional intelligence is a form of social intelligence that involves the ability to monitor one's own as well as another's feeling. Daniel Goleman (1998) found that "the single most important element in group intelligence . . .is not the average IQ in the academic sense, but rather in terms of emotional intelligence." The Levering, Moskowitz, Munoz, Hjelt, and Wheat (2002) studies of great places to work also found that companies with excellent employee relationships and social harmony enjoyed greater financial success than other companies in their industry.

The consultant focus on learning to leverage the knowledge of people in an organization decreases tension and allows the knowledge creation process to develop a healthier culture overall. The task of this chapter is learning to leverage knowledge through learning what's important in creating knowledge, and in linking knowledge to performance frameworks to create a new culture of self organizing self-educators.

Enabling knowledge creation

The task in learning to leverage knowledge is complicated by the need to first enable knowledge creation in the work place -- where so many barriers to knowledge creation still exist (Van Krogh et al., 2000). Many workplaces operate in a manner that denies the use of new knowledge or the possibility of learning from the future.

Knowledge creation is a dynamic process that can involve contributions from literally all people in an organization. Each member of a community has unique, personal knowledge, at least part of which is tacit and not easily explained to others. When managers bring workers together on a project, the challenge for everyone is discovering how to utilize the full potential, leveraging it to be more than the sum of what individual members know. Whenever individuals share their knowledge in a group, they must publicly justify what they believe. This public sharing can be quite difficult – fraught with self doubt, fear of going against community norms or established relationships, and the overall need to stand up for one's own ideas. In fact, justification plays a crucial part in knowledge creation and is what makes it such a highly fragile process.

In any organization, there are four severe barriers to justification in a group setting: (1) the need for a legitimate language, (2) organizational stories, (3) procedures, and (4) company paradigms (Berger & Luckmann, 1967). Like individual knowledge barriers, organizational barriers often arise because of natural human tendencies, but these barriers can also be strengthened because of a weak managerial attitude toward the use of knowledge and knowledge creation. This is particularly evident when it comes to numerous procedures and the required acceptance of limited company paradigms.

The current popularity of knowledge-management initiatives might lead one to believe that many firms are constructively addressing the barriers to knowledge creation. Yet it is much easier to talk about knowledge use than to "walk the talk." In addition, knowledge management as it is practiced in most firms represents a constricting paradigm rather than a transformative one. Von Krogh et al. (2000) noted several factors that contributed to a constricting paradigm; for example: some of these were 1) the emphasis on quantifying ever smaller pieces of information, 2) an obsession with measurement tools, 3) the use of terminology that may limit the free flow of ideas, 4) the rigid procedures established, and 5) the overarching assumption that knowledge can be controlled. All of the factors reinforce many of the barriers instead of dismantling them.

The links between knowledge enabling and creation The fragility of knowledge creation means that it must be carefully supported by a number of enabling activities, in spite of the obstacles. Knowledge enabling encompasses a specific set of variables: 1) instilling a knowledge vision, 2) managing conversations, 3) mobilizing knowledge activists, 4) creating the right context, and 5) globalizing local knowledge. Figure 14. The Knowledge Enabling Grid shows the knowledge creation steps. It is important that knowledge enabling involves both deliberate activities – those that can be planned and directed by management – and emergent ones, the unintended consequences of intended actions, or discovery after the fact of particular activities promoting knowledge creation. Overall, knowledge enabling should be thought of in a circular manner; it is always aimed at enhancing the knowledge-creating potential of the company. For the developing management consultant this may require developing new *sensitivities* to enable and create in the engagement.

An enabling context matters Knowledge creation puts particular demands on organizational relationships. In order to share personal knowledge individuals must rely on others to listen and react to their ideas. Constructive and helpful relations enable people to share their insights and freely discuss their concerns. They also enable micro-communities, the origin of knowledge-creation in companies, to form and self-organize.

Knowledge Creation Steps

KNOWLEDGE ENABLERS	Sharing Tacit Knowledge	Creating a Concept	Justifying a Concept	Building a Prototype	Cross-Leveling Knowledge
Instill a vision		√	√ √	√	√√
Manage Conversations	√√	√√	√√	√√	√√
Mobilize Activists		√	√	√	√√
Create the Right Context	√	√	√√	√	√√
Globalize Local Knowledge					√√

Adopted from © Von Krogh et al (2000)

Figure 14: Knowledge Enabling Grid
Adapted from © Von Krogh et al. (2000)

Healthy relationships purge a knowledge-creation process of distrust, fear, and dissatisfaction, and allow organizational members to feel safe enough to explore the unknown territories of new markets, new customers, new products, and new manufacturing technologies.

At a more basic level, several studies show ways in which people interact – cooperative sharing versus competitive hoarding, "join us" versus "not at my table" – these strongly affect the distribution of tacit knowledge. The sharing of tacit knowledge is especially susceptible to both individual and organizational barriers identified, and requires careful nurturing. Since knowledge is often equated with power and influence in a firm, knowledge "shielding" tactics can become daily practice (Pfeffer, 1992). The management consultant must acknowledge the hoarding of knowledge as one of the fundamental issues of modern business organizations, and that that is why the concept of care has such relevance. The importance of relationships in a business setting may seem obvious, necessary, and almost not worth mentioning. Yet as most management consultants know, difficulties often arise precisely because of "people problems." When productive knowledge-creation – the very engine of innovation in contemporary organizations -- is threatened, the bottom line can suffer. The creation and justification of concepts is influenced by the strength of relationships and the extent to which organizational members feel they can suggest new concepts and ideas, as well as convey and receive constructive criticism.

Most management consultants know "in their head" that the need for care of others may be met by helping others to learn, by increasing their awareness of important events and consequences, and by nurturing their personal knowledge while sharing their thoughts. But consultants, as a collectivity, do not act on what they know. In most cases, consultants are unclear about how to address the need organizationally.

What is needed to move ahead is social capital building – building trust, sharing of values, and developing mutual understanding. For the developing consultant to build social capital it means taking time and creating opportunities for people to interact to build trust. In many cases, it means confronting the myth that trust may not be developed because it is an intangible and hard to get "a hold of." Trust may be developed in almost any situation, if the need is verbalized among all involved and focused on. Tom Isgar (1993) says "I believe that trust can be developed rapidly and maintained, but that the team leader and the team have to *actively focus on trust building* rather than hoping that trust occurs as a result of time and experience [emphasis added]." Later in the text Isgar summarizes:

- Trust is built by focusing directly on it
- Taking risks is necessary to build trust
- Getting supported for taking risks builds trust
- Allowing yourself to be vulnerable increases others' trust of you
- Caring about each other is necessary to establish trust
- Letting go of negative incidents in the past is critical to trust building

The developing consultant has a double task in trust building. First, in building trust between themselves and the client, and second, in assisting the client to build trust among themselves in each setting. Building trusting relationships is critical in enabling knowledge creation.

In Figure 15. Knowledge Creation When Care is High or Low, Von Krogh et al. (2000) points out that knowledge creation can take two different paths depending on the extent that care is present. The two contexts shown are Low Care: Hypercompetition at its worst, and High Care: Indwelling and an enabling context. At one extreme – *hypercompetition* – care runs low, individual knowledge is seized, and hegemonies of knowledge are built and highly protected. In contrast, *indwelling* is about commitment to an idea, experience, concept, or fellow human being.

	Individual Knowledge	Social Knowledge
Low Care	SEIZING Everyone out for himself	TRANSACTING Swapping documentation or other explicit knowledge
High Care	BESTOWING Helping by sharing insights	INDWELLING Living with a concept together

© Von Krough et al (2000)

**Figure 15: Knowledge Creation When Care is High or Low
Adapted from © Von Krogh et al. (2000)**

In the text the authors suggest a practical guide in the workplace to "indwelling," which the consultant may use while working at knowledge creation at an organizational level. The use of the guide requires time and space in the organization. The seven steps are:

1. Review the knowledge vision
2. Identify sources of tacit knowledge
3. Identify the likely impact of this tacit knowledge on the vision and how accessible the sources are
4. Establish caring relationships with each source of tacit knowledge
5. Build up a common experience base with each source

of tacit knowledge
6.   Allow for numerous reiterations of steps 4 and 5
7.   Evaluate the results of indwelling

Indwelling is a path to take, and these steps are offered to aid the management consultant in helping the organization along the knowledge creation path, and in balancing strategy to create competitive advantage.
In conclusion, consultants need to give precedence to knowledge creation, realizing that they are enabling new knowledge to continually alter and adapt the advancement strategy and vision of the firm. The next section focuses on frameworks focusing knowledge use, and links knowledge to performance.

Using knowledge frameworks encourages navigation

Identification and definition of the key knowledge elements is the basis for understanding.   Further, it provides a usable language in communication. Successful navigation in the knowledge era depends on the use of a map of the territory. A map is invaluable in dealing with the complexity that abounds.   To get the map one must sort the ideas, knowledge, and experience of many thinkers in many fields to see apparent patterns. Bringing together differing theorist thinking exposes meaningful patterns.   Verna Allee (1997) developed a knowledge archetype as a basis for applying learning in an organization. Figure 16. The Knowledge Archetype shows a progression of knowledge that is seldom as neat in real life as depicted. However, it does provide a framework for the consultant to use as he/she assists the organizational navigation through the fast developing knowledge jungle.

- **Data** floats like so many whitecaps in a larger sea of information. Data becomes information through linking and organizing with other data
- **Information** becomes Knowledge when it is analyzed, linked to other information, and compared to what is already known
- **Knowledge** operates in the larger social context of Meaning, which encompasses archetypal patterns and forces, as well as our social and cultural biases and interpretations
- **Meaning** in turn, is embedded in the larger and more abstract realm of philosophy, which is the broad territory of assumptions, beliefs, and theories about how things work
- **Philosophy** and the systemic thinking that typifies this level are embedded in the yet more inclusive Wisdom perspective of values
- **Wisdom** enfolds our values and purpose. It encompasses the totality of our worldview
- **Union** is an open, all inclusive, expansive feeling state of oneness, enabled by the intellect that allows us to understand and change our values in relation to the ultimate good.

Figure 16: The Knowledge Archetype
Adapted from© Verna Allee (1997)

Knowledge is always changing. In an organization, knowledge changes around products, services, processes, technology, structures, roles, and relationships. No sooner is a pattern of knowledge identified than a new one seems to appear. Allee (1997) identifies some hard realities of organizational knowledge that the developing management consultant may wish to consider to put her at ease in the knowledge management process:

- Knowledge is "messy"
- Knowledge is self-organizing
- Knowledge seeks community
- Knowledge travels on language
- The more you try to pin knowledge down, the more it slips away
- Looser is probably better
- There is no final solution in knowledge management
- Knowledge does not grow forever – something eventually dies or is lost
- No one is really in charge
- You cannot impose rules and systems
- There is no silver bullet
- How you define the knowledge "question" determines what and how you manage

During the 1990's organizational learning-related activities were largely focused on the incremental improvement of existing processes. Most leadership teams are now facing a new set of business challenges that can rarely be successfully addressed with the traditional methods and concepts of organizational learning. Classical methods and concepts of organizational learning are all variations of the same Kolb- based (1984) learning cycle "Observe, Reflect, Plan, Act" where all learning is based on reflecting on the experiences of the past. However, several currently significant leadership challenges cannot be successfully approached this way because the experience base of a team often is irrelevant for the issue at hand. In order to do well in the emerging business environments, organizations and their leaders have to develop a new cognitive capability, the capability for sensing and seizing emerging business opportunities (Arthur, 1996) in the Other Learning Cycle "Seeing, Sensing, Presencing, and Enacting" commonly referred to as Learning from Emerging Futures (Sharmer, 2000). The other learning cycle refers to its capacity as the emerging discipline of *Presencing*. The term *Presencing* means to use one's highest self as a vehicle for sensing, embodying, and enacting emerging futures. The purpose here is to introduce the concept of *Presencing* as a leadership discipline for developing management consultants and leaders alike for navigation in emerging business environments. Figure 17. Comparative Learning Cycles depicts the two learning cycles discussed: Learning from the Experiences of the Past, and Learning from Emerging Futures. The latter, Learning from Emerging Futures' temporal source is the future, more precisely, the *'coming into presence'* of the future. This learning is based on sensing and embodying emerging futures rather than re-enacting the patterns of the past. Today's business environment presents most companies with challenges that require a new source and process of learning. These challenges are concerned with how to compete and to cooperate under the conditions of the new economy – that is, how to learn from a reality that is not yet embodied in manifest experience. The answer to "learning from a reality not yet embodied experience of the future" takes one to an analogy in managing the complexity of large-scale change (Scharmer, 2000)

Until today, most approaches to managing change have followed the basic sequence that Lewin (1946 defined. although different names and numbers of steps have been used in various approaches to change management, the underlying logic has remained the same – Lewin's terminology of *unfreezing, moving,* and *refreezing.*

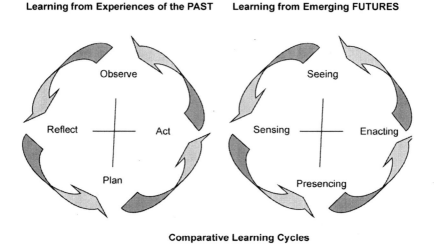

Learning from Experiences of the PAST   **Learning from Emerging FUTURES**

Observe

Reflect ——|—— Act

Plan

Seeing

Sensing ——|—— Enacting

Presencing

Comparative Learning Cycles

Figure 17:   Comparative Learning Cycles

Scharmer now redefines managing the complexity of large-scale change as an *organizational breathing cycle*. Imagining the organization as a living system (which it is) one can think of "uncovering" or unfreezing as the organization *inhaling*: taking the current reality into its consciousness, actually "breathing in."   Likewise, one can think of enacting as an interior-out process of converting a changed consciousness into practices and actions in "breathing out."   Accordingly, the Lewin model of unfreezing-moving-refreezing can be seen as one sequence within an ongoing process of *organizational breathing*. Further, clarifying the shift required in organizational breathing as learning cycles moves from the reflective learning. Learning from experiences of the past – to generative learning, learning from emerging futures. According to the Lewinian model, the highest leverage point is located at the stage of unfreezing. The key challenge for both consultants and leaders is at this stage: how to shift from reflective learning to generative learning – learning from emerging futures within the organizational breathing process as depicted. The management consultant must enable the shift by assisting a company to develop the capacity to challenge and change its own assumptions and beliefs. The shifting of underlying assumptions and beliefs can release tremendous new energy. The consultant must be able to model this openness and responsiveness to the environment – and to encourage, not dictate   to   the   client,   to   demonstrate   a   greater   openness   and responsiveness to the environment to instill the organizational breathing cycle. Often this can be accomplished by linking knowledge, learning, and performance in their active breathing experience.

Seeing patterns of knowledge, learning, and performance Knowledge and learning in groups and organizations is different. At the individual level, the way individuals receive, process, and communicate information usually work unconsciously. Individuals master advanced thinking skills through education, self-reflection, and discourse. An organization is composed of many individuals, and faces a significantly more difficult task when trying to master knowledge and learning. There is a quantum leap in complexity, stemming from the sheer numbers of people and groups who need very different kinds of knowledge to support their work. In addition, the communication and learning processes around information and knowledge are much more complex at the group level. Each mode of knowledge thrives on different communication modes. Each has its own language for problem solving. Further complications arise in times of stress and when time-frames are short. The sidebar "Understanding Team Learning" provides insight to team learning important to make a shift in learning cycles and the shift to an emphasis on performance.

Sidebar: **Understanding Team Learning**

Insight and understanding alone are not always enough to solve team performance problems. Every group of people is unique. Different groups require different solutions. In some cases, people just will not be able to work together successfully. Collaboration and cooperation require more than just understanding differences. It requires a variety of social and personal capabilities as well. Developing effective teams requires mastering a whole range of skills and team processes.

Team learning is different from team building. Team building focuses on interpersonal behaviors that improve communication and build strong relationships. Team Learning, on the other hand, is a more inclusive term that includes team building. Team learning involves both looking inward to create alignment and looking outward to build knowledge – together.

Team learning develops as members of a work group learn to *consciously* reflect on their own learning processes. Team learning is not something that is done to or for a work group. Team learning is not something people must do for themselves. If people do not know how to pay attention to their own group learning processes, then team learning will not move to more advanced levels.

Individual and team learning will happen whether people pay attention to it or not. However, if a group wants to maximize and deepen learning together, then it must be valued, appreciated, and attended to. Team learning is not mechanical, it is organic. Learning unfolds from the purpose and intent of the people involved. Team learning really begins when people ask, "What is it we are all here to do, and why do we want or need to do it together?"

To make a comfortable shift in "breathing in" to "breathing out" with a new activity, focus is required, the experiences must be conceptually linked demonstrating the relationship between specific learning and performance anticipated or needed. Based on the knowledge archetype, Verna Allee has produced a comprehensive reference chart in Figure 18. The Learning and Performance Framework. The chart links knowledge, learning, and performance, identifying the appropriate time perspective for each level. The chart is an invaluable tool for the management consultant to use in facilitating the learning required to manage change in an organizational breathing cycle. In the chart each aspect of knowledge or knowing has a corresponding learning activity that supports it. Learning leads to changes in behavior and performance. Since learning is demonstrated by improved performance, each learning mode supports a different performance focus.   Using this chart as a reference, the management consultant can link different types of learning to the performance challenge a manager or a team might face in the course of their work.

An example that Allee (1997, p.97) uses in the chart is focused on the Procedural Mode of learning and its related performance. "In an organization, superb procedural performance is demonstrated by consistency in handling step-by-step processes and procedures. The ultimate goal of those procedures is not of concern in this mode, just their efficiency.

Processes for converting tacit Procedural knowledge to explicit shared knowledge are straightforward. Procedural knowledge can easily be codified into written sequences, linear schematics, and quantitative measures.   Guides and technical manuals communicate written sequences. Linear schematics and flow charts capture each step of a procedure, such as filling out a form or machining a part. Simple conformance measures – such as quantity, length, speed, and temperature can easily be established, and checked for conformance. Learning processes focus around tactile skills, practice, and transfer of information in very tangible forms. Short-term time horizons mean a narrow and very specific performance focus."

Knowledge and Learning	Action and Performance Focus
DATA Instinctual learning *Sensing.* The data mode of learning is at the sensory or input level. Little actual learning takes place	**DATA** Feedback *Gathering information.* Receiving input, registering data without reflection.

Time Perspective: Immediate moment
Consciousness: Awareness

INFORMATION Single-Loop Learning *Action without reflection. Procedural.* Learning entails redirecting a course of action to follow a predetermined course. Learning is mostly trial and error.	**PROCEDURAL** Efficiency *Doing something the most efficient way.* Conforming to standards or making simple adjustments and modifications. Focus is on developing and following procedures.

Time Perspective: Very short (present - now)
Consciousness: Physical sentience

KNOWLEDGE Double-Loop Learning *Self-conscious reflection.* A larger perspective that involves evaluation and modification of the goal or objective, as well as design of the path or procedures used to get there. Learning requires self-conscious reflection.	**FUNCTIONAL** Effectiveness *Doing it the best way.* Evaluating and choosing between two or more alternative paths. Goals are effective action and resolution of inconsistencies. Focus is on effective work design and engineering. Aspects, such as process redesign.

Time Perspective: Short (immediate past and present)
Consciousness: Self-reflective ————MEANING

MANAGING Communal learning *Understanding context, relationships and trends.* Learning requires the making of meaning, which includes understanding context, seeing trends, and generating alternatives. From this perspective, it is possible to detect relationships between components, as well as comprehending roles and relationships between people.	**Productivity** *Understanding what promotes or impedes effectiveness.* Effective management and allocation of resources and tasks, using conceptual frameworks to analyze and track multiple variables. Encompasses planning and measuring results. Also attends to working roles, relationships, and culture.

Time Perspective: Medium to long (historic past, present, very near future)
Consciousness: Communal

PHILOSOPHY Duetero Learning *Self-organizing. Integrative or systemic learning* seeks to understand dynamic relationships and non-linear processes discerning the patterns that connect including archetypes and metaphors. Requires recognition of the embeddedness and interdependence of systems.	**INTEGRATING** Optimization *Seeing where an activity fits the whole picture.* Understanding and managing socio-cultural system dynamics. Focus is on long-term planning and the ability to adapt to a changing environment. Comprises long-range forecasting, development of multi-level strategies, and evaluating investments and policies with regard to long-term success

Time perspective: Long-term (past, present, and future)
Consciousness: Pattern

WISDOM Generative Learning *Value driven.* Learning for the joy of learning, in open interaction with the environment. It involves creative processes, heuristic, open-ended explorations and profound self-questioning. Allows for the discovery of one's highest capabilities and talents, purpose, and intentions.	**RENEWING** Integrity *Finding for reconnecting with one's purpose.* Defining or reconnecting with values, vision, and mission. Understanding purpose. Very long term time frame leads to deep awareness of ecology, community, and ethical action.

Time perspective: Very long-term (very distant past to far distant future)
Consciousness: Ethical

UNION Synergistic *Connection.* Learning integrates direct experience and appreciation of oneness or deep connection with the greater Cosmos. Requires processes that connect the purpose to the health and well being of the larger community and the environment.	**UNION** Sustainability *Understanding values in greater context.* Inter-generational time perspective evokes commitment to the greater good of society, the environment, and the planet. Performance is demonstrated in actions consistent with these deeper values.

Consciousness: Universal   Time Perspective: Inter-generational, timeless

Figure 18: Learning and Performance Framework
© **Verna Allee (1997)**

Each mode has its own language and uses different tools for problem solving. Specific success factors and best practices that are critical are addressed in the text. The management consultant is encouraged to develop his knowledge more fully before use.

Management consultants who are about learning to leverage knowledge focus their own capability and time usage before going on to assist the client in learning the same thing. The responsibility of the management consultant in learning to leverage knowledge is awe-inspiring. Beginning to explore and develop one's own learning to leverage knowledge only broadens the task in cultural change with each organization that the consultant engages.

<u>Creating a new culture of knowledge and learning</u> A culture of learning and knowledge sharing does not happen by accident. In fact, the old practice of hoarding knowledge is so deeply ingrained in business that changing the culture is a major component of shifting into a learning mindset. The key elements of a knowledge culture are a climate of trust and openness in an environment where constant learning and experimentation are highly valued, appreciated, and supported. Creating a new culture of knowledge and learning is clearly <u>not</u> the responsibility of every management consultant that undertakes learning to leverage knowledge in this era. But certainly each consultant must realize what door he or she is opening when you begin to work with developing the relevant " knowledge" territory.

To understand the difficulties in changing culture, it is important to know something about culture. To begin with, any culture is based on a set of assumptions and beliefs about how the world works. Edgar Schein (1999) has defined five categories of assumptions that make up the worldview: the nature of the environment, the nature of reality or truth, time and space, human activity, and human nature. If one would change a culture to support knowledge, then one must challenge the prevailing organizational assumptions and beliefs in each of these areas.   In addition, the question of how one understands knowledge as it relates to each of these areas must be addressed.

Culture change must be handled with great sensitivity to both the realities of the existing culture and the hidden aspects of the new culture that is emerging. It must be remembered that people are not naturally resistant to change. People change things all the time when they have the freedom to do so. People do resist being manipulated, and they do challenge mixed messages. It is also important for people to be collaboratively engaged in the creative process of the culture change themselves. Inquiry and experimentation around culture must involve as many people as possible. People need to find themselves in a new system. They need to understand their role. They need to understand how the rules of the game are changing and practice new behaviors. They need to understand the logic and assumptions that are operating and be free to challenge them. These are not only important in culture change, but in learning to leverage knowledge.

In summary, enabling knowledge creation in the workplace is a big step in learning to leverage knowledge – and quite an important one. Of great significance in enabling knowledge creation is the attention necessarily paid to developing trust and in caring for others in the context – in particular, stressing the importance of healthy caring relationships with all the members involved. These relationships need to be established with each source of tacit knowledge, as well as building up a common experience base with the source. Although these remain significant in establishing trust and caring in the knowledge creation situation they are basic in general for the consultant in establishing relationships for information sharing and work in the engagement – including assisting the organization manage complex change through a process of breathing in and breathing out.

There are many frameworks to choose from in linking knowledge, learning, and performance – and most importantly the management consultant is encouraged to select a comprehensive one, and to use it consistently – maintaining an openness to new learning at all times. The developing management consultant recognizes the new culture – leveraging knowledge, learning, and performance in managing complex change in living systems.

Chapter 8   Learning to Institutionalize Innovation

"We now stand on the threshold of a new age – the age of revolution. In our minds, we know the new age has already arrived: in our bellies, we're not sure we like it. For we know it is going to be an age of upheaval, of tumult, of fortunes made and unmade at head-snapping speed. For change has changed. No longer is it additive. No longer does it move in a straight line.   In the twenty-first century, change is discontinuous, abrupt, seditious . . .Global capital flows have become a raging torrent, eroding national economic sovereignty. The ubiquity of the Internet has rendered geography meaningless. Bare-knuckled capitalism has vanquished all competing ideologies and a tsunami of deregulation and privatization has swept the globe. The 20th century age of progress began in hope – it is ending in anxiety."

– *Gary Hamel, in* Leading the Revolution

At first, the idea of learning to institutionalize innovation is overwhelming in the complexities of the new age. However, the learning issues for the developing management consultant remain the same: *understanding* first, and then *mastering*. It is a time to be more hopeful than fearful, because the new era is presenting us with an opportunity never before available to humankind. For the first time in history we can work backward from our imagination rather than forward from our past. We can create new understanding to master. The gap between what can be imagined and what can be accomplished has never been smaller. Armed with this knowledge, institutionalizing innovation is possible.

Developing management consultants must understand the "whys" and "hows" of innovating.   Basically, as Hamel, Gharajedaghi, Ackoff, Argyris, Kelly, Kotter, and others state – in a new age the old ways no longer work. Different authors describe the new age differently. For example, Hamel talks of the Age of Revolution, and Gharajedaghi and Ackoff describe a multi-minded era where holistic Systems Thinking and a socio-cultural view of organizations is required. Argyris tells us that 21st century companies will not be managed as 20th century companies. Kelly spells out new rules for the new global economy, and Kotter describes leading transformative change in the 21st century.   The evidence before us is very clear in understandable terms. Innovation is required because the old ways no longer work. Continuous improvement methods no longer work – they are only steps on a slow road to irrelevancy. Consultants and others must begin new learning, unlearning, relearning, and learning from the future to innovate

Understanding innovation

To begin, the dictionary defines innovation as the act of beginning or introducing something new and different – being creative. Innovation as can begin with observing what the customer needs. Recall Kevin Kelly's (1996) new rules for a new economy where the first rule is *wealth flows directly from innovation*, not optimization. Hamel (2000) sees innovation as the destination, and further clarifies the issues for organizations in this quote:

"It is not knowledge that produces new wealth, but insight – insight into opportunities for discontinuous innovation. Discovery is the journey; insight is the destination. You must become your own seer. In a nonlinear world, only nonlinear ideas will create new wealth. Most companies long ago reached the point of diminishing returns in their incremental improvement programs. Continuous improvement is an industrial age concept, and while it is better than no improvement at all, it is of marginal value in the age of revolution. Radical, nonlinear innovation is the only way to escape the ruthless hypercompetition that has been hammering down margins in industry after industry. Nonlinear innovation requires a company to escape the shackles of precedent and imagine entirely novel solutions to customer needs."

The issue for both developing management consultants and managers is more "getting different" than "getting better". Recall the emphasis in Chapter 7 on the importance of knowledge creation for the management consultant in meeting new age requirements. Now, consultants must avidly pursue knowledge creation and innovation. First, for their own learning and experience of it, and second, in order to transfer this learning to the client in learning to change the organization. This direction is in sharp contrast to organizational learning and knowledge management – which only meets 20th century needs of the past. Radical nonlinear innovation is the only way to escape the ruthless hypercompetition. For example, understanding radical nonlinear innovation means understanding business concept innovation -- that is taking the entire business concept as the starting point for innovation –

rather than working with a product or service. Competition is no longer between products or services, it's between competing business concepts. Focusing on the business concept innovation refocuses for the management consultant the importance of beginning with an attitude of success. If the consultant is to be successful in a new age, he must shift his way of thinking too – to that of thinking in business concept terms. Further, to get the client thinking in business concepts makes the innovative difference. Understanding the role of innovation directs learning and mastering in new development.

Learning to innovate is first Learning to BE

To learn to innovate one must first Learn to BE in a new cultural context. Recall that learning to BE it is not a one-time learning experience. Learning to BE is a developmental task to be mastered anew in each context. Learning to innovate presents a new cultural context where the developing management consultant must learn and relearn again the capacity to *desire*. One must get a strong hold on a "sense" of desiring innovation. Understanding the importance of desiring is critical. In the cultural context, it is character building that creates value for innovation. Think about being able to innovate. Imagine what it feels like, what it tastes like, and what it looks like to be innovative. Observe others innovating. Shadow innovators – find out how they behave to innovate and when innovating – for the task is learning to be an innovator.

To successfully innovate time after time, one must do conscious and intentional unlearning to destroy the old tapes of continuous improvement, to discard the language and concepts that fueled continuous improvement and the successful experiences of the past. Recall that success is often the signal of failure, and begin to use the signal as indicating an opportunity to innovate. This process of unlearning takes some time – and it will continue for a long time, for it is difficult to simply erase language and associated experiences all in one swooping effort. The process of unlearning is not as simple as pressing the "delete" key. Even when you think you have completely erased all of the references and cues, you will enter situations that call for more unlearning, before going ahead to innovate in real time.

But as one becomes serious about learning to BE an innovator, it becomes even more clear that the classical methods and concepts of organizational learning represented by the Kolb type learning cycle –

learning from the experiences of the past – is not enough. One must consider learning from the future.

Innovation is Learning from the Future

Presencing, the new discipline of learning from the future, is as much a collective or organizational phenomenon as it is an individual or personal one (Scharmer, 2000). What this means for the developing consultant is working simultaneously on the personal and organizational level in *Presencing*, by working with the individual to learn from the future. *Presencing* signifies the process of coming-into-being of emerging futures and is highly dependent on understanding learning, change, and cognition. The issue for the developing management consultant is how to access the dimension of knowing and change that allows new patterns to emerge in order to identify what it takes to compete in the new economy. Figure 15. Four levels of Cognition and Social Reality Formation identifies two major processes: *awareness* and *will* – both necessary for success.

In accessing the deep levels of knowing (Scharmer, 2000) identifies four levels of cognition and social reality formation focusing the importance of knowledge creation and knowing. The four levels are briefly described here as a means of understanding steps for the individual to be able to presence :

- Level 1 Cognition is *downloading mental models,* involving jumping immediately from paying attention (perception) to projecting one's (habitual) judgment. Actually this is re-enacting one's old mental models and habits of thought. All deeper and more profound cognition and knowledge creation require the suspension of this habitual judgment, thus opening space for a deep and profound encounter
- Level 2 Cognition is *reflection and reinterpretation,* and is based on a higher quality of paying attention, i.e., on seeing, reflecting on the phenomenon, and allowing the appropriate judgment to form. On this level, cognition does not operate by simply downloading mental models but rather by modifying and adapting existing mental constructs according to the perceived situation and its reinterpretation at hand

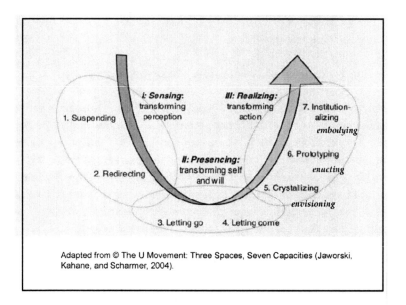

Adapted from © The U Movement: Three Spaces, Seven Capacities (Jaworski, Kahane, and Scharmer, 2004).

**Figure 19.   Four Levels of Cognition and Social Reality Formation
Adapted from © The U Movement: Three Spaces, Seven Capacities
(Jaworski, Kahane, and Scharmer, 2004).**

- Level 3 Cognition is *imagination* is based on a deeper quality of attention that allows one to sense the phenomenon from within. The switch from "seeing" (level 2) to "sensing" (level 3) is redirecting attention from the object to the source.   Level 3 cognition does not focus on objects, as in the prior two levels, but on the coming-into-being of these objects.   This is a level of consciousness in which the knower actively participates in bringing forth the world of which he is a part. Level 4 Cognition is primary knowing – *presencing*.   It is where the quality of attention is at its highest and most subtle level, which allows it to become one with the intention of the emerging whole. This level of cognition is *"primary knowing of wisdom awareness.* The discipline here is to become aware that mind and world are not separate but arise together as aspects of the same informational field. Mind and World are not separate since the subjective and objective aspects of experience arise together as different poles of the same act of cognition – are part of the same informational field – they are already joined at inception (Rosch, 1999)."

Gharajedaghi (2006) on the same point says, "Objectivity, after all, is collective subjectivity."

At this point, after most have completed the first three stages – seeing, sensing, and presencing, they consider the new learning complete. However, Scharmer (2000) points out that at best the job is only half complete. The first half of the cycle shown in Figure 19 concerns accessing experience and becoming aware, and the second half of the cycle involves forming, inspiring, and enacting will. The second part reflects the primacy of will, and its importance in learning from the future. Three aspects of will formation are briefly described below to solidify importance of the second half of the cycle

- *Envisioning:* The capacity to develop a clear vision and a 'laser focus" for implementing this vision involves operating from a cognitive space that is different from the three spaces mentioned: seeing, sensing, and *Presencing* Enhancing the quality of aspiration, vision, and intention has always been at the heart of entrepreneurial leadership, and included in Senge's (1990) disciplines of Personal Mastery and Shared Vision

- *Enacting:* Social reality only exists insofar as it is enacted by people. Seeing, sensing, *Presencing*, and envisioning will not make a difference unless they translate into action. Brian Arthur (2000) sees the way to operate in the new economy as a sequence of (1) observe, observe, observe, (2) allow inner knowing to emerge, and (3) act in an instant. Acting from the inner self, Arthur (2000) says, "In oriental thinking, you might just sit and observe and observe – and then suddenly do what's appropriate."

- *Embodying:* In an age dominated by globally acting organizations and institutions, social changes become sustainable only as they become institutionally embodied in organizational routines. Thus institutionalizing focuses the shift toward creating the organizational contexts, and infrastructures that will allow the new to continually unfold

In summary, the U-shaped process of transformation shown in Figure 19 is an example where everything happens twice. The upward journey of the second part of the U-shaped process reverses the themes and gestures of the downward journey during the first part of the U-shape process. For example, the gestures of suspending, turning inward, and letting go of the first part of the process are reversed in the second part by the gestures of letting come, turning outward, and embedding. In many ways, making transformational change similar to the ongoing process of organizational breathing, but both only as one sequence in the process of breathing change into the organization, stabilized at the end of each sequence.

What's important for the management consultant to understand is the transformational "switch" which applies to the individual-collective relationship, and to the self-world relationship.   Goethe's (1985) description of the self-world relationship is: "Man knows himself only to the extent that he knows the world, he becomes himself only to the extent that he knows the world, he becomes aware of himself only within the world, and aware of the world only within himself. Every object, well contemplated, opens up a new organ within us."

The cognitive capacities that individuals and communities can open up for themselves are of two types: One focuses on reflecting the enacted reality of the past – the *reflective mind*, and the other is in accessing the generative sources of co-creating something entirely new – the *intuitive mind*.   That is what *Presencing* is about.   *Presencing* is a birth-giving activity. It is about bringing oneself into being as one access the sources of one's highest creativity. The experience of *Presencing* is twofold: co-creating and giving birth to a new reality and, at the same time, being transformed and born into a new world by the very same process.

In conclusion, *Presencing*, as depicted in Figure 19, provides a step-by-step U-shaped cycle showing the individual and the collective the stages to innovate, and what is necessary to institutionalize the innovation. Embedding or institutionalizing is a step that ends the upward second part of the cycle. As a culture, this is a stage we have not invested in the past. Possibly, this is because we did not have to be concerned about sustainability. However, now we cannot depend only on learning from the past, and we must clearly emphasize learning from the future. It behooves the developing management consultant to focus the manifestation of will in envisioning, enacting, and embodying to institutionalize innovation.   The task of mastering institutionalizing innovation is the focus of the next section.

Mastering institutionalizing Innovation

Mastering is to become skilled or proficient, as well as successful in the performance of a specific set of knowledge. For example, innovation and the sustainability of innovations. To address mastering in learning from the future, three tools used in the process of *Presencing* are developed. These tools map some different qualities of attention. Tool 1 is at the individual level, listening on the collective level defines Tool 2, and Tool 3 is languaging and the organizational, leadership practices.

Tool 1: Listening

While most organizations and individuals are pretty good at listening 1 (downloading), and many companies have mastered listening 2 (seeing), few organizations and groups are really skilled at listening 3 (inquiry) and rarely reach listening 4 (*Presencing*) as shown in Figure 19. Shifting the Locus of Listening. Figure 20 maps four different places from which systems operate. In Listening 1 the place of attention is with myself (I-in-me). What I hear is what I already know. Thus, Listening 1 is simply the activity of *downloading* and reconfirming my old mental models and prejudices. I know that I am using my Listening 1 skills if a situation confirms all my mental models and prior assumptions.

In Listening 2 the focus of attention moves from myself to the periphery (I-in-it). I pay attention to every word that is said. I pay attention to everything that might differ from my expectations and mental models.   This level of listening corresponds to the Level 2 cognition *seeing.* While listening to another person, I experience the other person as an "it," a thing, an entity that is separate from myself. I know that I am operating using my Listening 2 skills when I hear something that surprises me, when I am discovering something new "out there."

In Listening 3 the experience of the other person shifts from being an "it," a thing, to being a "you," a human being (I-in-you). All dialogue experiences include this subtle switch from seeing the world through my own eyes to suddenly seeing the world through somebody else's eyes. In terms of cognition the shift is from Level 2 cognition (seeing) to Level 3 (sensing). I know when I am operating using my Listening 3 skills when I have gone outside the boundaries of my organization and become one with another person, if only briefly.

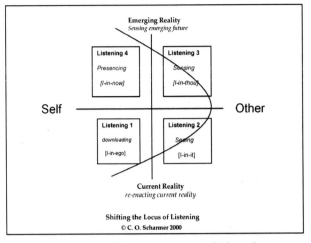

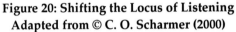

Figure 20: Shifting the Locus of Listening
Adapted from © C. O. Scharmer (2000)

In Listening 4 the source of attention moves yet another step upstream to the ultimate source through which the Self and you (thou) come into being (I-in-now). At this level, the separation between I and you fully collapses into the self-transcending experience of flow and spherical expansion. In terms of cognition the switch is from sensing to *Presencing*. The difference between the two is that sensing taps into emerging futures in one's environment while *Presencing* uses one's highest self to sense and embody what is about to emerge. I know that I am using my listening skills when the boundaries between myself, and the other person have collapsed and when my locus of listening has shifted towards listening from the whole. To use more tangible criteria, after the conversation I have become a different person, being more who I truly am.

As organizations move further towards an innovation-driven economy, additional capacity to operate from levels 3 and 4 will become a major source of competitive advantage. The developing management consultant is urged to practice using dialogue skills, and to create opportunities for Listening 4 skills to develop in *Presencing* (I-in-now). At first, both of these listening skill development experiences may feel uncomfortable and different. That is a good sign, and one should be encouraged to utilize each more. Figure 21. Inflection points between the four levels of Listening to focus on the underlying territory where redirection of attention is required – and allows people to move across the spaces identified in the four areas. For example, Figure 17 shows how the inflection points correspond to the different modes of listening. Moving from Listening 1 to Listening 2 involves passing over the threshold of *suspension*: suspending the politeness of habitual talk. Moving from Listening 2 to Listening 3 involves passing over the threshold of *redirection*: redirecting one's attention from exterior (things) to interior (the coming-into-being of things), from listening to exterior statements to listening from the inner place where speech acts are first articulated, or to put it in a more radical way, to listening from inside the self of another. Finally, moving from Listening 3 to Listening 4 involves passing over the threshold of emptiness: letting go and surrendering to what wants to emerge.

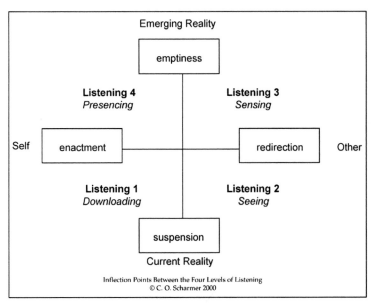

Figure 21: Inflection Points Between the Four Levels of Listening
© C. O. Scharmer (2000)

In the next section the perspective on *Presencing* is switched from the individual (listening) to the collective (languaging).

Tool 2: Languaging Many change processes fail because they are unable to sufficiently uncover the current and emerging realities of a system. Often the quality of conversation is unable to capture the system's complexity. Without adequate dialogue, people are unable to express their tacit, taken-for-granted assumptions about how the system really works, or doesn't work.

Figure 22. Languaging: Four Fields of Conversation outlines a process archetype developed through many consulting, action research, and community-building experiences (Isaacs, 1999). The model is based on four generic stages and fields of languaging.

- Field 1: is *talking nice*, reproducing or "downloading" an existing language game

- Field 3: is *reflective dialogue*, redirecting one's attention to the assumptions that underlie our points of view; inquiring into the underlying assumptions of current reality and sensing emerging realities

- Field 2: is *talking tough*, adapting the language game to what is really going on in the minds of the participants; addressing and debating the real issues

- Field 4: is *generative dialogue*, going through the space of emptiness and arriving at a timeless sphere and source that reconnects us with our highest potential, both individually and collectively; *Presencing*.

Conversation moves through the four fields. In each quadrant, the speech acts (Searle, 1969) differ in how they relate to the rules of the language game in which they operate. For example, *rule-repeating* (talking nice), *rule-adapting* (talking tough), *rule-intuiting* (reflective dialogue), and *rule-generating* (generative dialogue) speech acts produce different kinds of conversations. Each allows the conversational field to operate from a different place.

When thinking about change, each level of unfreezing or uncovering reality requires a particular language mode. For example, uncovering the third level of reorganization (reframing) requires using *reflective dialogue* (Field 3).

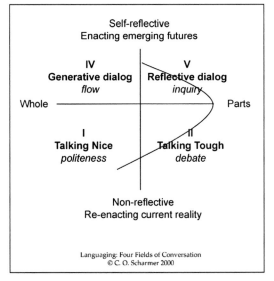

Figure 22: Languaging: Four Fields of Conversation
© C. O. Scharmer, (2000)

Uncovering the fourth level of organizational reality (common will) requires *generative dialogue* (Field 4). The challenge in leading change is to help people, teams, and organizations get "unstuck" from the first field (*talking nice*) and to develop the capacity to move with ease across all four fields of conversation as needed in a particular situation.   For the developing management consultant the task is first to gain the capability of using Fields 2, 3 and 4, and then to develop the flexibility of use demanded by the situation.   The latter requires leadership on the part of the consultant to first model intervention in the system to shift the place from where the system is currently operating.   This leadership in intervention is the subject of the next section.

Leadership is shifting the place from which a system operates Shifting from politeness (Field 1) to reconnecting what we *think* with what we *say* (Field 2) requires *suspending* the old ways of communicating as shown in Figure 19.   Inflection Points for Shifting the Locus of Conversational Fields.   In other words, say what you think; confront other actors with obvious contradictions between what they say and what they do. Moving from a Field 2 conversation (debate) to a Field 3 conversation (reflective dialogue) again involves shifting the tacit field structure of conversation.   In a debate, each individual advocates his or her own point of view.   In contrast, in reflective dialogue participants shift from advocating their own opinions to inquiring into the assumptions that underlie them.   That shift involves **redirecting** the collective attention from exterior to inner sources and assumptions.   The principal leverage for the consultant/intervener is to reconnect what people think and say with what they *see* and *do.*   It does not help to say "I just noticed that everybody seems to be engaged in blaming others rather than reflecting on their own responsibility.   Why don't we try to use reflection and inquiry."   This intervention will almost certainly fail because it only *talks* about *reflective inquiry.*   Instead of reflecting on his own impulses, the consultant/intervener blames others.

Moving from reflective to generative dialogue again involves a shift. This time, the shift involves moving across the threshold of *emptiness* and surrendering to the flow of the emerging new (*generative dialogue* or *Presencing*).   In *Presencing*, the place where *I* operate is identical to the place where *we* operate. It emerges from the presence or the coming into being of the larger whole.   Sometimes, this level of conversation occurs after many days of common work, as intentional quietness or sacred silence (Isaacs,1999).   When it happens, the experience of time slows down, and the speech acts change from speaking based on reflection to speaking from what emerges in the here and now.   This level of reality experience is *synchronicity,* where the boundaries between I and thou seem to completely disappear.   Generative dialogue, like reflective dialogue is based on reconnecting what we think and say with what we do and see.   The difference is that in Field 3 one acts first and reflects second, whereas in Field 4 the two happen *synchronistically* (action = reflection).

The drama of dialogue plays out according to these four types of conversation.   They differ in the degree of complexity that they are able to capture and represent. The more easily teams and companies are able to move across the four fields of conversational action, the more they will succeed in unfreezing and accessing the deeper and more subtle levels of learning and change.

The essence of moving from Fields 1, 2, and 3 to Field 4 (I-in-now) is not only to shift from Type I learning (reflection) to Type II learning (*Presencing*) but also involves a profound aesthetic experience.   At the heart of this experience is a spheric expansion and enhancement of one's own experience of self in the whole – which is not only phenomenal in itself, but very energizing to experience.   Often as musicians play to the whole   concert   hall   report   this   type   of   spheric   expansion   and enhancement. Professional athletes often report similar experience where there is instantaneous learning with zero feedback delay – that is, one operates from two places or spheres simultaneously. One, from the peripheral sphere of one's own organization, sensing what is about to emerge, and second, from within one's organization at the very same moments that they perceived the actions from the outside. During these instances of high performance the self operates both outside and within one's own organization. These synchronistic experiences may not be able to be planned for by everyone, but they should be able to be recognized and taken advantage of when they happen. For the developing management consultant Field 4 experience is important to consider as a high potential with high payoff to the individual involved – be it himself or the client.

Tool 3: Leadership Practice In any change, leadership is key. Initially, the consultant may have to provide leadership in learning from the future and he must develop leadership within the organization. The third tool, leadership practice, is invaluable. Leadership maybe practiced in a leadership laboratory (Jaworski & Scharmer, 2000). The leadership laboratory helps to make operating in learning from the future work in the context of large organizations. The key idea of the laboratory is to provide leaders with an opportunity to explore and nurture four interrelated and interwoven environments of thought and action.

The first environment is about seeing and sensing, taking the participants outside the boundaries of their organization. For example, as consultant one might conduct field visits to new economy companies or other places where people can sense and experience the emerging new.

The second environment is about retreat and reflect – an elevated space for thinking, where the point is to enhance the quality of thinking together, specifically to advance from sensing to *Presencing*. For example, the laboratory might arrange to take managers on a multi-day retreat in Santa Fe (or an emerging art area). There, they would begin by crystallizing the learning from field visits, put the different images of emerging realities together, and use this as a body of resonance for *Presencing*, the emerging new, both individually and collectively.

The third environment is a kind of business incubator designed to help entrepreneurs turn their ideas into powerful innovations and embodied actions. Hamel (2000) is very clear that what matters in the new economy is not return on investment, but return on IMAGINATION. How a company or an individual gets return on imagination is by rewarding imagination. For example, Royal Dutch/Shell started in late 1996 developing the Game-Changer process (a type of new business incubator) to make venture funding available to employees at all levels who were willing to put their ideas up for testing. Of Shell's five largest growth initiatives in early 1999, four had their genesis in the game changer process.

The fourth environment is accomplished through a high level social learning and unlearning to discover and interpret "assumptions" that are blocking successful performance – otherwise, the culture may not be changed despite a very significantly designed intervention. Gharajedaghi (2006, p.183) discusses "dissolving the second order machine" as consisting of two separate, yet interrelated processes: self-discovery and self-improvement.   First one must identify what is relevant and supportive to the shared vision of a desirable future, and second, one must diagnose what turns out to be part of the "mess" and therefore obstructive to progress and development. The latter must be removed. The experience of the fourth environment is often overlooked and leads to failure in the tool application.

Through experiments similar to Royal Dutch/Shell it is clear that there is an innovation solution that may be used to develop innovation as a capability. In an organization, the developing management consultant may use the business incubator concept to create design rules for innovation, develop innovation as a capability through developing innovation skills, innovation metrics, information technology for innovation, and management processes for innovation. The business incubator is creating a practice space to bring emerging futures into reality. It is a practice field with high payoff.

Leadership practice is a tool that helps managers to deeply connect to the emerging futures outside the organization in the first environment (Space 1), and within (Space 2) and to bring them forth into reality (Space 3). Practice may be necessary in all of the environmental spaces to address the challenge of innovating in organizations. It is clear that developing management consultants, as leaders, need to develop a new leadership capacity in *Presencing*. *Presencing* is both a collective/organizational and an individual/personal experience in which the self becomes the gate through which the new comes into reality. It is the discipline of bringing one's full self into presence and using one's highest self as a vehicle for sensing and bringing forth new worlds. Choosing learning from the future – *Presencing* – is choosing the high road. A choice with high payoff, but not easy – for it requires new learning, unlearning, and relearning to successfully institutionalize innovation.

Value of Institutionalizing Innovation for Learning to LEARN

Institutionalizing innovation is necessary and purposeful in Learning to LEARN. Actually, by institutionalizing innovation the cycle of learning is generative. That is, the learning system used in this text: Learning to BE, Learning to LEARN, and Learning to DO becomes a natural generative routine. Initially it becomes natural for the developing consultant to use with himself/herself, and then it becomes quite natural to facilitate the learning of others. The Consultant's 2-step Learning Tool described in Chapter 6, is fully implemented and becomes a useful routine. Certainly, the tool may be adapted and expanded in different contexts. For example, to be successful in the context of innovation, the developing consultant focuses more on Learning to BE and Learning to Learn – Learning from the Future – *Presencing* bringing into being new realities. Unlearning – letting go of much of what he has thought about and what he has actually practiced – and now needs to change to be able to Learn to DO. *Presencing* takes the learner to open door of Learning to Do through application of the learning.

The challenge in the use of the learning system, as in a number of other situations, is to go ever faster in the cycle of learning, to go ever deeper, and to become more agile in reaching effectiveness each time. The budgeting of one's time and knowledge utilization in the cycle is an individual one. It is a matter of individual choice. As long as this choice is available in organizations, individuals competing against themselves will continue to shorten the cycle by going faster and faster -- but only to a point! This point (sometimes called the point of no return or diminishing returns) is a signal of success and a clear signal to change.

Recall for a moment that Kevin Kelly (1998) described the cycle as one of "find, nurture, destroy," and that it happens faster and more intensely than ever before. Thus the full challenge becomes clearer, than when the point of speed and intensity has been reached they can no longer be increased – it is the signal to destroy, and start anew in innovation. Knowing this gives reason to be working on several areas of innovation at the same time, so time is not lost in having a long start up time in putting a new cycle of learning to innovate in place again. This type of sophistication comes both to the individual and to the collectivity in time, and with experience.

In summary, these are challenging times for the developing consultant – and his clients. The new learning system of Learning to BE, Learning to LEARN (including *Presencing*) and Learning to DO is very exciting. It is filled with a desire to bring emerging reality into being. It is filled with a sense of unending – a feeling of forever – making it a very hopeful time.

Hope arouses, as nothing else can arouse, a *passion* for the possible. Hope is necessary to use the new system of learning from the future. *Hopefully*, the developing management consultant takes initiative to start the cycle – using learning from the future, making it happen. This, at first, may appear as an overwhelming task – and an unneeded responsibility to undertake. However, in innovating one is responsible only to self. All that matters is that you care enough to risk starting to learn from wherever you may be at the time, and go on from there.

PART 4:
UNDERSTANDING THE CHALLENGE OF LEARNING "TO DO"

> *A journey of a thousand miles begins with a single step.*
> *– Chinese proverb*

Understanding the challenge of Learning to DO in management consulting requires learning from an active intervention stance by applying the knowledge and practice from the context of the consulting engagement. There are many opportunities to learn and develop the numerous steps in the thousand-mile journey for the consultant leveraging intervention in the transformation process, using the four-phased consulting systems worldview. Most important for both the developing and seasoned consultant, is keeping an image of the whole journey in mind – and consistently moving toward the destination of successful goal attainment – essentially, achieving a coherent, enabling context for the implementation of the designed solution.

The fourth part of the book addresses the challenge of the consultant in Learning to DO – learning to facilitate the client to achieve an enabling context for implementation of the designed solution. The lead chapter, Learning to DO, explores the meaning in practice –focusing on the important business of application, the role of professional development, and on developing an intervention capability – the most powerful marketable competency available to the management consultant. The Consulting Systems Worldview (CSW), as depicted in Figure 19. is revisited in detail, focusing one chapter on each phase.

Transformation Process

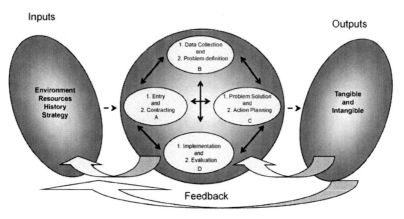

The Consulting Systems Worldview
© Marilyn E Harris, 1996

Figure 23: The Consulting Systems Worldview (CSW)

The subsequent four chapters define and describe the key interventions required for success in each phase, and apply the learning to two exemplary cases: Long Island Company and the Columbus Medical Association found in the appendix.   Each case uses a different methodology. These cases were selected to illustrate a comparative approach addressing intervening power dynamics for the developing management consultant. The avid management consultant is alerted to read and study the cases and the methodologies before studying the chapters which follow. A chart summarizing the key interventions of the phase accompanies each chapter.

Chapter 10 entitled "Effective Intervention in Entry & Contracting" defines the means of undertaking the first important phase in the CSW. The phase is important regardless of the level of consultant involvement during Entry, and in developing the contract with the client when many of the expectations are set relative to the entire contractual relationship. Savvy management consultants focus on understanding what has been contracted especially if they were not initially involved. The consultant is advised to first "know thyself" in order to make a winning presentation relevant to success in the consultation. In a successful phase 1 the issues of interdependency, self-organization, and choice are focused on relationship-building to develop a workable contract that opens the door to phase 2.

In the next chapter the focus is on "Effective Intervention in Data Collection & Problem Definition." The consultant is strongly encouraged to separate problem definition from problem solution – a common error of many 'would-be-successful consultants.' Further, the chapter concentrates on a Systems Thinking approach to problem definition by taking the learner through problem formulation in a three-phase process: 1) searching, 2) mapping, and 3) telling the story. The value of this approach is underscored by the participation of the stakeholder, saving considerable energy and cost to the client in subsequent phases.

Chapter 13 focuses problem solution and action planning to reach the defined solution. Once the solution is identified and the 'second order machine' is dissolved, action planning begins, identifying the myriad steps required for a successful implementation. A critical part of action planning is to develop plans for evaluation to measure success in the implementation.

Chapter 14 is "Implementation and Evaluation" and completes the highly interdependent four-phased cycle. Further, it is the test of all the previous efforts. The challenge here is to follow the plan step-by-step, evaluating regularly to keep on course in the thousand mile journey – but more importantly reading the feedback from the evaluation and making adjustments accordingly in application of the many challenges in Learning to DO.

Chapter 9   Learning "TO DO"

The Cracked Pot

A Water Bearer in India had two large pots; each hung on each end of a pole, which he carried across his neck. One of the pots had a crack in it, and while the other pot was perfect and always delivered a full portion of water at the end of the long walk from stream to the master's house, the cracked pot arrived only half full.

For a full two years this went on daily, with the bearer delivering only one and a half pots full of water to his master's house. Of course, the perfect pot was proud of its accomplishments, perfect to the end for which it was made. But the poor cracked pot was ashamed of its own imperfection, and miserable that it was able to be a bitter failure, it spoke to the Water Bearer one day by the stream, "I am ashamed of myself, and I want to apologize to you."

"Why?" asked the bearer. "What are you ashamed of?" I have been able, for the past two years, to deliver only half of my load because this crack in my side causes water to leak out all the way back to your master's house. Because of my flaws, you have to do all of this work, and you don't get full value from your efforts." the pot said.

 · The Water Bearer felt sorry for the old cracked pot, and in his compassion he said, "As we return to the master's house, I want you to notice the beautiful flowers along the path"

Indeed, as they went up the hill, the old cracked pot took notice of the sun warming the beautiful wild flowers on the side of the path, and this cheered it some. But at the end of the trail, it still felt bad because it leaked out half of its load, and so again it apologized to the bearer for the failure.

The bearer said to the pot, "Did you notice that there were flowers only on your side of your path, but not on the other pot's? That's because I have always known about your flaw, and I took advantage of it. I planted flower seeds on your side of the path, and every day while we walk back from the stream, you've watered them. For two years I have been able to pick these beautiful flowers to decorate my master's table. Without you being just the way, he would not have this beauty to grace his house."

Each of us has our own unique flaws; in a sense, we're all cracked pots, but if we will accept it, we can learn from our flaws and learn to work with them, capitalizing on a marketable competency. In a global economy, nothing goes to waste.

Learning to DO is learning to manage complexity in the application of knowledge and skills in the context of a consulting engagement. Learning application is learning to scientifically intervene systemically in a specific context. The cracked pot story focuses several important points guiding action in application. For example:

- Importance of an attitude of success
- Relevance is more important than perfection
- Tedious, timely preparation is critical
- Recognition and respect of "context"
- Conscious focus on goal directed intervention
- Actively identifying the marketable competency

In today's world, Learning to DO must be more formalized for the management consultant -- more so than in the water bearer's world. Until recently, application learning – however and whenever it occurred – was equivalent to the professional development of the consultant. With the overwhelming growth and resulting competition in consulting, professional development takes on more meaning – requiring structured study, development, and practice intervening to consistently sophisticate interventions and to satisfy the relevant goals in the consulting context. Recently, the trend is to develop university based courses using action research to bridge theory and practice. Large consulting firms have developed their own course of study and training, perfecting a "consulting company approach."

Learning to DO is Application

Learning to DO is leveraging one's knowledge and skills to accomplish a specific change goal – actually implementing systemic transformation processes. That is application. Application is quite complex and quite challenging. Initially, it involves understanding <u>how</u> the job to reach specific goals gets done, and then leading the organizational application in project implementation -- from beginning to end – in a manner reflecting context specific means to reach a relevant end. What makes application so tough is that it occurs in many different contexts. In fact every organization has an individual context to consider – and some large organizations may have many different contexts to consider within the boundaries of the organization, and dependent on the nature of the industry.

In management consulting, application is defined as both an art and a science. The art is bounded by one's attitude and experience to achieve a sense of beauty of the whole, while the science deals with the systematic application of knowledge and skills required in a systemic approach, both within the constraints of a fast developing profession. Application is about developing an attitude of success, using frameworks to structure, and learning to intervene successfully – over and over again – throughout the entire action research process during the engagement.   In reality, application is ever testing and ever challenging the consultant's professional fiber in many different ways in each engagement.

Application begins with an attitude of success In this sense, application actually begins before entry --while preparing oneself to consult in Learning to BE.   Recall from the earlier discussions that the developing consultant must work on realizing the value of an attitude of success and developing the capability to desire – and to require a fresh attitude of success for each new application. This type of preparation will begin to make the necessary attitude of success a routine consideration long before one actually comes into contact with the client or the problem. There may be several times during the engagement that the consultant may have to refresh his attitude by a brief return to Learning to BE to strengthen earlier resolve.   It becomes increasingly important to maintain and develop an energetic attitude of success for the management consultant *and* the client alike. In the beginning the consultant must keep working at developing and actively sharing this form of "excitement" in a variety of ways – by the energetic way you walk, the excitement in your voice, and the "innovative ideas" expressed in the content of your communication.

Remember that the maintenance of this joint excitement in the approach you and your client take is often the generative energy required to move forward in the project. It is not only important to maintain momentum, but the means to this momentum is often eased by the desire to BE – to BE excited by the progress -- small as it might be. In Learning to DO, the real challenge is in maintaining and developing the attitude that exudes true excitement and energy throughout the application.

It is a challenge to consistently converse in an exciting fashion about change in the application, and an ongoing challenge for the consultant to demonstrate creativeness and innovation in their communication. Recall that innovative conversation is generative dialogue (fourth field) in languaging. Generative dialogue is a form of innovative conversation that aids the listener in "uncovering the fourth level of organizational reality – common will or *Presencing*," learning from the future. For the listener, this is entry into an exciting new way of learning. Excitement in the learner may incite a circular process of energy in the application. This type of energy is valuable for both the client and the consultant in the application, for this type of energy supports an attitude of success.

Application is hard work Successful application results from respecting the immediate feedback on an intervention and the evaluation of success for a specific series of interventions. For example, after each major event planned in the application, evaluation should take place – and the results of the evaluation must be addressed at that time. It is not sufficient to explain why it happened or rationalize the results. The consultant must take into account what happened and what didn't happen, and make a decision to correct it if in his/her estimation the event has not been successful. Then, this calls for additional explanation, planning, and intervention to deal with the difference that has occurred. It is this scrutiny of all the events and the ensuing decision to re-plan action – the hard work of application. It is also tedious – for evaluation must be systematically applied and not just used when the consultant may "feel" it is necessary or she/he wants to do something different for whatever reason. Catching even a small variance early on can make a significant difference in the outcome. This is one of the times that "the earlier the better" applies.

Timing in application is important The timing of any application should be worked out in advance with the parties involved in each phase of the implementation. The timing of application should be at the client's convenience whenever possible.   The client needs to be present to examine the change as it happens.   The client's presence aids learning to change, and adjusting to change during the application.   If there has been some misunderstanding or miscommunication on the matter at hand, it is usually easier to clarify, correct, or justify at the time – than to leave until later to unbundle and clarify the issue.   Application focuses the need for clarity and direction that aids timing (scheduling) in the application. Developing skills in time management aid both the developing consultant and the client to succeed in the application.   Often, someone else has planned the scheduling of the segment of the application at an earlier time.   The initial scheduling effort must be reviewed, and possibly rescheduled to fit the needs of the present time.   Appropriate timing in the scheduling of the application provides energy to change.   It is important to adjust timing fast enough that it acts as a stimulus to change, not as a burden detracting from successful completion.

Learning to DO requires Professional Development

Generally, professional development is formalized in a curriculum defining a course of study within institutional boundaries and practice beyond the walls of the institution, preparing graduates to deliver a special expertise to the society.   Currently, in the field of management consulting, this is not the case.   In addition, professional education of consultants is not well defined.   In reality, it takes many forms and on many occasions, persons "hang out their shingle," without formalized training or professional development.   At best, they may have assisted or shadowed a senior person for a short period of time – or used consultant-vendors in their previous business as models.   Many consultants do not know there is a history to management consulting and do not recognize the significance of "management" describing consultancy (see Chapter 2 for detail).

Addressing the problem circumscribed by the lack of professional development in the field, many of the large consulting firms have developed training programs for their own consultants.   For example: McKinsey & Company, Accenture, and Price Waterhouse Coopers all provide extensive in-house training for new staff in select strategies.   In addition, books are now appearing that work at understanding and implementing the problem-solving tools and management techniques of one of the world's top strategic consulting firms, e.g., The McKinsey Way (Rasiel, 1999, and The McKinsey Mind (Rasiel & Friga, 2001);   yet, these do not provide professional education for management consultants in a fast growing industry – recognized for the dollars changing hands in payment of consultants around the world.

Developing a framework for professional education In retrospect, it appears that many entities have dealt unsuccessfully with the business of professional education and development of the management consultant. Often these efforts have been from a selective approach without considering the holistic aspect of professional development. Comparing the past efforts with Gharajedaghi's (2006) description of professional education may be instructive to the field of management consulting. He contends that professional education should not be constrained by a formalized curriculum or period of time, but rather the needed professional education emerges out of a survey of the professional needs and desires – of management consultants. Professional education should not be constrained by the use of traditional classroom formats. Instead it is facilitated by solid experiences using the concepts of learning, research, and practice cells. From the survey, plans and programs result that can be created which match the management consulting business requirements and developmental potentials. The best option is often realized through apprentice models of training, using indigenous experts with proven competence in the needed areas. Through this type of mentoring the needed technicians and professionals may be developed. The professional group may then forge alliances and affiliations with known colleges and universities in order to get its programs accredited. Within these structures performance criteria and measures are identified that demonstrate the professions' use. Highly successful outputs are measured by several variables: 1) active widespread interest in learning is generated, 2) the demand for graduates of the program, 3) the evidence of multi-dimensionality in participants and in the resource utilization, and finally 4) in the cultural vitality. The succinct description which follows provides direction for defining a professional education in management consulting.

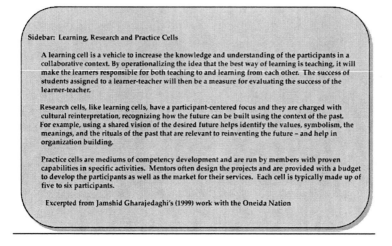

Sidebar: Learning, Research and Practice Cells

A learning cell is a vehicle to increase the knowledge and understanding of the participants in a collaborative context. By operationalizing the idea that the best way of learning is teaching, it will make the learners responsible for both teaching to and learning from each other. The success of students assigned to a learner-teacher will then be a measure for evaluating the success of the learner-teacher.

Research cells, like learning cells, have a participant-centered focus and they are charged with cultural reinterpretation, recognizing how the future can be built using the context of the past. For example, using a shared vision of the desired future helps identify the values, symbolism, the meanings, and the rituals of the past that are relevant to reinventing the future – and help in organization building.

Practice cells are mediums of competency development and are run by members with proven capabilities in specific activities. Mentors often design the projects and are provided with a budget to develop the participants as well as the market for their services. Each cell is typically made up of five to six participants.

Excerpted from Jamshid Gharajedaghi's (1999) work with the Oneida Nation

Defining professional education for management consulting. The four parts to develop the professional education component are:

1) Defining the professions' needs and desires,
2) Identifying mentors to use practice models and develop apprenticeships to learn,
3) Creating plans and programs to match the business potential
4) Developing the appropriate accreditation and certification along with appropriate performance criteria and measures

This may take a few years to accomplish, as in other professions – for example medicine, law, nursing, accounting, and teaching. It takes time to deliver developmentally sound programs that contain all four factors.

In terms of defining the professions' needs, there have been many sporadic attempts by organized groups – including consulting firms, institutes, business schools, universities, and colleges to define needs and desires of management consultants. These data gathering efforts have been designed to meet the needs of a specific group, not a fast developing profession. As management consultants themselves become more organized as a profession they may capitalize on many of these preliminary efforts through existing societies, such as The American Society for Training and Development (ASTD) or new comprehensive organizations with purposeful intent.

Mentoring, using practice models and apprenticeships, has long been a part of a consultant's development. Historically, many management consultants have Learned to DO at-the-elbow of a seasoned consultant within the context of a live consultation. Many have learned to DO first as 'junior consultants" accompanying the seasoned consultant.

There are many cases where a seasoned consultant, acting as a mentor, produces a robust learning experience through the integration of theory and practice. A seasoned consultant who wants to develop marketable competency in others is key when mentoring for successful interventions that deliver measurable results. Mentoring focuses critical skill development in relationship building, so relevant in establishing the sociocultural model in organizations. This type of experience clearly showcases at-the-elbow learning as a valuable experience in bolstering the management consulting profession in the 21st century.

Many seasoned and developed consultants shy away from research, thinking that it has little to do with the professional education. On the contrary, research is the basis of documentation and measurement. Both documentation and measurement are critical skills in consulting.

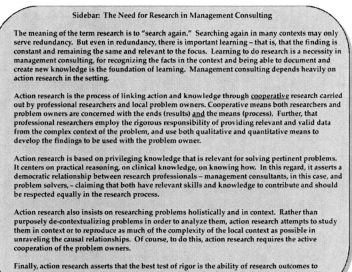

Sidebar: The Need for Research in Management Consulting

The meaning of the term research is to "search again." Searching again in many contexts may only serve redundancy. But even in redundancy, there is important learning – that is, that the finding is constant and remaining the same and relevant to the focus. Learning to do research is a necessity in management consulting, for recognizing the facts in the context and being able to document and create new knowledge is the foundation of learning. Management consulting depends heavily on action research in the setting.

Action research is the process of linking action and knowledge through cooperative research carried out by professional researchers and local problem owners. Cooperative means both researchers and problem owners are concerned with the ends (results) and the means (process). Further, that professional researchers employ the rigorous responsibility of providing relevant and valid data from the complex context of the problem, and use both qualitative and quantitative means to develop the findings to be used with the problem owner.

Action research is based on privileging knowledge that is relevant for solving pertinent problems. It centers on practical reasoning, on clinical knowledge, on knowing how. In this regard, it asserts a democratic relationship between research professionals – management consultants, in this case, and problem solvers, – claiming that both have relevant skills and knowledge to contribute and should be respected equally in the research process.

Action research also insists on researching problems holistically and in context. Rather than purposely de-contextualizing problems in order to analyze them, action research attempts to study them in context or to reproduce as much of the complexity of the local context as possible in unraveling the causal relationships. Of course, to do this, action research requires the active cooperation of the problem owners.

Finally, action research asserts that the best test of rigor is the ability of research outcomes to transform situations in desired directions. The validity of action research is found in its ability to achieve desired goals.

Consultants, firms, and academic groups have not consistently demonstrated an ability to contribute towards creating plans and programs that meet the business potential. This is probably due to not understanding the needs and desires of the developing community of emerging consultants, and being trapped in a history of automation rather than innovation. That is, many consulting firms, both large and small, attempt to design a package – making it their trademark – that can solve literally all problems, in different organizations and settings. These are often called "canned" programs or approaches. Many firms offer some form of the canned package to each client regardless of the individuality of the context or the apparent need. These canned programs do not meet the systemic requirements of defining the problem in each context, by assuming what worked earlier and achieved success, will work equally well and provide success again in the same way. Consultants must remember that the "art of playing the game successfully changes the game itself and results in a new competitive game (Gharajedaghi, 2006, p.7)." Recall the earlier discussion on success and the change of the game. This is an important point worth reviewing – that the game is changing and one must always start as if in a new competitive game.

Once again, in terms of developing appropriate accreditation and certification, considerable work has been done by a few independent institutes and organizations. For example, the Institute of Management Consultants (IMC) of about 3,000 individual members in the United States, is in turn a member of the International Council of Management Consulting Institutes (ICMCI) which represents 30,000 Certified Management Consultants (CMC) worldwide. Successful accreditation in IMC results in the designation of CMC, to be used by management consultants in practice. Certification includes a recertification process every five years. However, performance measurements and criteria are limited.

Measurement of performance is still a difficult matter in management Consulting. Some organizations such as IMC use consulting case reviews and time in the field as a measurement, while many firms still use billable hours as a key indicator. Measurement variables are still crude, and yet to be designed and implemented within this rapidly developing field. The new measures need to be eclectic, and they need to be both objectively and subjectively devised and applied in the context of consulting. For, "objectivity, after all, is only collective subjectivity (Gharajedaghi, 2006, p.210."

In summary, the classification of management consulting as a profession, and based on the four components defined, still has some distance to go. It is clear that successful classification as a "profession" is highly dependent on management consultants -- both individually and collectively addressing the issues involved in professional education in

Learning to DO.   The capability to intervene to create a profession remains a significant challenge.

Developing Intervention Capability is Central to Success

Developing an intervention capability is a necessity for the aspiring consultant, for success is now a requirement. There are several challenges immediately apparent as one begins to examine an intervention capability. The challenge in "developing" suggests a series of events to be learned and practiced. For example: the ability to stop action and to change direction of the ongoing action demonstrates capability in consulting intervention. Intervention is a key skill, and like many others it is an emergent property, demanding constant work to continue its existence and hone its development.

The real value of emergent properties is that the property itself is in a position to be consistently improved and developed. Many projects do not successfully reach established goals due to the lack of skillful intervention capability applied in a timely fashion. Just as likely to fail, is the misnomer that one great intervention at the right time is all that is needed. That worked fine when we lived under the 'Great Man Theory' and one great intervention could turn the tide and make the significant difference. Now, in the midst of chaos and complexity the competent intervener realizes that one must go back time and time again, and that it is necessary in some cases to make the same intervention several times until the goal is reached.

On many occasions, specifically in chaotic ones, it is as if the intervener was not heard the first time. In reality, there is so much white noise in the field that it is easy for the consultant's intervention not to be heard – or in fact, only partially heard. Even when it is heard on some occasions, it may not be perceived or understood – it doesn't get into the brain in a meaningful way to cause learning on the part of the client. Therefore the intervener must develop the many skills of good communication and constantly check to be sure that they have been understood – and the client has actually had the opportunity to learn in the situation.

In communicating, context is very important. The closer one is to the responsible position for action as the receiver, the more likely one is to pay attention to the intervention message.   That is, the intervening message in the context must be delivered to a person(s) who can do more than just stop-action in the present. The receiver must be able to gather the valid data and information in the situation, be capable of making a free and informed decision, and be able to develop commitment to specific actions in the situation – thereby following through on the primary tasks of intervention (Argyris, 1970).   At the same time, the receiver may need to involve others, attempting to get their full attention. An intervention is empowering to those who take advantage of it. The receiver has the power to change direction, to move closer to being helpful in the setting. Of course, they may also choose to not take action – only stopping the past action momentarily. The consultant-intervener must be prepared to provide the relevant and valid information needed to help the client move forward in the best direction.

Recall the earlier discussions on intervention where the intention of the intervener must be clear in the statement and the opportunity must be created to examine the situation anew in order to jointly create the best move for the future. This is a time when the intervener excites people in the immediate context to become democratically involved, invites those involved to participate in examining valid data to the question, make some decision, and then develop commitment to act.   The consultant-intervener must be clear in their mind first, before stopping the action. For example, once clear, they may say: "Let's stop the action at this point and reconsider where we are going. Is there a better way to move at this point? What additional information do we need to answer that question? . . . and so forth."

Ability to intervene is the most important skill for the consultant-in-action   Being able to intervene appropriately is one of those big rocks that is critical to put in your jar. Many say that the intervention capability is the marketable competency of the management consultant.   That intervention capability is how the consultant is known to the world – by how they intervene in the situation. Seemingly, intervention skill appears to be more important than results in choosing a consultant, for if the interventions are not good and timely there will be no results. It is important to plan the key interventions and to consider the best timing for each one before actually intervening. The first macro intervention is really important – it sets the tone and the expectations for others. It is important to follow-up on the initially focused macro intervention, until all involved are truly ready to listen and consider new action in the context. The context of the intervention is important to provide direction and insight that structures the situation, with the primary tasks of intervention for the best results.

Indicators of need for an intervention It is important to recognize some of the signals that a consultant intervention may require. When the consultant spots a situation that seems to be repetitive, that is, no visible progress – this is prime area for intervention. For example, when one person seems to be repeating the same thing over and over – and is apparently unheard. There clearly is a block in the working situation to be removed. On some occasions, the consultants may find themselves in the position of not being heard -- there is a problem that is blocking communication.   The problem must be identified and dealt with. However, poor communication is usually just the symptom that is obvious, and not the problem to be identified.

Another indicator is when the client reports progress, or that everything is "OK," but cannot demonstrate any progress in practice. In a sense, the client seems to be marking time. This usually indicates a problem concerning direction or next steps. The consultant needs to stop the action and find out where the problem is located, but in a non-threatening and non-punishing way.

To successfully intervene, time after time, an overarching framework is needed for the management consultant. In the next section we will revisit the Consulting Systems Worldview (CSW) to use as a framework for intervention throughout the consulting engagement.

Defining a Framework to Guide Intervention

In revisiting the Consulting Systems Framework the focus is on understanding the four sequential phases as a framework for intervening during a consulting engagement. The worldview framework focuses on the whole and makes one aware of the phases as interdependent components in the transformation process.

A Four-Phased System with Interactive Elements Figure 25 focuses the transformation process and the interactive functioning of the interdependent phases of consultation: Entry & Contracting, Data Collection & Problem Definition, Problem Solution & Action Planning, and Implementation & Evaluation.

Reviewing Ackoff's (1997) definition of a system reinforces the importance of Systems Thinking in viewing the whole.   Further, it clarifies the focus on the importance of interactions of the elements in the four phases.

A system is a whole defined by one or more functions, that consist of two or more essential parts that satisfy the following conditions: 1) each of these parts can affect the behavior of properties of the whole; 2) none of these parts has an independent effect on the whole; the way an essential part affects the whole depends on what other parts are doing; and 3) every possible subset of the essential parts can affect the behavior or properties of the whole but none can do so independently of the others.

Transformation Process

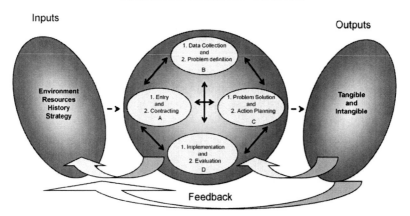

The Consulting Systems Worldview
© Marilyn E Harris, 1996

Figure 24: The Consulting Systems Worldview

Developing consultants are advised that the most important perspective for applying this understanding is that a system is a functioning whole and cannot be divided into independent parts and still be effective.   When applied to the transformation process in the Consulting Systems Worldview [CSW], this means that all four phases are part of the functioning whole system and must be addressed systemically in an iterative fashion.

Many consultants fail in transforming the organization simply because they only address parts of the transformation process in the Consulting Systems Worldview, and not the whole – as in the four interactive phases shown here. The whole includes all four phases and it is the consultant's responsibility to recognize it as the whole even when the focus may be on one of the phases at any given time.

When one does place the organization in the context of the whole, the set of problems may be identified quite differently.

The defining properties of a functioning whole system are in the interactions of its parts. Many consultants find it easier to focus on individuals, in contrast to the interactive process and the relationships. Many authors (Lazlo (1972); Deming (1975); Gharajedaghi, (1985)) point to the problems of an organization as lodged in the system, and not in the individuality of the actors or participants of the organization. Further, Gharajedaghi points out that each social system or organization manifests certain characteristics and they retain these characteristics even if all members are replaced. Organizations are beginning to realize that the true costs of downsizing are astronomical – including the "hidden costs" in lowered morale of those remaining, and future costs of recruitment and training; furthermore, they find that downsizing does not solve their system problems.

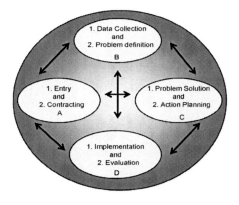

The Consulting Systems Worldview
© Marilyn E Harris, 1996

Figure 25: The Transformation Process of the Consulting Systems Worldview

In summary, the sociocultural system is a set of elements linked almost entirely by the intercommunication of information. It is seen as an organization of meanings emerging from a network of interaction among individuals.   The essential focus is on the information-bonded intercommunication in the network of interactions among individual relationships.

Sidebar: Designing an Ideal-seeking System

The state of a social system, at any given time, is defined by the four independent variables of structure, function, process, and the environment. Understanding the state of the system in a systems view is where social structure is seen as a temporary expression of relations between a system's components and its environment. This structure is ever changing in a dynamic fashion, based on the capacity of the culture in social learning.

These relations can be observed only in the context of its total functions – in the generation and dissemination of knowledge, power, wealth, values and beauty – and the process of its change. Therefore, instead of trying to describe social structure in terms of being, we have to understand it as a process of becoming and understand the concepts of culture and social learning.

Understanding the social structure component as an ongoing process of becoming leads to exploring what this process of becoming effects. First, where specifically is it evident and how may it be addressed? Second, how may it be intentionally used by the consultant in the creation of learning for the client? Gharajedaghi (1985) says that: " It is essential to note that by emphasizing the learning process, the systems approach to idealization is not to design an ideal state, but an ideal-seeking system."

First, the management consultation must recognize the importance in seeing the social structure outcome as a process of becoming; this is first evident in the culture of the organization in shared image or mental model development. Addressing the process of becoming in the organization may first require changing the understanding of the concept of change to that of an *ongoing process*, deriving its energy from the interaction of the elements of the system.

Second, it may be wise to address the creation of shared images in the organization and how that may be developed in social learning. That is, the organization's creative ability to meet the challenges of continuously emerging desires and ideals, which demands conscious and active adaptation, not a passive acceptance of events.

In summary, this may appear clear conceptually, but initially putting it into practice using the Consulting Systems Worldview (CSW) is a challenge. The several chapters of this fourth part of the book focus each phase comparably using real cases: Long Island Company and the Columbus Medical Association.

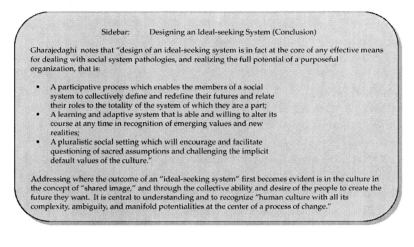

Sidebar: Designing an Ideal-seeking System (Conclusion)

Gharajedaghi notes that "design of an ideal-seeking system is in fact at the core of any effective means for dealing with social system pathologies, and realizing the full potential of a purposeful organization, that is:

- A participative process which enables the members of a social system to collectively define and redefine their futures and relate their roles to the totality of the system of which they are a part;
- A learning and adaptive system that is able and willing to alter its course at any time in recognition of emerging values and new realities;
- A pluralistic social setting which will encourage and facilitate questioning of sacred assumptions and challenging the implicit default values of the culture."

Addressing where the outcome of an "ideal-seeking system" first becomes evident is in the culture in the concept of "shared image," and through the collective ability and desire of the people to create the future they want. It is central to understanding and to recognize "human culture with all its complexity, ambiguity, and manifold potentialities at the center of a process of change."

Using the CSW Framework in Cases

Using the CSW framework in consultation on specific cases is a new challenge in each case. However, having a framework and clear steps spelled out is helpful. In attempting to demonstrate more fully the four phases of the Consulting Systems Worldview, two different methodologies are used, with Systems Thinking as the structure to work through the two cases to shed light on each phase. The methodologies selected have been in use for decades and represent time-tested and theoretically-based approaches. The use of methodologies selected is intended to integrate knowledge and skills of the management consultant in the sophistication of their experiences in the four interactive phases of the Consulting Systems Worldview.

In preparation, the developing consultant is encouraged to read the Appendix introducing the methodologies and the cases used to Learn to DO before reading Chapters 10 – 13. These chapters include a detailed discussion of the individual phases in the Consulting Systems Worldview and focus Systems Thinking concepts in general, and then the specific methodology related to each case used. At the end of each of the subsequent chapters there is a chart summarizing the key interventions in each phase .

In this section the developing consultant may gain experience with real cases, working at applying intervention knowledge and skills. The cases may be reviewed several times considering new opportunities in skill leveraging and development.

Choosing Options in Application

It is ideal to begin at the beginning and to work systematically and iteratively through the four-phase Consulting Systems Worldview framework defined and used here. However, many times that is not possible for one reason or another – often beyond the control of the developing consultant. Sometimes a consultant may be brought in to finish up someone else's work, and companies do not like to pay to go over what they think is already done – and for good reason, from their perspective. However, the consultant-just-employed to do the job must carefully review what has been done – attempting to fill in any glaring gaps, in an effort to avoid problems later on and to protect his own integrity and ethical approach.

On other occasions, the management consultant may join a team already in operation and the team does not want to start over from scratch to bring the consultant up to speed. In both cases, it may be shortsighted to jump over the initial phase (s) and just go to work, as requested. It is always worth the time to begin at the beginning. It is another time where it is worthwhile to "go slow, to go fast."

However, in several cases you may not have the luxury of billing the client for your learning time. Nevertheless, filling in the early "cracks and crevices" with the necessary information and knowledge and, at a minimum, reviewing the steps taken to get to this point will have high payoff for the management consultant. In many cases, this will provide the information that is required to finish the consultation with a high degree of success, meeting the requirements of 21st century consulting.

These different events create options for using the Consulting Systems Worldview. Actually, there are at least four different pathways or options that one may take into account when considering the full use of the four-phased approach:

- The first and very common alternative is to begin right after the first phase in Entry & Contracting. Many times this first phase is completed by executives and/or the legal team that do not appear to have an active interest in the work of the newly executed consulting agreement

- A second alternative is inclusion mid-phase 2, in the midst of Data Collection & Problem Definition. Many times, after beginning quickly, it is realized that more hands are necessary or professionals in data collection and problem definition will aid the project overall. Often someone is needed who can articulate the "system of problems" or the "mess" in a politically attractive way to the stakeholders. A presentation is needed that can get the stakeholders involved and challenged to succeed under the dominant circumstances

- The third position is at the end of phase 2, Data Collection & Problem Definition, where many times the client may need a "different face", or a different set of skills to move into Problem Solution & Action Planning, working with employees and stakeholders in a different way than the earlier phase

- A fourth place is at the beginning of the fourth and final phase, Implementation & Evaluation, for some of the same reasons as in other cases, but also to have someone who was not part of the actual Problem Solution & Action Planning. Many believe that an outsider may do a better job of Implementation & Evaluation

There are pros and cons to all of these positions and it is wise to consider them before one jumps into the project at any midway position.

Whenever the consultant does not initiate the Consulting Systems Worldview approach, for whatever reason, it is wise to set a period of orientation for yourself to the project and to see what has gone before you. What are the major decisions and how well has each been implemented?

If important aspects have been omitted, the consultant should pose sufficient questions to understand what is missing from the whole; when the project has been viewed holistically you can make a judgment regarding how to proceed. It is not wise to be adolescent in this case, going along with the crowd or going it alone, but to act in a mature fashion, raising questions which challenge the underlying system principles that should be directing action.

For example, Ackoff argues for synthesis in contrast to analysis (Wardman, 1994, p.3) saying that "no amount of quality analysis will ever be able to give the reason for cars now being sized to fit a family of four." In explanation analysis of the part will never yield the answer to a problem of the whole, as in this case. Thus, it is important to keep the whole system in mind and how the focal point in question is how the focused part relates to the functional whole. The temptation is to analyze and analyze because that is what we are familiar with; we have worked with the sociocultural model a shorter time and have not become comfortable with synthesis in many cases. Analysis in lieu of synthesis will not yield useful information for the developing consultant; the project must be viewed as a system before determining the best starting point.

In conclusion, all consultant actions should move from a theoretical base, and in this case, the Consulting Systems Worldview. When moving from theory, you can be much more confident, because in reality one bases their actions on the knowledge and experience of many others who tried and tested the same issues. It becomes easier and easier to defend a theoretical base as more and more people -- employees, clients, and colleagues -- are learning more each day, and as Learning to DO becomes clearer in each application.

Chapter 10   Effective intervention in ENTRY & CONTRACTING

The first phase may be the most important in the four phased consulting process. In phase 1 the tone of work is set and the foundation for the client-consulting relationship network is built – basic to the many significant relationships in a holistic approach. For these reasons, the savvy management consultant knowingly initiates Entry & Contracting with an attitude towards success that permeates all of the interactions in the phase and apparent in each intervention. The consultant initially creates an up-beat climate for transformation, and ensures that this climate develops throughout the engagement, with each client interaction.

Often, the interaction between the would-be-client and the consultant is subtle and political. However, the "dance at the beginning" is performed and sets the parameters for the rest of the consulting effort. Often, what is difficult to know is exactly when Entry begins. In many cases, the first consideration of a consultation is through an informal event – a chance meeting, a telephone call on another issue, a party or celebration of a different matter. The developing consultant must be alert to these opportunities and always be intentional about "beginning," even when the event is informal and not directly connected to a new consultation.

The shaded position of the first phase is focused in Figure 22. The Management Consulting Process - Phase 1: ENTRY & CONTRACTING in the Transformation Process.

Transformation Process

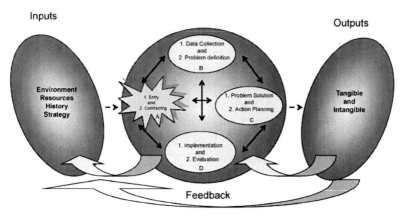

The Consulting Systems Worldview
© Marilyn E Harris, 1996

**Figure 26: The Management Consulting Process - Phase 1: ENTRY &
CONTRACTING in Transformation Process
© Marilyn Harris, 1996**

Why ENTRY & CONTRACTING are important

Phase 1 is influential in establishing a necessary interdependence in the client-consultant relationship that is crucial throughout the four-phased transformation process. The American Heritage Dictionary defines interdependent as "mutually dependent." In reality, being mutually dependent applies to the whole range of states throughout the engagement. For instance, early in the relationship the client may be very dependent on the consultant, whereas later on it may become more of a "50:50" as both the client and consultant learn how to best use their resources in given situations. It may be a 90:10 ratio at one time, and shortly thereafter a 30:70 ratio. In a healthy interdependent situation the exact variance and ratio does not matter, but the two are mutually working to meet the goals identified. It is a wise move for the consultant to articulate the value of an interdependent relationship early in the Entry process and describes the possible fluctuation in the ratio. It is important to note that in mature relationships there is healthy cooperation working toward clearly identified transformational results.

In Phase 1, the consultant has the first opportunity to demonstrate an attitude of success. One must keep in mind that although it is important for the consultant to demonstrate an attitude of success throughout all four phases, it is most important to start the process in Phase 1. Demonstrating an attitude of success is seen as an input into the transformation process. The output task is to develop an interdependent (client-consultant) partnership yielding a working agreement. It is important to realize that the client must also demonstrate an attitude of success and to change significantly, in most cases, to be a part of a developing interdependent relationship that is capable of gaining transformational results.

The task to build interdependent relationships must be identified by the consultant before starting Phase 1 because it is key for a successful consultation. The consultant must realize that transformative results will not be successfully achieved in a sustainable fashion without developing a highly interdependent relationship. The important point to keep in mind is that all of Phase 1 may be accomplished without actually having a consulting contract. The actual agreement for transformative change may not come until the end of the first phase. This may be paradoxical in much of the consultant's earlier experience. However, in most cases, the consultant's commitment to transformative change works as a driver in defining the parameters and goals of the contract for change.

A common concern of the developing consultant during this period of time is working without remuneration. To be sure, the time and effort are always considered in the contract, so that the remaining three phases actually cover the cost of the first phase. In that sense, it is encouraging to the developing consultant to be more effective and influential in this first phase in terms of moving to closure with a contract, thus not accumulating several unpaid first phases. The developing consultant will be fortunate, initially, to close on about 25% of the entries he may begin.

In order to achieve success in gaining the contract the consultant needs to be able to describe an interdependent partnership that successfully addresses transformative change in the client environment. In summary, for the developing consultant this means that he/she must be clear about "being" a consultant, and know their role in presenting the transformative change process to the client for "buy-in." Additionally, he/she must be able to explain the necessity of developing interdependence in the client-consultant working relationship and to help define rather clearly what the deliverables might be (in broad terms), and what the real costs of such an effort may be.

Generally, Entry and Contracting are seen as one phase with two distinct components. One is Entry, and the other is Contracting. Both components are considered *processes*. A process is a series of events or tasks required to experience the whole component.

The task of this chapter is to conceptually clarify the two components, define the critical tasks of each component, and recognize the iterative, interactive, and interdependent aspects of the components as well as with subsequent phases. To clarify, the critical tasks in Entry and Contracting are considered separately. The next section applies the learning to two cases in light of the actual interventions made in practice. In the final section, Emerging Opportunities are considered as future challenges for the developing consultant.

Entry

Entry refers to the first stage in the first phase of the consulting systems process. It is considered as the formal consulting entrance into an organization. In many cases, this first contact may be casual and informal in nature – nevertheless, it is still considered the formal entrance into the organization. Entry in itself is intended to be explorative and informative to both the client and the consultant. The purpose of entry in consulting is to develop the necessary relationships with the client to make an agreement or contract that will help the organization as a whole to transform, or to significantly improve in some aspect of its operation.

It is important to recognize the consulting value of a good Entry into the organization. Most consultants recognize that a positive entry into an organization has many values. For example, it saves time later in the total consultation, it improves the quality of the interaction in the consultative process, and it identifies key transformative results early. Many future doors may be opened through an outstanding entry experience.

Many seasoned management consultants, known by their successful experiences, deal routinely with Entry only as a business experience solely designed to get the contract. In these cases, the consultant may be well known and their reputation precedes them. One should be alerted that this "knowing of a reputation" may not be enough or sufficiently focused for the specifics required in each context. The developing consultant is cautioned not to depend solely on a reputation, although one must constantly be working on developing reputation in each context.

In larger firms, an officer or a partner may do both Entry and Contracting as one task, attempting to guarantee a quick and clear close on a large contract. Following the close, the contract is handed over to a junior to fulfill. When the developing consultant is in the position to follow a seasoned consultant, managing officer, or partner in fulfilling the contract, the entry should be carefully reviewed, as frequently many important factors may have been agreed upon that are not part of the written contract.

An example from recent experience focuses the importance of gaining the knowledge regarding entry. A fellow consultant was reporting on the findings of their study of the McKinsey Consulting method. He said that in a recent study of 2000 past McKinsey consultants, trainees reported on the most important factor in their McKinsey training. New consultants had the opportunity made for them – they could call any Mc Kinsey consultant anyplace in the world and describe what happened to them in a similar consulting situation. The McKinsey consultant is required to get back with the caller within 24 hours and to fully talk through the whole engagement from beginning to end. The fellow consultant, an ex McKinsey consultant himself, corroborated the information with his own experience in the firm. He reported that this "requirement to call another McKinsey consultant" proved to be the most important and invaluable experience in his consulting. Learning from another what went on during Entry not only influenced the rest of the consultation, but reinforced the importance of improved positive upbeat entry. It made entry smoother, for in a sense entry was rehearsed and compared to many others so it was no longer a new, loner experience. The calls prepared the new consultant for things that might happen in that entry, and prepare for things not thought of earlier.

Critical tasks to perform in entry

In searching the experience of consultants in entry there are three critical tasks that are identified. The first is presenting yourself as a consultant. Realizing the importance of the first impression, and how that first contact may affect the remaining phases in consulting systems process, the developing consultant may wish to rehearse entry tasks before actually meeting the client. The second is in "expectation setting" about relevant norms and boundaries that apply to the future consultation. The third focuses on development of a healthy relationship where cooperation is possible in the first phase.   Healthy relationship development refers to the earlier references on interdependence and information-bonded relationships, described in the first chapter in how the game is changing.

Presenting yourself One of the most difficult realities for the developing consultant to understand is that when "ideas" are presented to a client, the consultant is perceived as presenting him/her self. During this time, the client comes to conclusions about what makes the consultant tick, and why they are there.   Even though the consultant may indicate a different ownership of the idea -- that it belongs to someone else or to the firm, the consultant is perceived as putting forth their own ideas that they now support and must defend. Unfortunately, there is no way of making a neutral presentation.   The consultant must be able to put the idea or proposal forth and to support it completely based on him/her self in the present moment. Doing this successfully means knowing yourself well and being able to match the facts to questions raised in the situation. The fact remains that you are presenting yourself, although not directly as in giving your "name, rank and serial number," but by how engagingly one makes the presentation of relevant concepts related to transformative results in the situation.

When the management consultant is part of a consulting group or a larger firm, there may be general guidelines and opportunities to "shadow" a seasoned professional consultant and to rehearse before any effort is made to present oneself or the company in Entry.   However, when that is not the case, it may be wise to review your answer to the questions noted below in preparation for presentation to the client – not necessarily in this order:

- What seems to be the problem, or system of problems
- What knowledge or experience do I have in the same or similar industries that may be beneficial
- How do I want to refer to myself? For example: as a professional management consultant, as a social systems engineer, as a management specialist, as an associate in a firm, or by some other role classification

- What relevant background do I want to share? Formal education, practical education, on the job learning, or other knowledge and experience
- What kind of data collection may be necessary
- Who should be involved? Should there be inside teams, outside teams, or both
- How many data collection efforts should be planned or how much time in analysis, synthesis, and report writing is needed
- How time is needed to do a complete job including implementation
- How much time do I have? At what cost
- Why do you and your company want to work with this client? Essentially, why problem solve, and why transform at this time?
- What outcome and benefits will result from this consultation for the client and the consultant

Clearly, these questions go beyond entry, but the consultant must be fully prepared when entering the situation, having thought through many of these questions so there is not a fumbling for words, concepts, or conclusions in the meeting. *Presencing*, and anticipating the future is important. Advance preparation places the consultant in a stronger position to respond to the client at the meeting in contrast to going in "cold." There is a tremendous advantage that is gained from studying cases of other consultants and their use of specific methodologies. In fact, this type of advance study presents an opportunity to create your own "practice field" for preparation.

In this explorative phase the client is usually assessing whether they can relate well with the consultant and whether the consultant's previous experience, knowledge, and values displayed are applicable to the present situation. At the same time, the consultant is assessing the probability of relating well with the client, the motivation and values of the client, the client's readiness for transformative change, and the extent and depth of the client's resources to support a change effort.

Setting expectations Expectation setting is the opportunity to influence the client to "stretch" in the consultation to meet the 'changing game' defined by the double paradigm shift. This is the time when the consultant helps the client *understand* – in the present,– the different requirements for transformation. He helps the client to understand why transformation is necessary now, in contrast to the past. He/she helps the client realize the importance of all four phases in the consultation, so the consultant can be available to help in the implementation – where many small problems crop up in the performance of new tasks. They may help the client realize the value of participation of the stakeholders in the beginning – how, for example "we fail not because we fail to solve the problem we face, but because we fail to face the right problem" (Ackoff, 1984). That in fact, the people closest to the problem – the stakeholders -- may be very important in defining the right problem. It may be wise to point out the importance of communication, and how we must increase clarity and the amount of knowledge communicated to succeed. It is also wise to make clear that as a consultant you are striving for success, that you are interested in innovation and learning from the future, and the value for the client. This is a time when the consultant wants to lay out in broad terms what his implementation for the engagement – so there are no surprises and you as the consultant are off on the right foot in developing a healthy interdependent relationship.

Developing healthy relationships In understanding the importance of relationship development it is important to focus on the member interaction rather than the individuality of its members. It must be remembered that it is through the "interactions" that a relationship is developed. The focus is not on the individual, nor their traits – but instead it is focused on the information and knowledge transfer in the interactions between the people relating.   Thus, for the developing consultant it is important to interact with the client in such a way that the relationship is developing in the direction of agreement on results from the consulting engagement.   A healthy working relationship may be defined as one where there is agreement on common perceptions, management of conflict, and movement toward purposeful results.

During the Entry portion the consultant is seeking understanding and agreement on many basic aspects in the consulting engagement, and is attempting to build a foundation for a continuing relationship. Establishing and developing a trustful relationship built on joint participation is worthwhile to prevent misunderstanding and conflicts later. It is clear that all conflicts and misunderstandings may not be prevented, and there should be means to manage those at the time they occur. It is worthwhile to take time in the beginning to develop a healthy relationship that is based on understanding and agreement for a number of factors that capitalize on "people input.' People are very important in attaining success in the consultation. Kent and Anderson (2002, p. 24) state "that technology will take any organization only half as far as it needs to go. The people in organizations take them all the way to success." It is worthwhile to go slow at first in developing the key relationships through numerous interactions valuing people, in order to go fast later on in the implementation phase.

In summary, the consultant presents him/her self as an energized person who is interested and very capable in facilitating the work of the client to dissolve the problem or system of problems identified. The client must believe that they and their organizational problem is understood. In the presentation the consultant needs to do some important expectation setting affecting the parameters of the contract and future work. Finally, during this period of entry the consultant has focused on developing healthy interaction between him/her self and the client valuing people. It is worthwhile for the consultant to keep these three markers in mind as they move through a rehearsed practice entry toward contracting.

Contracting

The contracting component of the first phase is the development of a relatively clear understanding of just how the client and the consultant will proceed to create "deliverables" that meet or dissolve the systemic problem. The understanding is usually recorded in a formalized agreement called a "contract." The contracting provides direction for intervention in implementation, in a list of deliverables that provide measurement of success and the basis for learning, change, and innovation.

Critical tasks in CONTRACTING

Contracting may be an elaborate process accomplished by a contingency of lawyers, a simple one-page letter of agreement, a handshake, or something in between. The developing consultant is encouraged to put something in writing as a matter of reference for use throughout the engagement. The type of contract really depends on the requirements of the client and consultant organizations, and the extent and depth of the systemic issues. The critical tasks include identifying the human and material resources needs on a scheduled time line for the consultation, agreement on the priority of new learning for the client and the consultant, and documenting the agreement in a contract for the engagement. Further, in all contracts there should be a clause that allows for change for any reason, as long as the reason is put in writing and given a period of time to be considered before the change is activated or the contract is terminated.

Developing a timeline noting deliverables In developing the contract it is necessary to project a timeline with activities to be carried out to reach the agreed upon goals. It may be sufficient to develop a timeline along the lines of Figure 23. Example: A Projected Timeline for A Systems Intervention. It may be necessary to fill in more detail as in Figure 28. Example: A Schedule of Activity Projected.   Figure 37 shows the detail required for the whole project. It is necessary for the consultant to detail the activity at the level that provides full understanding to the client and aids cooperation subsequently in implementation.

Developing a schedule of activity identifying resource utilization Before developing the contract the consultant and the client need to develop a schedule of activities which identifies resources and materials required by the consultant and the client to produce

A Systems Project in State Education

Initial Meeting to review and customize the Plan (to be arranged)   1 hr

Timeframe	Activity	Total Contact Days
3 mos.	Phase 1: Designing the Intervention Process	
	One day to organize and develop plan for State	1 da
	One day to select stakeholders	1 da
	Stakeholder Training Sessions to Formulate & Design	
	Four – 2 day sessions (2 sessions per mos.)	8 da
3 mos.	Phase 2: Formulating the Problem and Phase 3: Designing the Solution (Concurrently)	
	Yields one iteration of the State 'system of problems' And a design to be implemented	
	2 teams meeting in two – 2 day sessions/mo	12 da
1 mos.	A second iteration is needed (at minimum)	12 da
5 mos.	Phase 4: Realization and Preparation for Design Implementation	
	Pilot preferably in one regional area Minimum	20 da
1 Budget Yr.	Full Implementation	
	(Design implementation for full Dissemination)	48 da
1 Budget Yr.	Measurement and Implementation in the rest of the State	24 da

N. B. Project budget for first year is at $ xxx/mos. And $xxxx for first year, payable a month in advance. Please note this is a generic timeline, specific dates applied on acceptance.

Figure 27: Example of a Projected Timeline for a Systems Intervention

the deliverables. It identifies the amount of time involved by all staff – on site and off site. After these basics are defined in a Gantt Chart [see example in Figure 24. Schedule of Activity Projected], costs may be more easily assigned and justified.

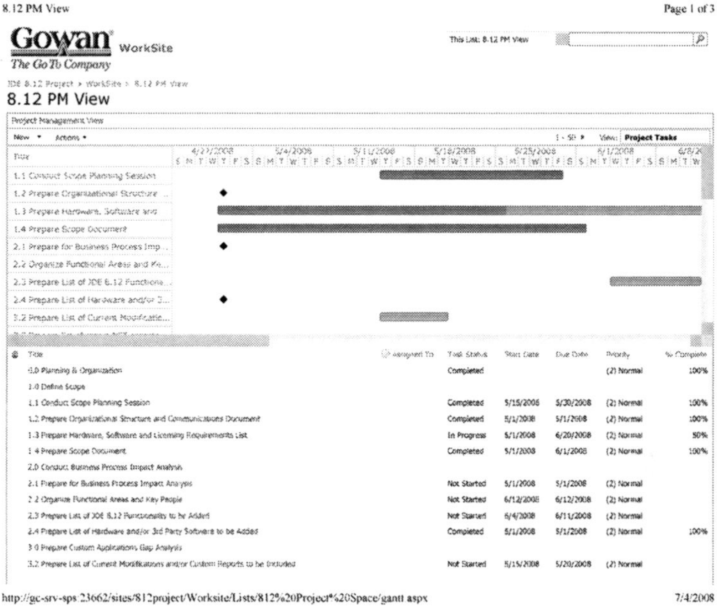

Figure 28: Example of a Schedule of Activity Projected

It is common to underestimate the time that it takes to implement a project fully, particularly when there are several people involved over a long period of time. For that reason, it is important to plan and check the work of the scheduler, to be sure that you have included sufficient time and cost for the anticipated resource need. In addition, one may wish to include a contingency clause that allows for expansion, if necessary, during the time of this agreement in the development of a subproject or new unrelated program that may be important to the success of the main project.   It appears that as complexity increases it takes longer to successfully move through this first phase in Entry and Contracting to meet the goals of the project.

Developing the contract Once the human and material resources have been identified, for both the client and consultant, and the schedule of activity has been developed, costs may easily be attached to these documents in preparation for preparing the terms of engagement, commonly referred to as an agreement or contract.   The developing management consultant is encouraged to carefully respect these steps and to put something in writing, as it can serve as a reference throughout the engagement.

A New Perspective on the First Phase

The most important factor in the first phase is that the consultant gain an understanding of the consulting task before him, and figure out how he will confidently address the task. To accomplish this, the developing consultant must be comfortable with his own image as a consultant and his professional development for the consulting task.   Most assuredly these factors will be communicated to the client.   It is a good idea to do some rehearsing of this first meeting, prior to coming in contact with a potential client.   One might rehearse several different beginnings, creating a repertoire of alternatives to choose from – thus being prepared when the occasion may occur without previous notice.

It is also necessary to understand the importance of establishing an initial foundation for an information-bonded relationship with the client. Additionally, the entry phase is an opportunity to help set the client's expectations for success throughout the future phases.   This opens the client to "stretching" the boundaries in problem definition, in problem solution, and in action planning in preparation for implementation. It is worthwhile to walk the client through the anticipated phases and begin to prepare them for a more participative approach.

In the contracting phase the consultant needs to identify the resources needed for the client and the consulting organization to carry out the change project successfully. It is during this time, that the priority of new learning needs to be addressed.   Finally, the agreements should be documented in a contractual arrangement, which may vary from a simple letter of agreement to an extensive contract covering the many aspects in great detail.   The developing consultant is cautioned to get something in writing and to provide a timeline to work through the phases.

First Phase Process Summary Chart

The critical tasks and outputs of the consulting process are summarized in Figure 29,_The Management Consulting Process Phase 1: Entry and

Contracting. It is noted that the depth and necessity of each task outlined in the chart depends on the context of the situation being considered. In each phase some tasks are emphasized in bold to focus their importance. The emphasized tasks may be considered key in the series, but will not produce success when used singularly. In summary, the tasks listed are interdependent, interactive, and iterative, requiring considerable effort to complete successfully. The outputs are a management tool and may be used by the developing consultant to evaluate the phase – was this output achieved? To what degree?

The first phase process summary chart may be used in two ways – "before" and "after." Before beginning the phase, the chart may be considered in planning and preparation, as a checklist to identify what one should do. After completing the phase the consultant may use the list to review the actions undertaken on each task. Each step may be reviewed by constructing a five-point scale at the end of each statement. Each scale ranges from 1 = not considered at all, to 5 = fully used and practiced successfully. Initially, there may be only very few "5s." In reflecting on the findings from the small evaluation attempt, the consultant may find that not enough time was devoted to preparation of specific items. This is a common conclusion. The factor of time needs to be carefully dealt with, not compromising quality of the effort in the service of time. The consultant needs to reflect on his findings so as to identify places and means to continuously improve on the next effort in Entry & Contracting. There may be considerable learning from redesigning what you just did and by thinking through the whole process again. The learning gained from this retrieval may be mentally stored for another occasion.

Periodic evaluation of the consultation process is useful in developing the consultant's individual learning system of Learning to BE, Learning to LEARN, and Learning to DO. As the consultant becomes more familiar with each part of the system and the relationships involved, he/she may use the learning system more freely in assisting the client in learning.

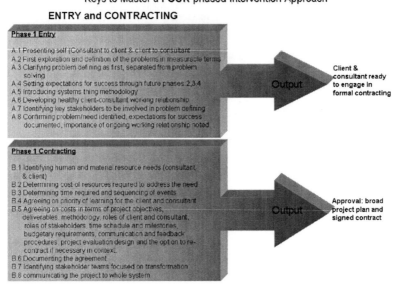

The Consulting Systems **WORLDVIEW**
Keys to Master a **FOUR** phased Intervention Approach

ENTRY and CONTRACTING

Phase 1 Entry

A.1 Presenting self (Consultant to client & client to consultant)
A.2 First exploration and definition of the problems in measureable terms
A.3 Clarifying problem defining as first, separated from problem
     solving
A.4 Setting expectations for success through future phases 2,3,4
A.5 Introducing systems thing methodology
A.6 Developing healthy client-consultant working relationship
A.7 Identifying key stakeholders to be involved in problem defining
A.8 Confirming problem/need identified, expectations for success
     documented, importance of ongoing working relationship noted.

Output

Client &
consultant ready
to engage in
formal contracting

Phase 1 Contracting

B.1 Identifying human and material resource needs (consultant
     & client)
B.2 Determining cost of resources required to address the need
B.3 Determining time required and sequencing of events
B.4 Agreeing on priority of learning for the client and consultant
B.5 Agreeing on costs in terms of project objectives,
     deliverables, methodology, roles of client and consultant,
     roles of stakeholders, time schedule and milestones,
     budgetary requirements, communication and feedback
     procedures, project evaluation design and the option to re-
     contract if necessary in context.
B.6 Documenting the agreement
B.7 Identifying stakeholder teams focused on transformation
B.8 communicating the project to whole system

Output

Approval: broad
project plan and
signed contract

**Figure 29: The Management Consulting Process – Phase 1: ENTRY &
CONTRACTING
© Marilyn Harris 1996**

Gaining Perspective from Applications

To gain the full perspective in application in this chapter, the two cases, The Long Island Company (LIC), and The Columbus Medical Association (CMA) in the appendix, must be reviewed first. If the developing management consultant has not taken advantage of this opportunity, the application experience in this chapter and subsequent chapters will be found lacking.

Application in The Long Island Company (LIC) In this case, entry and contracting was established upfront between the owners of LIC and the newly selected management consultant. It was evident during Phase 3 of LIC's development that the Company was experiencing some slowing and stagnation in development. The entry and contracting was performed by one individual through a series of interviews with the owners understanding and defining the scope of the engagement. The focus of the interviews coincided with contracted consulting services defining LIC's current state, desired state and obstacles inhibiting its further growth. The critical components of entry and contracting were completed supporting a viable go forward strategy.

The three major components of entry at LIC included the consultant's presentation of self, expectation setting and relationship development. It was important to the LIC owners that the management consultant had a reasonable understanding of their organization, as well as the industry in which it operated. The selected management consultant had a longer tenured relationship with one of the owners which assisted in establishing credibility with the other owners. Through a series of discussion with each of the owners, expectations were clearly established regarding the current obstacles and what was desired from the consulting engagement. This is when the aspect of defining its current state, desired state, and identifying potential obstacles inhibiting development were clearly articulated. The process in these initial discussions with the owners was the basis for a healthy relationship being developed prior to the commencement of the engagement. These discussions provided the management consultant with a much clearer perspective of the relationships between the three owners.

During the contracting process, the management consultant worked with the owners at LIC to establish a clear timeline of milestones, requirements for the use of individual resources at LIC, and agreement on the assignment. It was important to the owners at LIC that this initiative be concluded in an expeditious manner. A timeline reporting milestones was completed and approved. The requirement to interview key stakeholders in the organization was defined which resulted in a series of three interviews for each stakeholder. The interviews focused on LIC's leadership, organizational culture and functional development. Lastly, a detailed project plan containing resource requirements and a description of deliverables was agreed upon between the owners and the management consultant.

Consistent with the CSW framework, the entry and contracting at LIC resulted in the establishment of a clear understanding of the task at hand, as well as the identification of the required tasks to perform to the LIC owner's satisfaction. This outcome was reinforced through a series of discussions with the owners that resulted in an information-bonded relationship before execution of the consulting engagement.

Application in The Columbus Medical Association (CMA) Columbus Medical Association and its affiliates — the Columbus Medical Association

Foundation, the Physician's Free Clinic, and the Central Ohio Trauma System—operate as a collective organization in terms of high level goals, learning practices, and organizational development. The greatest level of change had occurred after the CEO was hired in 1999. Anxious to document their learning and development journey to support continued evolution, the CEO responded to a researcher's request to analyze the organizational changes and provide insight into future development pathways. In this respect the researcher acted as a consultant to CMA (from this point forward the researcher will be referred to as a consultant so as not to confuse the reader). A third party referred the consultant to the CEO and vice versa. The initial contact was made by email and quickly followed by a telephone call for mutual introductions and to explore the needs of the organization. Following this introductory contact between the consultant and the CEO to confirm interest, these two individuals met to plan the subsequent research and analysis phases through a series of planning meetings. Expectations for success as well as boundaries for scope, confidentiality, and organizational access were discussed and agreed in these planning meetings. Stakeholders were identified as the employees, the board members, the CEO, and external members of the Franklin County community. The consultant described an interview process with various employees and stakeholders, and was provided a comprehensive list of potential participants. The consultant then contacted 20 individuals and made plans to conduct the hour-long interviews in person during a weeklong visit to the CMA facility. Interview questions covered leadership, communication, organizational structure, strategy, and learning practices.

The CEO, an avid lifelong learner, was already well acquainted with the systems perspective and conversations during the contracting process confirmed that Systems Thinking is an integral part of the organizational development to be documented, and integral to the continued success for the four affiliates.

The three major components of entry at CMA included an initial contact with the CEO establishing alignment of goals and outcomes, and an active partnering with the CEO and boards of directors to ensure that all of the organizational goals could be met simultaneously. A key element of the entry and contracting phase was establishing trust with the organization and its employees and stakeholders. As a result, the consultant was provided unfettered access to the participants, publicly available organizational documents, and unstructured conversation with employees and stakeholders. The CEO was provided an estimate of time required for interviews and analysis, as well as a timeframe for completion and follow-up with the organization. An important aspect of the contracting phase was the consultant's promise to return to the organization to share the findings and recommendations with the entire employee base and interested board members.

Consistent with the CSW framework, the entry and contracting at CMA resulted in a clear and aligned set of expectations between the consultant, the CEO, and the board members. These expectations were documented in a letter of agreement between the CEO and the consultant. This part of the contract was fulfilled with a written report of the analysis, findings, and recommendations presented in person by the consultant at the CMA facility.

Emerging Opportunities

Emerging opportunities in consulting may be identified as the problematic areas or the "rough spots" that remain in Entry & Contracting, once you have worked through the experience. Unfortunately, many developing consultants pass these rough spots off as areas that need continuous improvement – not realizing that the area under scrutiny is actually an emergent property that requires constant *generative* processes to continue existence. In this case, the processes that support the property may be in need of new learning and moving to a higher level. For example, in *Presencing* these are the listening and languaging tools shown in Chapter 8. Understanding comes from applying the systems concepts related to emergent properties – not putting the process aside or simply saying that it is in need of improvement. To maintain an attitude of success throughout and to be successful one must recognize emergent properties as emerging opportunities. In *Presencing,* some current examples for the developing consultant may be in presenting oneself, in setting expectations, and in developing healthy relationships, using the tools identified earlier and moving to new levels through *presencing.*

In many cases, developing consultants have failed initially to make clear the aspects of an emergent property or to identify other system principles to the client. This makes it doubly difficult to deal with one's own problematic areas, but also those of the client – which in many cases may be very similar. Even when consultants have made the point to their clients, they often fail to heed the "understanding" they themselves touted. Further, they tend to see areas defined as dilemmas and/or challenges as areas to be blocked off and not worked. They then tend to avoid addressing them in the future. Several of these will be addressed here, in order to alert the developing consultant to them as areas of emerging opportunity. These are areas where it may take considerable *innovative new learning* to change.

A common scenario for developing consultants to avoid is falling captive to accepting a "deal" to consult without any exploration or study of the situation. For example: A consultant is told of a problematic situation and offered a relatively handsome dollar amount for agreeing to take the job at the time.

This often happens in what the client considers "crisis-like" situations. It is difficult to avoid "grabbing" such a contract immediately. One is encouraged to always consider the self-learning that is possible from addressing the "contract" offered in the studied fashion and avoid accepting a "pig in a poke." On first presentation it is difficult to know what is included and what is excluded. It is much wiser to display both ethics and business acumen to apply some study and assessment on the consultant's part before answering. When costs are undetermined in advance, the consultant usually finds him/her self "doing more for less." The client, in these instances, is thinking of what they have available in dollars to address the problem identified (which may not be the problem in any case) and the client is not thinking about the actual cost of problem dissolution. The main thing to keep in mind is to address even this first phase *jointly,* with at least two people – the consultant and the client. Accepting the status quo may telegraph to the client that the consultant is not into a whole system approach, and further that they may not have access to the latest technologies to assess the problem or to problem solve in the contract.

Who takes initiative in beginning – the consultant or the client – is a political problem. Many times the consultant must raise a question to provide the opportunity for the client to take initiative. This is also a question of balance and identifying who has the expertise to move at this point. The basic tenet to respect is in building a joint approach; balance in participation is important (right from the beginning). Often identifying the expertise needed to move ahead is a way of initiating consideration, which is not as threatening as just taking action. When one is identified as having the expertise in hand, one should make that public and ask to share the expertise.

In the past, the consultant has frequently had the knowledge of the process steps and the expertise to continue. This has caused the client to be unnecessarily dependent and unable to take initiative,   while at the same time, the client may have always been seen as the "starter" and the authority. It is important in these settings to start by making a deal to work jointly throughout, and to strongly enforce this right from the beginning. By always sharing in advance, the client is knowledgeable of the proposed activity and can have input into the thinking and planning; this paves the way for joint action. It is important, once again, ***to go slow to go fast.***

Developing emerging opportunities in this first phase depends heavily on the consultant communication and the presentation of self in a short amount of time. It may equate to learning for both the client *and* the consultant by modeling the critical tasks in the service of development of a healthy relationship, and by raising the value of people input. Entry & Contracting provide the opportunity for the consultant to communicate systems concepts that are important for the client to hear, and to begin to jointly practice the beginning work in the consultation. In this first phase, there are many opportunities to set up "Rules of the Game" together that will work best in this consultation. These should be continuously reviewed for emerging opportunities as the consultant and the client develop a healthy relationship in practice, as they move through this phase and into subsequent phases.

Chapter 11   Effective Intervention in Data Collection & Problem Definition

"Misconceptions about reality display self-fulfilling qualities.   Unless uncovered and dismantled, they outmaneuver and outlive assaults aimed at uprooting them.   The obstructions that prevent a system from facing its current reality are self-imposed.   Hidden and out of reach, they reside at the core of our perceptions and find expression in mental models, assumptions, and images.   These obstructions essentially set us up, shape our world, and chart our future.   They are responsible for preserving the system as it is and frustrate its efforts to become what it can be."

— Jamshid Gharajedaghi (2006)

What's so important about Data Collection & Problem Definition

The components of phase 2 are basic and critical tasks that provide the valid knowledge base for problem definition in the management consulting engagement. Defining the problem first, before solution, is basic in achieving success. Ackoff says that we fail not because we fail to solve the problem we face, but because *we fail to face the right problem* [emphasis added]. It is important to identify the valid knowledge to define the right problem. Figure 30. The Management Consulting Process - Phase 2: DATA COLLECTION & PROBLEM DEFINITION in the Transformation Process graphically shows the shaded location of the phase. The purpose of this phase is to use relevant and valid knowledge, both known and developed, to *identify the problem or system of problems* to dissolve.

Transformation Process

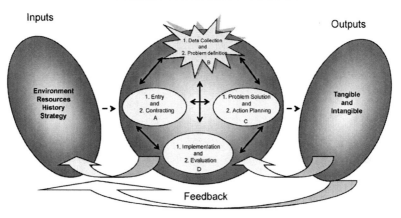

Inputs

Outputs

The Consulting Systems Worldview
© Marilyn E Harris, 1996

**Figure 30: The Management Consulting Process - Phase 2: DATA
COLLECTION & PROBLEM DEFINITION
in the Transformation Process
© Marilyn E Harris, 1996**

Paul Friga, a former McKinseyite, says of the McKinsey problem solving process, that the consultant is directed to frame the problem at the first meeting with the client. That is "Solve the problem at the first meeting – the initial hypothesis. The problem is not always the problem." At first, the McKinsey directions sound good, and supportive of Ackoff's statement. However, listening carefully to the meaning of the words it is clear that McKinsey, in this instance, is into problem solving, not *problem defining*. The process of defining the problem must be deliberately separated from problem solution, as depicted in the Consulting Systems Worldview (CSW). Phase 2 components include Data Collection & Problem Definition, while Phase 3 components are Problem Solution & Action Planning, demonstrating a clear separation in *definition* and in *solution*.

Moreover, problem defining may take precedence over data collection or at minimum as Gharajedaghi (2006) recognizes, that data collection is an integral part of "formulating the mess." The problem defining [formulation of the mess] is a three-phase process of (1) searching, (2) mapping, and 3) telling the story.   This approach makes sense in the complex and chaotic contemporary settings – settings in which most management consultants are asked to intervene in today's world. Pursuing the three step approach to problem definition adds credibility to the consultant, for in this case he is working with the stakeholders to bring order from chaos, involving them in defining and owning the problem.   Stakeholder involvement increases overall effectiveness in the second phase.

Critical Tasks in DATA COLLECTION

Data Collection has become very sophisticated in a complex world. With the advent of the information society, data are collected, manipulated, and stored quite automatically. The relevant issue in problem definition is not just the collection of data, but the collection of the right data by the right people at the right time to immeasurably effect problem dissolution. The latter, in problem dissolution is the desired outcome of data collection. The critical tasks in data collection are searching out the data with the stakeholders, mapping the problem including finding and dismantling the second order machine, and developing the story of the problem.

Data collection in Systems Thinking terms is formulating the problem. In pursuing the formulation of the problem, understanding of the term "mess" is primary. A mess is a system of problems. It is the future implicit in the present behavior of the system, the consequence of the system's current state of affairs. The essence of the mess is the systemic nature of the situation. It is not an aggregate representing the sum of the parts. A mess is an emergent phenomenon produced by the interaction of the parts. Formulation of the mess requires understanding of the essence of the behavioral characteristics of social phenomena. Gharajedaghi (2006) states that a mess is neither an aberration nor a prediction, but the following:

- The natural consequence of the existing order, based on false assumptions that nothing will change
- The product of success rather than failure, the consequence of a belief based on the fallacy that if X is good, more X is even better
- An early warning system reminding the actors that if things can go wrong they probably will

- An exaggeration intended to highlight the critical issues that may become the seed of a system's destruction in the future
- Messes are very resilient; they have a way of regenerating themselves. It is this quality that makes a mess an intractable phenomenon. The prevalent powerlessness and impotency in dealing with the mess lead to the inevitable denial on which messes thrive
- Finally, the mess is not defined in terms of 1) deviations from the norm, 2) lack of resources (time, money, and information), or 3) an improper application of a known solution
- The mess is formulated to achieve the following aims:
- Provide a perspective that sets the relevant host of problems in the proper context
- Develop a shared understanding of why the system behaves the way it does and generates a shared understanding about the nature of the current reality among the major actors
- Minimize the resistance to change and maximize the courage to act by making the real enemy publicly visible and believable
- Identify the areas of greatest leverage, vulnerability, and/or possible seeds of the system's destruction
- Make a convincing case for fundamental change and set the stage for effective redesign. It may lead to despair without an intent to redesign

It is clear that pursuing mess formulation is a challenging approach that may use considerable time and energy on the part of the developing management consultant. However, it is worth the investment because defining the problem through the three-phrased process leads to formulation in a way that the problem may be *dissolved* and therefore stays solved. In our complex world solving the problem once is necessary, for there is neither time nor money to continually solve the same problem over and over, as we have in the past. This makes the process of searching, mapping, and telling the story to define the problem especially valuable.

Searching out data with stakeholders Searching is the *iterative examination* that generates information, knowledge, and understanding about the system and its environment. The searching phase of problem defining involves three kinds of inquiry as shown in Figure 31 Iterative Process of Inquiry.

1. Systems Analysis: To develop a snapshot of the current system and its environment that describes their structural, functional, and behavioral aspects without making a value judgment
2. Obstruction Analysis: To identify the malfunctioning in the power, knowledge, wealth, beauty, and value dimensions of a social system
3. System Dynamics: To understand the interactions of critical variables in the context of the following: time, the totality and the interactive nature of the change within the system, and the system's environment

Gharajedaghi (2006) says that the three inquiries – systems analysis, obstruction analysis, and system dynamics – evolve iteratively. With each successive cycle of iterations, a higher level of specificity is achieved. In the first iteration, the task is to get a feel for the whole, define the system boundary, identify important variables, note areas of consensus and conflict, and identify gaps in information, knowledge, and understanding. Between iterations, gaps are filled when possible. The subsequent iterations verify the assertions made in the previous iteration, obtain agreement on significant issues, and develop models to understand the behavior of the system.

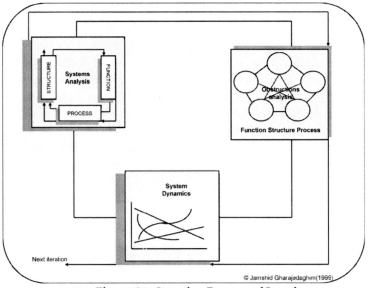

Figure 31: Iterative Process of Inquiry
Adapted from © Gharajedaghi (2006)

Time is the most important factor in a search process. A group might have just a day, a week, a month, or a full year to formulate the set of problems. The available time defines the level of generality and the degree of specificity that can be achieved. However, the available time should be allocated to each part of the inquiry to permit a pass-through cycle to understand the holistic nature of the situation as well as identify the significant elements of the mess. This pass-through cycle should be done at least twice to gain maximum value and leverage.

Having completed the first iteration of the systems analysis, the obstruction analysis, and the system dynamics, it is important to pause to make sense of what we've already learned. We need assumptions to be able to develop a tentative holistic picture. Subsequent iterations will clarify, verify, and modify this picture. The initial picture is used primarily as a guideline for what we need to know in more detailed iterations. In developing one's searching techniques, the serious management consultant should study Gharajedaghi's (2006) work – description of systems analysis, obstruction analysis, system dynamics tables; these are offered as guides and examples of the types of questions that may be examined in the search process. These forms should not take over the content. Remember, this is an iterative process and the user should avoid getting lost in the jungle of information. An important guide is to generate enough information so you can establish the relevancy of each variable under consideration. Even using this guide systematically, one may be overwhelmed with information that may initially appear incoherent. It is important to maintain perspective that is gained through the iterative search process.

Mapping the problem The search phase usually identifies a large number of obstructions. To make sense of these obstructions, it is necessary to synthesize them into a few categories so their interactions may be examined to understand the essence of the mess. This process involves grouping various phenomena into categories or subsets, then identifying themes, each of which is the emergent property of its constituent elements.

Gharajedaghi (2006) says the generation of these themes usually requires an interactive discussion to achieve a shared understanding of the grouping criteria. Each theme should be 1) defined clearly so there is no confusion about what it represents and 2) substantiated in terms of its prevalence. Themes should not reflect isolated occurrences. A litmus test for the validity of the themes is that when presented to relevant stakeholders, a clear sign of recognition results the equivalent of an "aha!" experience.

Finally, after all relevant themes are identified and substantiated, the relationships (interactions) among the elements must be addressed. Each theme is normally a mini mess in its own right, however, for the purpose of studying the interactions, initially each theme is treated as a self-containing whole. In subsequent iterations, if a theme emerges as the central concern we would break it down further into smaller components so their interactions with the other elements of the mess can be properly represented.

It is often helpful to develop pictorial representations of the interactions among themes as in Figure 32. Mapping the Mess, borrowed from Gharajedaghi (2006, p.135). It will be used to graphically represent the four themes identified: viability of market niche, product division culture, product potency, and operational effectiveness. "This type of diagram can be read by tracing the lines of interactions as follows: As a substitute product gradually gains acceptance, a gradual loss of product potency results in decreased market demand. In a divisional culture, the identity of any division is defined by the viability of its market niche. Any threat to this niche constitutes a threat to that division. Therefore the first reaction to this unpleasant reality is denial.

The division, to protect itself, repeatedly issues exaggerated forecasts, which prove false and damage its credibility. This increases the pressure to improve sales by reducing cost at any cost. But the change in the marketplace demands a redesign to improve product potency. Meanwhile, pressure to produce immediate results encourages short-term remedies. An ineffective operational system, under this pressure, is not capable of redesigning the product, so it patches minor changes onto the existing product. This further increases the cost, reducing the sales and, most unfortunately, granting precious time to the competition to solidify its position. The vicious circle thus continues (p.136)"

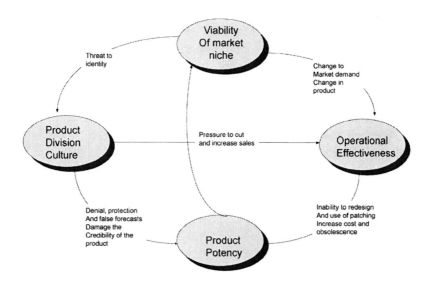

Figure 32: Mapping the Mess adapted from
© Jamshid Gharajedaghi (2006, p.136)

In mapping the mess it is important to underscore the nature of interdependency and the dynamics of the situation.   This requires remembering the assertion regarding the counterintuitive behavior of social systems. To appreciate the nature of counter-intuitiveness one needs to recognize these assertions:

- An event (cause) might have more than a single outcome (effect)
- Cause and effect are separated in time and space (time lag)
- Cause and effect can replace one another (circularity)
- Effects, once produced, might have an independent life of their own. Removing the cause will not necessarily remove the effects

Finding the second order machine Most importantly, mapping the mess is the heuristic process of defining essential characteristics and the emergent property in the existing set of problems. It involves finding the "second order machine" residing within the system. A second order machine is a set of commonly held assumptions about organizing principles that on the surface appear very simple and look quite harmless. Yet, residing at the core of the organization's collective memory, they are responsible for making the system what it is and behave the way it does. They are very powerful, despite their seeming innocence, and they act as self-fulfilling prophesies. This unanticipated consequence of the existing order produces paralyzing properties that create inertia, prevent change, and frustrate attempts to make significant improvements. Gharajedaghi (2006, p137) clearly states that to achieve an order-of-magnitude improvement in any system's performance, the second-order machine has to be recognized and dismantled.

Although this may appear to the developing management consultant as an unnecessary sidetrack -- to dismantle the second-order machine – success depends on the ability to separate those core assumptions essential for our existence from the ones that are obstructive and dysfunctional. Recall that "success is the devil called by another name. What used to work in the past comes back to haunt us. It is said the most stubborn habits that resist change with the greatest tenacity are those that have worked well for a space of time and have led to the practitioner being rewarded for those behaviors (p.49)".

Success in dismantling the second-order machine "depends on the ability to separate those core assumptions essential for our existence from the ones that are obstructive and dysfunctional. Even then, the pursuit of a successful strategy for change cannot be externally imposed. The only chance of effecting a cultural transformation is when the pick-and-choose process is attempted selectively, iteratively, and participatively. Selectivity, iteratively, and participatively are difficult in practice, but critical to success".

Cultural transformation and the dissolution of the second-order machine consist of two separate yet interrelated processes of self-discovery and self-improvement. Initially, they involve identifying what is relevant and supportive to our shared vision of a desirable future and, subsequently, diagnosing what turns out to be part of the "mess" and therefore obstructive to our renewal and progress. Accordingly, successful cultural transformation will involve 1) making the underlying assumptions about corporate life explicit through public discourse and dialogue, and 2) after critical examination, gaining a shared understanding of what can happen when defaults that are outmoded, misguided, and/or downright fallacious are left unchanged. The process is a high-level social learning and unlearning. Only by the very act of discovering and interpreting our deep-seated assumptions can we see ourselves in a new way. The experience is liberating because it empowers us to reassess the purpose and the course of our lives and, through that, be able to exercise informed choice over our preferred future.

The serious management consultant, who wishes to contribute to cultural transformation and lasting change must take careful note of dismantling the second-order machine. The important aspect is that in this second phase, even before going on to the third part, one must be aware of, and intervene, to dismantle the second-order machine. This is a touch job to bring to light and to assist the client in high-level social learning and unlearning as required here. At minimum the process and the rationale to dismantle the second-order machine must be understood at this time by both the client and the consultant. The implications of not recognizing the second-order machine and of not moving to dismantle it are disastrous, and should be avoided at any costs. The developing management consultant is encouraged to read and reread this section on mapping the mess until they gain a full understanding and desirous of developing the ability in practice of implementing the high level social learning and unlearning to dismantle the second-order machine.

Developing the story of the problem The challenge is to create a shared understanding of the current reality and its undesirable consequences, thus creating a desire for change. The story should consider stake, influence, and interest of the relevant stakeholders. It should not assess blame or make people defensive. The mess should be presented as a consequence of past success, not as a result of failure. Remember, the world is not run by those who are right, it is run by those who can convince others that they are right.

Often members of an organization, more often than not, are aware of the nature of the mess; in most cases they are simply not allowed to talk about it as completely as during the formulation of the mess. What they really don't know is whether management is aware of the mess or not. Usually sharing the mess brings a sigh of relief and a willingness to confront it.

In conclusion, it is very important to jointly search, map, and tell the story. It is not believable if the consultant does it alone, or even if the client does it. To be believable, it must involve all the stakeholders in the search to gain understanding, in the mapping to represent the understanding of the interdependency and the complexity identified in the search, and to learn to articulate the complexity in telling the story.

Critical tasks in PROBLEM DEFINITION

Publicly defining the problem is telling the story. Publicly telling the story is important.   Recall that Gharajedaghi (2006) says defining the problem is not a prediction, it is an early warning system. According to Ackoff, "The future is not contained in the past, most of it is yet to be written."   Gharajedaghi (2006) points out that proper packaging and communicating of the message is as important as the content of the message itself.   Formulating and disseminating the problem is as significant a step as solving it. More often than not, knowledge of the problem shared helps dissolve it. A believable and compelling story that reveals the undesirable future implicit in the current state has to be developed. Assume that things will go wrong, if they can, all at the same time. It is important to try to produce a resonance and show how a system breakdown can occur, and already has in many cases.

Although the critical tasks in Problem Definition revolve around preparing to tell the story in the organization, the two other critical tasks of this component are equally important.   Preparing the individual sessions to reach the whole organization is very important.   These sessions to communicate or tell the story of the problem confront the "quick fix" mentality and help all employees at every level understand the complexity involved in the problem. These sessions must not only define the problem, but include dismantling of the second order machine identified. People must understand how important it is to remove these attitudes and behaviors in order to change.   Lastly, the actual communication and understanding organization-wide of the problem now fully defined is the third critical task to be undertaken. This sharing of the defined problem must, at the same time, communicate a readiness to move into problem solution and to create a generative spirit fostering new energy to move forward.   This is a necessary step because the conversations, dialogue, and presentations are new to many.   These presentations represent a digression from the past. Employees must be encouraged to participate, become involved, and contribute, through dialogue, their support of the problem definition. It is necessary to create an excitement about reaching this point and at the same time create a readiness to go on to problem solution.   The developing management consultant may generate excitement by focusing on Learning to BE in a new environment. Creating desire to solve the complex problem now identified.   Genuine excitement about the current involvement of the stakeholders in defining the problem provides new energy to go forward.

A new energy is required to form the problem solving teams to action plan.   Often the stakeholder teams generating the problem definition have run out of energy and must be replaced by new problem solving teams.   The problem solving team must be sufficiently energized to complete the tough task of solution planning.

A new perspective on DATA COLLECTION & PROBLEM DEFINITION

Gaining a new perspective on data collection is not easy, for the sophistication of the electronic era masks the complexity and chaos in the reality of the context.   It is no longer fair game to purposely decontextualize problems in order to analyze them.   Decontextualizing places the problematic situation in a sterile laboratory situation, devoid of reality.   Gummesson (2000) says that the management consultant's number one challenge is in his/her access to reality.   A consultant's ability to carry out work on a project is intimately tied up with the availability of data and information that can provide a basis for analysis and synthesis to reach conclusions.   The use of technically advanced and computerized quantitative techniques to process data will be in vain if the real-world input is flawed.   Even if the methods of collecting and processing data are sophisticated, the well-known adage "garbage in, garbage out" cannot be discounted.

Thus, data collected in the context by the stakeholders is a necessity. When the management consultant examines the realities of the context there are many factors that confront understanding.   Understanding the context and communicating about it in a summary fashion provides a still greater problem -- where to begin, what language to use to communicate – what constitutes data, what frameworks apply to knowledge, or learning in the context.   The most important aspect for the management consultant is to decide on a methodology that will involve all of the stakeholders and address the whole.   For the management consultant to carry out this key task requires considerable skill in communicating, coordinating, and cooperating with many different segments of the relevant stakeholders.   Often, to keep the stakeholders in communication until some learning has occurred is an all consuming task.   The wise management consultant addresses the triple challenge of communication, coordination, and cooperation in a timely way -- but much in advance of the operationalization of phase 2.

In terms of the methodology selected, the management consultant is encouraged to use an interactive methodology that includes all of the relevant stakeholders in the whole system. The data collected must be managed to address problem definition rather than problem solution. The management consultant is cautioned to separate problem definition from problem solution while avoiding client time pressures which compresses problem definition into problem solution one – for the consultant is then in a position of a "quick fix" unable to advise the client on the interdependencies to be addressed in transformative change. Instead of seeing the second phase in the traditional two component view, the new perspective tightly fits data collection and problem identification into a single smooth operation energized by the learning of the stakeholders who are involved.   The new perspective uses a methodology that "formulates" the mess, addresses problem definition positively, and identifies key themes that are relevant to be addressed and understood.

In considering the time required to identify the system of problems in an interactive methodology one may say that the amount of time is too much for most systems to be able to allocate to problem identification. However, when one consults the designed time required as shown in Figures 27 (in Chapter 10) one sees that for example that 20 days are required for one iteration to get the problem identified *and* a solution designed – with two different stakeholder teams operating -- one on problem identification, and the other on problem designed solution. The twenty days includes eight days of training.   Twenty days may be considered as one month's effort when compressed. One to three months is not considered abnormal or a large amount of time for data collection and problem definition, particularly when one is dealing with the culture change required in transformative efforts. It is important to note that the amount of time used in phase 2 needs to be considered as well as how one will address the time used. Essentially the time is used in gaining understanding of how to successfully operate now that the game has changed.

Recall in the discussion of how the game is changing, that Gharajedaghi says that "the dominant language of our time produces only a partial understanding of our reality and relates only to parts of our being, not the whole of it. We need a holistic language, a language of systems that will allow us to see through chaos and understand complexity. A language of interaction and design will help us learn a new mode of living by considering various ways of seeing, doing, and being in the world. We can then design new methods of inquiry, new modes of organization, and a way of life that will allow the rational, emotional, and ethical choices for inter-dependent, yet autonomous social beings." Successfully reaching the goal in the engagement is heavily dependent on the management consultant's capability to assist the client in developing a new language that will be symbolic and useful in gaining understanding of the change required to successfully improve. It is equally important to assist the client in understanding interdependency and in recognizing its critical value in the success of the engagement and the overall transformation process.

In summary, implementing the new perspective in DATA COLLECTION & PROBLEM DEFINITION is first developing a crucial holistic language that communicates, and provides for coordination and cooperation in the whole system. Once, the need for development of this new language is understood, the relevant concepts and practice may be learned. The management consultant must be courageous in learning, and unselfish assisting others in learning to change and in actively accomplishing change. Finally, developing a new language takes precedence over all in the management consultant's Learning to DO. This new language development takes the developing management consultant back to Learning to BE and Learning to LEARN in a new world, now existent. The central issue may be developing courage to learn, and to share the need to learn and do things differently in the present and in the future.

Second Phase Process Summary Chart

The key tasks identified in the process summary for the second phase in Figure 29. The Management Consulting Process – Phase 2: Data Collection and Problem Definition are comprehensive, iterative, and overlapping due to the complexity of defining the problem in the situation. As pointed out in the first phase summary, the key tasks are interdependent and will not produce success when performed in a singular fashion. Likewise the phases are interdependent and the second phase is interdependently involved with the other three, which further complicates the interactive process. In mastering the process of intervention in Learning to DO it is important to not only fully understand "interdependence" – but to actively recognize interdependence in practice with the client, recognizing the requirements and its value at the time.

The second phase process summary chart is graphically displayed in Figure 33. The second phase process summary chart may be used much as in the first phase, in a fashion both before and after. The management consultant is encouraged to reflect on the findings from the evaluation in the use of the Second Phase Process Summary Chart. They are encouraged to identify the exact positions and means to take advantage of emerging opportunities in the second phase and in the total four phased intervention in the transformative change process.

The Consulting Systems **WORLDVIEW**
Keys to Master a **FOUR** phased Intervention Approach

Phase 2 DATA COLLECTION and PROBLEM DEFINITION

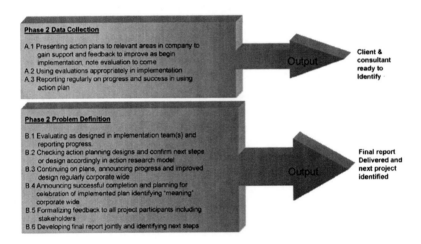

Figure 33: The Management Consulting Process – Phase 2:DATA COLLECTION & PROBLEM DEFINITION
© Marilyn Harris 1996

Gaining Perspective from Applications

To gain a more robust perspective on application in this chapter, the two cases in the appendix must be reviewed first. If the developing management consultant has not taken advantage of this opportunity, the application experience in this chapter and subsequent chapters will be found lacking.

Application in The Long Island Company (LIC)   In the LIC case, the data collection and problem definition was performed by one individual through a series of three interviews with selected stakeholders. The focus of the interviews was to examine the alignment between three defined interview constructs 1) leadership, 2) organizational culture, and 3) functional maturity. Written documents were also collected and analyzed to triangulate with the verbal perspective.

LIC began as a sheet metal manufacturer and survived in a shrinking environment.   After an organizational transition; father to sons, a product line of metal cabinets for information technology equipment was introduced. This transformation from a sheet metal fabricator resulted in exponential revenue and profit growth. The exponential growth required additional manufacturing capabilities, as well as an extended employee base. LIC began to experience layers of complexity in managing the growing volume of employees, servicing an expanded and diverse customer base, and controlling the organization on the whole.

In the last few years, the vision became distorted; certain roles within the organization were not clearly defined; and, an emerging need for more sophisticated business processes became evident. LIC's growth stagnated and the owners decided that new leadership was required. In early 2008, the owners engaged a new President to reinvigorate the vision, instill appropriate processes to support the organization and re-energize LIC development.

Simply affirmed, the problems that exist at LIC include re-establishing a clearly articulated vision for its next business cycle. The owners of LIC will need to identify and inspire processes that can support new development.

In this case, the data collection was brief and clear in the brief consulting engagement barely covering two phases in the Consulting Systems worldview phased intervention approach. LIC acknowledged that the need is to go beyond the discovery and problem definition, choosing to perform other aspects of the transformation through the new President/COO identified from outside the organization.

Another Case In contrast, the Columbus Medical Association case involved the examination of a not-for-profit service organization. The data collection interviews elicited open ended responses to reveal information and perspectives that would not surface in a quantitative approach. The interviews solicited the opinions of a variety of employees and board members. The content provided a view into the company history, values, traditions, and the most significant changes and norms apparent now.

The data provide background information about the Columbus Medical Association (CMA) which began in 1869 as a professional association for physicians in Franklin County, Ohio. In the period 1869-1958 the organization had a singular focus—professional support and advocacy for local physicians. In 1958 the Columbus Medical Association Foundation (CMAF) was created to provide medical education. In the 1990s the Central Ohio Trauma System and the Physicians Free Clinic were added, expanding the service offering to state and local stakeholders outside the medical community. Today these four affiliates operate as separate entities with unique missions and separate governing boards, but share a common chief executive officer and office space. Between 1869 and 1999 the organization was led by a series of executive directors with traditional hierarchical management skills. This hierarchal structure changed in 1999 when it became apparent that to sustain it would be better served to have a CEO lead all four affiliates.

CMA and its affiliate organizations have made tremendous strides in how they interact with each other, and in how they cooperate with stakeholders in the community. CMA's positive change is evidenced by a highly creative staff, hiring practices that foster a learning culture, leaderful behavior by all staff members, and a cooperative partnership with local citizens for improved health care; increased interaction with the community; and, foster improved focus on individual leadership among the staff. With the new vision the collective organizations began to evolve

The consultant is charged with creating a roadmap of sustainability. CMA understands that it will need to retain the thriving learning culture while achieving a rapid level of change in business processes and stakeholder needs in the next phase of work.

Emerging Opportunities

As in the first phase, seeing the emerging opportunities is important. For example, in data collection, not only the technique but the methodology has changed drastically in the last decade. It used to be that literally tons of data were necessary to convince management of needed change. Now "transformation" is on the lips of every employee and employer, and collecting the data and defining the problem progresses with the stakeholders through increased participation in a systemic approach.

However, consultants are still concerned about how much data to collect in any given situation. For example, many questioned if the LIC consultant's few interviews with key people were enough in the data collection situation. The answer clearly depends on how representative the sample is and how well the interviews collect the necessary data. When going through formulating the problematic mess – in searching, mapping and telling the story one should proceed in data collecting toward the formulation until one is able to "tell the story," and to recognize the second order machine that is blocking action. Sometimes, it is necessary to go back and do more data collecting to meet the need identified.

Participation is very important in data collection and problem definition. Developing the skill to open up communication in the stakeholders to gain the desired data and to be able to map and tell the story is part of the art in getting fuller participation. Developing skill in co-consulting, that is -- getting the participants to consult with others on their contributions and thinking on the issue is another strong factor. Finally, the skill in co-determining the outcome or decision is important. All three represent areas of emerging opportunities to raise client participation in each engagement.

Undoubtedly the biggest area to seek emerging opportunities is in recognizing the second order machine. There are problems in discovering and in communicating the misconceptions about reality. It is working through the obstructions and becoming more able to face the current reality.

This is a task for the consultant as well as the client in each consultation: Identifying the right problem to define continues to be a challenge as complexity and chaos are on the increase.

Seeing the emerging opportunities in the second phase depends heavily on the consultant leveraging his leadership in a way to avoid creating dependency in the client, but in contrast developing cooperation and leadership skills in the client population. It is important that participants begin to value their contributions and see that they have much to offer in searching, mapping and telling the story.

It is critical that participants and stakeholders "own" the story that defines the problem. It takes innovative capability for the developing consultant to assist the client in such a way as to develop these capabilities, so as they may reside in the client system after the intervention.

Chapter 12
Effective Intervention in PROBLEM SOLUTION & ACTION
PLANNING

Why is ACTION PLANNING so important in
PROBLEM SOLUTION

Problem solution and action planning, the two
components of phase 3, require the use of new
knowledge, new skill sets, and abilities to be
successful. In phase 3 the focus is redesigning the
organization's structures, processes, and
functional outputs so the organization can actually solve the problem.
What's important to realize is that the old structure, function, and
processes of the organization will only reproduce the same problem.
People cannot change unless the system that supports them changes. In
addition to designing the system change, the actors must design the
action plan for the organization – a step by step plan to solve the
problem.   An action plan is the road map to the destination of the
solution. Action planning is most important, for without a road map one
might never reach the problem solution in a complex world.

Phase 3, designing the solution, identifies the key elements to be
changed in the structure, the processes, and the functional output to
move toward successful solution in the system as a whole before
anything else. Second, in the action planning component sequencing the
implementation activities appropriately in a formalized plan enables
definition of action steps and evaluation of the plan in the context.
Figure 34 Phase 3: Problem Solution & Action Planning in the
Transformation Process frames the solution process and identifies
evaluated action steps to be taken during implementation.   For
implementation to be successful, evaluation of performance must be
designed during the action planning phase. Periodic evaluation promotes
staying on course to successful implementation of the problem solution.
Errors or omissions can be recognized at the time of evaluation. The
purpose of this phase is to outline an iterative design process producing
problem solution, and then to sequentially plan participatively for the
implementation of the design. This is a tall order!

Transformation Process

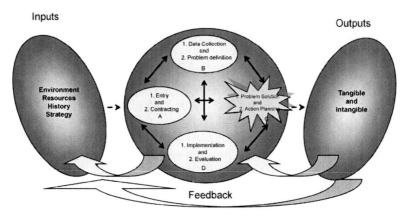

The Consulting Systems Worldview
© Marilyn E Harris, 1996

**Figure 34: Phase 3 Problem Solution & Action Planning in the
Transformation Process
© Marilyn E Harris, 1996**

Critical tasks in PROBLEM SOLUTION

In terms of business understanding, the management consultant must be able to define and understand the idealized design process sufficiently to lead the stakeholders in the process of developing an idealized design to graphically define the business architecture of the new system. For example, one must be skilled in defining the business purpose, defining the client's business, and helping define the strategic intent, the measures of success, and the core values. The understanding must be at a level where the alternatives in practice are easily available for the consultant, thereby being free to "inspire" and "excite" the stakeholders to define a vision of the future.

Lastly, in presenting the idealized design solution to others, one must be able to articulate -- using the terms and make meaning for others who are involved, outside of the developmental process. Developing and selling an idealized design is inspiring others to fully undertake "buy-in" to action planning.   This is a complex challenge for the developing management consultant.

Defining business purpose, strategic intent, and core values Before beginning to design a solution the stakeholders start with the concept of a "clean slate." That is, the stakeholders designing the organization assume that the system to be redesigned has been destroyed overnight, but that everything else in the environment remains unchanged. The designers begin with the challenge to design the system from scratch. The clean slate assumption is often difficult to operationalize, for as designers we are often still hung up with many of the misconceptions that haven't been brought to light and dealt with in some way. However, literally starting with a blank sheet is necessary to get an idealized design of a purposeful system. Further, an idealized design takes several iterations. The design team is made up of stakeholders who are to redesign the new system from scratch, and are to:

- Produce an order of magnitude improvement in the throughput of the system
- Create a shared understanding among the critical actors
- Generate ownership and commitment because people are more likely to implement an idea when they had a hand in shaping the solution
- Dissolve conflict and create win-win solutions (Management consultants management of a multi-minded system requires the ability to dissolve conflict, to see problems as opportunities and to be able to work through the problem)
- Convert obstructions into opportunities

The idealized design is of the next generation of the system replacing the existing order. It is a design subjected to three constraints: technological feasibility, operational viability, as well as learning and adaptation.

The design process starts with creating an idealized design of the solution. An idealized design is a process of operationalizing the most exciting vision of the future that the designers are capable of producing. "Operationalizing the most exciting vision of the future" is a challenging undertaking for any management consultant – seasoned or developing. To meet this challenge one must first go back to Learning to BE, energizing oneself as momentary leader in the situation – in this case, inspiring others to create an exciting vision that can be operationalized. It is also equally important for the consultant to assist the client stakeholders involved in becoming excited about creating the most exciting vision of the future. Without the energy born of excitement one will at best get only a mediocre vision of the new organization to be designed.

To define the purpose or the mission of a business enterprise is the most important task of designing business architecture. To understand purpose, one needs to deal with four basic concepts: definition of the business, strategic intent, the measure of success, and core values.

Business is usually defined in terms of a know-how or technology, which is transformed into a set of tangible products or services and delivered via a predefined access mechanism to a selected group of customers or markets. The systems architecture defines the nature of relationships between technology, product, and market. It is, therefore, a direct consequence of the way business is defined.

Designing an idealized design It is important to realize that idealizing is not dealing with a far-out future. Idealized design is not forecasting the future or using a crystal ball. The idealized system is designed to be self-sustaining in the current environment. An iteratively developed idealized design will have sufficient sources of variety to learn and adapt to possible emerging environments. Figure 35. Schematic Outline of a Design Process is an overall guide to development of the iterative process, and outlines the process of designing business architecture.

Idealization usually starts with design of the systems architecture. Architecture is a general description of a system. It identifies its vital functions, active elements, and critical processes. It consists of a set of distinct but interrelated platforms. Each platform represents a dimension signifying a unique mode of behavior with a predefined set of performance criteria and measures. Figure 36. Systems Architecture graphically shows the architecture of a health system, as an example. The systems architecture identifies the value chain, the critical dimensions of the health-care system (in this case), and the way it relates users to providers in the health-care system.   In order to create a system architecture that will realize the expectations and desires of the stakeholders, the designers recognized the necessity of employing multidimensional schema.

Such architecture is intended to dissolve the existing problem as well as transcend it by developing a vision of the next generation of a health care system. The architecture represents a platform from which the health care system's distinctive value chain would evolve. The value chain identifies all of the elements of the health care system and their relationships along a market dimension (access and care systems), and output dimension (health delivery modules), and an input dimension (core knowledge and shared services). This multi-dimensional framework not only helps the designers understand and

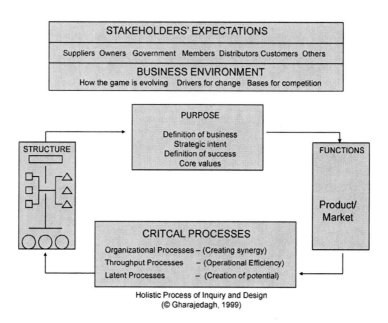

Holistic Process of Inquiry and Design
(© Gharajedagh, 1999)

Figure 35: Schematic Outline of a Design Process
© Gharajedaghi (2006)

differentiate each component of the system, but also establishes the components' relationships in such a way that an integrated and cohesive whole can emerge.

To design a systems architecture, the system's boundaries must be defined and the environment in which it intends to operate must be appreciated. Design is an iterative process. Each iteration addresses the system as an integrated whole. All three aspects of function, structure, and process are considered in each iteration. In successive iterations, more detail and specificity are incorporated into the design. The first iteration concentrates on developing the specification of the system's desired properties. In proceeding, the necessary understanding and definition of interdependencies among desired specifications in terms of complementarity, compatibility and conflict is required.   In order to dissolve differences in conflicting requirements it may be necessary to reconceptualize. In the second iteration, an initial sketch of alternative designs is produced to show how desired properties could be realized. The state of the art is explored and alternative design elements that could produce one or many of the required functions are developed.

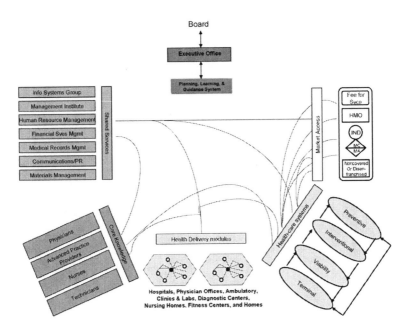

Figure 36. Systems Architecture
© Gharajedaghi (2006)

Presenting the idealized design In the third iteration, different elements of a design are selected and integrated to produce a single design that satisfies all concerns. This provides sufficient elaboration on the initial design to achieve consensus.   After testing for operational viability, necessary details will be developed in subsequent iterations of the design process.

The third iteration serves as an integrator to produce a useable idealized design to share with all the stakeholders and to gain acceptance before going on. Once again, this is an important time for the developing management consultant to *"go slow to go fast."* It is absolutely critical to gain full understanding and agreement to the idealized design. This is a time when excitement for the idealized design must be generated, for a good deal of energy is needed to go into the second component of the phase: – action planning. The action planning phase takes a considerable amount of time to complete and it is tedious in its specificity.

Critical Tasks in Action Planning

Often when a drawing of the business architecture exists, as in Figure 32. stakeholders think the solution is identified – that, the real work is done. Not so! Actually, it is rare that staff or employees can take action to implement the solution based on the business architecture drawing. The ideal situation may be that in the third iteration, if not earlier, some of the key persons who will be involved in the actual implementation may participate to gain understanding and to generate ownership and commitment to the designed changes identified. It is common knowledge that people are more likely to implement an idea when they have had a hand in shaping the idea-solution. Their involvement is also important because they have more hands-on knowledge and experience and more fully understand the boundaries and limitations in the real world. In action planning there are three critical tasks: identifying the macro steps, identifying the micro steps of each macro step, and designing the evaluation in advance before the plan is tested in reality.

The membership of the action planning teams remains the same once they are constituted. Initially, in constituting the teams, some members that were involved in the phase 2 problem-definition process may wish to follow through in phase 3. The continuing members provide continuity and communication capability on the spot about important aspects to be considered in the planning of the implementation of the idealized design. All of the action-planning process, including design of the evaluation component and the reality testing of the plan, are to be completed prior to any implementation. This has value for the overall process in terms of assuring the problem designers (which in many cases may be different than the action planners) that there is practical relevance in their solution design as well as being implementable. Completion of the action plan prior to implementation also prevents a too common reaction seen in: "Ready, Fire, Aim!"

The consultant's skill in leveraging the three critical tasks in the action plan, first macro planning the key aspects of the plan – and then developing micro steps with the action planning teams, and designing evaluation mechanisms to be used in implementation -- is a challenge. When action plans are complete they must be reality tested with potential users and debugged to be of real value.   Because evaluation in implementation is new and untried, the consultant and the potential implementation personnel are encouraged to rehearse the evaluation steps in this component – thus improving the implementation before it begins

Empowering action planners   Empowering, by creating "desire" to action plan is critical.   "Desire" and ability are both important in action planning; but desire is more critical in getting started. The consultant and the client must both go back to Learning to BE and create the desire – specifically the desire to action plan.   The energy and excitement that come out developing or redeveloping that desire is necessary in the action planning phase to confront the tedium and the complexity involved in defining a new future.

The greatest challenge for the management consultant in action planning is mobilizing a team to provide a formalized plan (product). The product must be useable with a wider audience of staff and employees of the organization. To successfully mobilize the team, the management consultant must be able to empower the team members identified, and gain their full participation in evaluative action planning and reality testing the plan before implementation. Recall the earlier discussion on empowerment – the important outcome is duplication of power.   Recall that in the discussions on participation – the communication, co-consultation, and co-determination are necessary for results.   The wise management consultant uses the metacompetencies to empower the action planning process.

Identifying macro planning steps   Action planning begins with a presentation of the solution design made by the people involved in developing it and communicating it to the whole organization. The presentation of the accepted designed solution functions to bring everyone on board with the same graphic picture and description of the solution for the action planning component.   From the presentation of this graphic picture, the action planners fashion outcome goals for their process, and also fashion several sub-goals that will be important to achieve to reach an implemented solution.   These two steps may be accomplished in a meeting of the whole using brainstorm processes to generate beginning statements, then refining them through a reporting out process, based on small group review. For example, in the case of Butterworth Health Systems the systems architecture as shown in Figure 33 is the graphic display that macro planners need to understand. The architecture represents a platform from which the distinctive value chain would evolve. The value chain identifies all of the elements of the health-care system and their relationships along a market dimension, output dimension, and input dimension. The macro plan is a multidimensional framework that not only the planners understand and use to differentiate each component of the system, but also establishes the components' relationships in such a way that an integrated and cohesive whole can emerge in a value-adding system.

Ordinarily, the management consultant manages this macro planning process in a single meeting in a large room that can house 30-40 participants. The number of goals that come out of the meeting define the number of micro planning teams that may initially be required. However, some goals may require several separate but interrelated micro plans to accomplish the desired outcomes.   For example in the Butterworth Health Systems macro goals, there may be one in defining the market access which would require at least six separate, but related micro plans including fee for service, HMOs, Independents, Medicare, Medicaid, and Non-covered customers.

Identifying micro planning steps The micro planning begins with teams using one of the identified macro goals to define the sequential steps required in implementation. Usually, there are more goals than teams, thus teams may take nested or like goals to plan. For example, one team may want to take all six of the separate goals around market access noted earlier – possibly doing several micro plans for each one dependent on the requirements to meet the goal. One can see very quickly that this micro planning can become a very complex task in itself. In most cases it takes some understanding to be clear what exists and what may need to be developed or created and how to work these different aspects together. Once some of these basic decisions are made, the team can begin to fill in the micro planning format as shown in Figure 37. Micro Planning Format for Implementation. The planning team members are cautioned early in their work that often the implementers fail because too little is planned or considered important to plan for a successful implementation.   This is where knowledge of the industry and the specific business is important. Planners are encouraged to initially brainstorm, then sort, winnow down and sequence by date to implement.

A helpful rule of thumb that is that each micro planning format should include at least ten different events to accomplish the specific goal, spread out over a reasonable time. One of these events should be evaluation of progress on the goal.

for MACRO STEP # State goal to be accomplished by date:				
Date Step completed Amt. of time req.	Define micro step and Identify sub-steps	Responsible person	Materials required	Location
	1.			
	2.			
	3.			
	4.			
	5.			
	6.			
	7.			
	8.			
	9.			
	10.			

Action Plan

Figure 37: Micro Planning Format for Implementation

In using the format, one begins by identifying the events to take place in the Events column. One is cautioned to have only *one* "person responsible" to carry out the event. Many may be involved in working on the event, but only one person is responsible. Next, the order of the events should be noted by putting date and time in the first column (the format may be redone in order of occurrence). The details of location, materials required, and assessment may be filled in at a later time.

Often, event planning of micro goals may be done in skeleton form until all of the relevant plans are integrated in a master time line for that goal. One then sees that corrections need to be made to avoid having the same person responsible for two different events which may occur at the same time. This is an iterative process, moving back and forth coordinating and considering options. Once the major decisions are made in the planning sessions, the whole plan may be computerized which aids follow-through.

Designing evaluation in micro planning

Overall, there is no question that evaluation adds value for the consultant as well as the client. For consultant and client, evaluation may appear to be one more step that makes the whole process cumbersome. This may be true in their reality, certainly at first – but evaluation becomes more and more integral to success, and therefore becomes more important to both the client and consultant. However, one should become clear that evaluation is a necessity in implementation. Evaluation is part of the action research cycle. Evaluation may be either qualitative, quantitative or both in type and design. There are many times that a qualitative approach may be effective in implementation.

The management consultant is encouraged to understand the importance of evaluation for himself and for the client -- and to realize that evaluation requires an effective measurement system. An effective measurement requires dealing iteratively with two elements: performance criteria and performance measures. Both of these require knowledge and specificity about the new dynamics of the situation. Much of the knowledge required is gained through redesign during the third phase.

Performance criteria are the expression of what is to be measured and why – for example, how success is defined. The selection process involves identifying dimensions and/or variable(s) relevant to an organization's successful operation. Relevancy is the most important concern in selecting performance variables. Traditionally, the overriding concern had been accuracy of measures. Unfortunately, it is said that the more accurate the measure of the wrong criteria, the faster the road to disaster.

It is much better to have an approximation of relevant variables than to have precise measurement of the wrong ones. Thus approximation is an important means to develop a means to reach the end. Accuracy of measures in evaluation was a 20th century concern, while healthy approximation in evaluation is a 21st century concern.

Performance measures are the operational definition of each variable, that is, how each variable is to be measured specifically. For example, if identifying "capacity utilization" as a performance criterion, then turnover ratio might be designated as its measure.   A procedure for calculating turnover ratio is needed. An important consideration in selecting any measure is its simplicity.   The cost of producing a measurement should not exceed the value of the information it generates.

Initially, the definition of evaluation and its measurement elements in management consulting contracts does not appear to be inhibiting or blocking use. At most the management consultant must spend some high quality input in defining measurement in the specific situation early in the development process. Operationally defining each variable may take some time, but it can be done rather easily when addressed in familiar settings.

The problem that appears for many consultants is that in many cases one is measuring an emergent property. Recall some of the earlier discussion on emergent properties being the spontaneous outcome of ongoing processes. Life, love, happiness, and success are not one-time propositions; they have to be reproduced continuously. If the processes that generate them end, the phenomena will also cease to exist. One of the challenges for the management consultant is being able to understand a property in terms of process of becoming in contrast to describing only in terms of being.

A common example that demonstrates effective measurement factors is in the understanding that an all star team is not necessarily the best team in the league, and it might even lose to an average team in the same league. What characterizes a winning team is not only the quality of the players but the quality of the interactions among them – the latter is evident in the process of becoming. Emergent properties cannot be measured directly, but can be measured only through manifestation. Unfortunately, using a single manifestation can prove misleading, and very costly. Measuring an emergent property by its manifestation must be done along several dimensions.

Stated in everyday language, the measurement challenge is twofold – first, in identifying the right processes of becoming (such as life, success, learning, failure, and others), and second, considering the variable as acted out (manifest) along several dimensions. Measurement for the contemporary consultant is a challenge. The first challenge is in identifying the right "processes of becoming" for the client to measure. The second challenge is being able to describe the relationship of the several dimensions to each other and to the outcome in meaningful terms. In the end, the management consultant together with the client may be clear about what factors must be improved, redirected, halted, or changed to be successful. What may be even more important is the generative evaluation that might be designed through a cooperative client and consultant relationship – for as one may recall generative evaluation has much more payoff to the system in the ethical results achieved at the same time.

Designing Evaluation of an Intervention Kreutzer and Wiley (1996) offer a means of evaluating a planned intervention prior to implementation to improve on design before application. First, the designer must know the purpose of the designed intervention. Second, using a three axes framework as shown in Figure 38. Design and Evaluation Framework, the designer of the intervention may evaluate up front 1) conceptual integrity, 2) process effectiveness and 3) Meaning/Rapport. The Design and Evaluation Framework should be used In the planning stages to evaluate the design of the intervention against the purpose of the intervention. When used in this way, it can help structure the process and indicate where resources should be placed for maximum effectiveness. For example, if the purpose is to build an expert model, the need for user buy-in would not be as necessary (low Meaning/Rapport), and the need to understand the model-building process would not be important (very low process effectiveness). However, Conceptual Integrity would have to be at the highest level, meaning that axis would need to be rated very high.

All the interventions designed need not address all three axes equally. In fact, there may be some natural conflicts between the framework axes. For example, if the project involves designing a model high on Conceptual Integrity, such as a complex mathematical model, it may not be possible to make the model building process visible (Process Effectiveness). Overall, the designed interventions should maximize effectiveness. Combining the effectiveness on the different axes for the strongest benefit will create a more meaningful macro intervention.

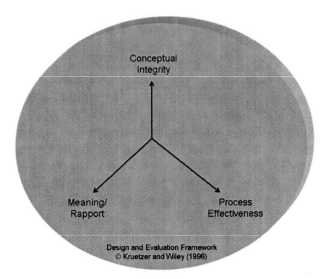

Figure 38: Design and Evaluation Framework
Adapted from © Kreutzer and Wiley (1996)

These definitions may help to clarify each axis: Conceptual Integrity captures what is happening in reality, is self consistent, may be validated and calibrated, as well as supports double-loop learning. Meanwhile, Meaning/Rapport   engages group enthusiasm, improves group understanding, creates results ownership, implementation buy-in, as well as supports a change in the mental models of the group.   Process Effectiveness makes the process explicit and visible, creates shared team meaning, uses industry specific vocabulary, and defines parameters based on available resources such as time, money, space, etc.

The beauty of using the design and evaluation framework in assessing the design of an evaluation is that the same framework developed in the planning stage may be used after implementation, testing the actual use of the design in practice.   The Design and Evaluation Framework as shown in Figure 38. can be used to measure the impact and effectiveness of the intervention by comparing the design intent to the actual results as shown in Figure 39. Design Intent versus Actual Results. This not only aids design but leverages learning in the implementation, first testing whether the intervener accomplished the intent, and providing direction for next steps.

In perspective, it becomes quite clear that evaluation design – identification of what is to be measured (success, failure, viability, life, etc.) and the operational definition of the variables manifested in different dimensions is not only quite important, but critical in Learning to DO in the action planning component. It is critical to insure that the appropriate activities are planned that produce the basis for the measurement required in the situation. The evaluation design and the measurement function are not a simple procedure to design and integrate into the action planning process.

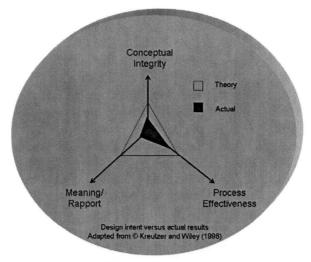

Figure 39: Design Intent versus Actual Results.
Adapted from Kreutzer and Wiley (1996)

It is critical to insure for the learning of the consultant as well as the client. Management consultants and clients who have cooperatively mastered the evaluative design in action planning and use of the evaluation, report overall success and realize success more often. Clients are happier, for often they can tally outcomes in dollars saved, or productivity gained from the change(s).

Reality Testing in Action Planning Once completed, the plan must be reality tested with at least one other user group for debugging – identifying things that might go wrong or would not possibly be able to be carried out given the knowledge available in the situation.   For example: when the action plan being reality tested reveals that the date of a large kick-off of a new program that is planned coincides with absence of the manager leading the change due to a planned holiday, the overlapping of these two events must be resolved.   This type of consideration and change is called "debugging" a plan.

Reality testing happens at least twice in the early life of the action plan – in the initial presentation as noted above; and most likely one other time when individual micro plans of macro events are fit together across the whole organization. There may be overlapping dates, location usage problems, and the like – which must be checked out and resolved to the best advantage of all involved. Each action plan should contain several points for progress assessment throughout the change effort. In reality testing, each action plan may be tested against Kotter's Eight Steps to Transforming Your Organization, which is detailed in Chapter 5.

Finally, the merging of all of the planned micro steps in a master action plan is posted for study, with consistent review and progress updates, while changes are registered in the macro intervention in the system. Each time a micro event is executed, the responsible person for that event along with the management consultant should review the success of that intervention in light of the evaluation. This assessment should be noted on the displayed action plan.

It is interesting to note that many times micro action plans are successfully completed in less time than actually forecast. Many organizations have computerized the project planning and display once it is first worked out – and can easily show progress and success visually. The management consultant is cautioned not to use a project planning program to do the initial planning, for the very human contribution may be diluted due to the focus on technology.

In conclusion, action planning is seen as an exhilarating time because it is so close to implementation.   However, to be keenly remembered and acted upon it is the consultant's responsibility to keep the exhilaration high, for the task is tedious. Most clients have been anticipating implementation of solutions from the very beginning. The anticipation tends to heighten emotions during this time and raise anxiety for the impending closure to problem solving that is experienced in implementation.

A New Perspective on PROBLEM SOLUTION & ACTION PLANNING

The challenge of phase 3 is dramatic. The management consultant and the client must work cooperatively to manage the chaotic situation, and to clarify the complexity of the solution design.   This must be accomplished in a way that relevant action in implementation may be planned for in the current phase, and successful action may be taken in the final phase of implementation and evaluation.

Cooperation is key in addressing the dramatic challenge of phase 3. A cooperation that is based on mature interaction is gained in the first two phases. Both the developing consultant and the client must keep their eye on the solution design, remaining focused on constantly maintaining compatibility between the means and ends to successfully cooperate to complete the problem solution and the action planning.

Third Phase Process Summary Chart

The key tasks identified in the process summary for the third phase in Figure 40. The Management Consulting Process -- Phase 3: PROBLEM SOLUTION & ACTION PLANNING are comprehensive, iterative, and overlapping due to the complexity involved

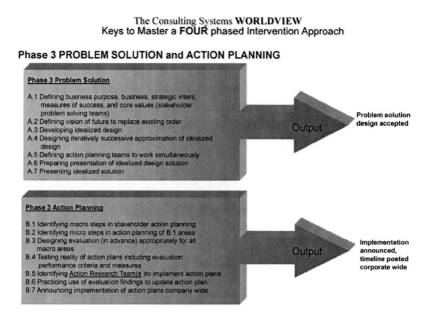

Figure 40: The Management Consulting Process - Phase 3: PROBLEM
SOLUTION & ACTION PLANNING
© Marilyn Harris, 1994

in designing the solution and planning for action in the implementation. It is important to note that the key tasks are interdependent and will not produce success alone. Likewise, the phases are interdependent. The third phase is interdependently involved with the first two, further complicating the interactive process. In mastering the design process in action planning it is not enough to understand "interdependence," but to actively practice it with the client, publicly recognizing the value and the requirements at the time.

The third phase process summary chart may be used both before and after the phase, reinforcing learning in the phase. The management consultant is encouraged to reflect on the findings from evaluating the Third Phase Process Summary Chart – identifying the exact positions and means to create emerging opportunities in the third phase and in the overall four phased intervention in the transformative change process.

Gaining Perspective from Applications

Application in The Long Island Company (LIC)   In the LIC case, problem solution and the development of an action plan was created after understanding the problem in leadership, organizational culture, and functional process perspective. Consistent with the CSW framework, next steps in micro planning included major functional business processes, the organizational functional unit intent, and the core values.

The management consultant realized it was critical that new thinking be involved in the design and development of an idealized design. The idealized design at LIC was necessary to not only sustain some its past revenue and profit growth, but more importantly focus on LIC's ability to readily adapt to a changing competitive landscape. The changing competitive landscape for LIC included global competition, as well as the shrinking manufacturing environment in the US. An iterative systemic and holistic approach was required to properly frame the competitive environment. Once defined, it was necessary to simplify the design for LIC so it was easily understood and achievable at all levels.

It became apparent to the owners at LIC that appropriate action planning for the idealized design was a formidable challenge. The management consultant drove the establishment of a macro plan to achieve the desired state that was identified. The initial defined plan did not include the micro planning steps, nor was there the recognition of the value of the action planning in advance. At this point it became the task of the new leader to action plan and to plan for evaluation of the action plan at appropriate times; first teaching others the fine points of action planning, and then to commence in the fourth phase: implementation and evaluation.

Application in The Columbus Medical Association   Following a comprehensive analysis of the interview data from CMA and its affiliates, the consultant organized her observations into categories of structure, culture, change, and leadership influence. CMA had already identified problems and organizational goals when the boards of directors hired a CEO to oversee the four affiliates. To make recommendations for continued development and evolution the consultant first documented progress to date relative to the goals established in 1999. Through interview data and increased cooperation with the external environment it was obvious that increased Systems Thinking, concurrent leadership throughout employee ranks, a focus on generative learning, and engaged executive leadership were strong influences in transformative change. The first portion of the analysis chronicled the changes from initial problem resolution to the new current state. CMA had implemented numerous changes including improved communication with new dialogue techniques, voluntary learning sessions in the form of a book club and visits from authors to discuss change, Systems Thinking, and co-created value, annual strategy retreats, work objectives for leaderful behavior, and ongoing, interactive discussions with the community about affordable and sustainable healthcare. The consultant noted that the progress to date could be strengthened if organizational members and stakeholders could visualize the changes on a continuum of development and transformation; the progress was plotted on the U Curve (Scharmer, 2007) and discussed with the organization.

From the current state perspective, the consultant worked with the CEO to make some recommendations to positively impact continued development and sustainable cycles of transformation. Several existing strengths were observed that established a strong foundation for perpetual cycles of positive transformation: 1) new values and norms in the organization that favor a systems perspective and a desire for learning, 2) a comfort level with a healthy balance of stability and continual change, 3) genuine interest in cooperation that will serve the community.

With a solid transformation in place, the organization was well poised to generate successive levels of positive change. The collective affiliates now recognize that their efforts at learning, communicating, cooperating, and strengthening leaderful behavior at all levels have allowed them to achieve greater success at an organizational and community level. Acknowledgment for their accomplishments increased their self-confidence and inspired their resolve to continue learning and development. Going through this experience strengthened the resolve to action plan and to plan evaluation of success in advance. These are the current tasks taken on by CMA leaderful employees. The next challenge which becomes the new "problem" is sustainability – successive cycles of transformation that presence new opportunities and collective solutions to drive the organization forward in the future.

Emerging Opportunities

In summary, the value of action planning may be that a planned implementation is much more likely to be successful and accomplished in a shorter time, with fewer bugs. This does not mean that there will not be "bugs" in the implementation, or that there will not be changes made at the time on site. Neither can all of the bugs be planned away, nor can all of the needed changes be sufficiently identified prior to implementation. However, the time and organization provided in the action plan undoubtedly saves significant time and definitely results in a higher grade implementation.

The challenge for the management consultant in designing a solution and in action planning in the third phase, is to maintain the perspective of the whole. Seeking emerging opportunities to develop skill that directs the client to cooperatively work in teams to identify the solution *and* to organize the many steps in action planning and evaluation to be ready for Implementation in the next phase is a huge challenge. Maintaining the perspective and interventions appropriately to keep all involved energized and on track is a tall order, which must be consistently reviewed and continued in the midst of what appears to be a mess. This is often referred to as 'maintaining your cool, while providing clarification and direction' for others. For the consultant this takes a constant self-reminding approach, so as to maintain their own clarity in the situation. This clarity then frees the consultant to provide clarification and direction to others. As time goes on, the skill is modeled for the client to use, and it may be applied by the client – then assisting the consultant in the situation.

Seeking emerging opportunities in the third phase, builds on the skill development of the second phase – where the consultant is leveraging his leadership in a way to free the client to move into a leadership role during implementation. This means that the consultant, in phase 3, must turn over to the client full ownership of the solution design and the action plan including the evaluation aspect. It is important to capitalize on the opportunity afforded in reality testing, and later in rehearsing evaluation means for the client to gain confidence in their applications of their learning in preparation for implementation. It takes full advantage of emerging opportunities for the developing consultant to assist the client to develop these capabilities in phase 3

Chapter 13 Effective Intervention in IMPLEMENTATION & EVALUATION

Several years ago, a Fortune 100 corporation began a three-year, $2 million organization experiment. The goal was to gain a sustainable competitive advantage by learning faster and learning to change faster than its competitors.

The company planned to accomplish this using a "secret weapon" -- Systems Thinking – that would enable management teams throughout the organization to achieve measurable improvement in organizational performance. It seemed plausible to the core project team that the organization could measure its learning in return on capital employed.

But when they assessed the results of the effort several years later, they had to admit that, although there were many successes at the project level, the change program did not achieve the organization-wide impact they originally intended. The problems seem to be centered around implementation.

While much effort had been put into selecting issues that were critical to the organization, and to designing robust models around those issues, scant attention had been placed on transferring the learning to a larger context. As a result, the insights had little impact beyond the original project teams.

How is the ultimate challenge in implementation met

"Making it happen" is the implementation challenge. Undoubtedly the greatest challenge of the whole consultation is bound up in the success of phase 4: IMPLEMENTATION & EVALUATION. Phase 4 is where the major change designed or called for is implemented and tested in the organization in real time. However, as the case of the Fortune 100 corporation experiment so aptly points out – the implementation phase is definitely rooted in earlier phases.   There is a critical and strong interdependent connection to the earlier phases

To be successful, implementation cannot begin after the project design is completed. It must start before the initiation of the project – as the management consultant and client first discuss expectations, anticipated outcomes, and measures for success in Phase 1: Entry and Contracting – and implementation must be considered and integrated into every step of the process in Phase 2 and Phase 3.   Designing for success need not be an academic exercise, but rather accomplished through an on-the-spot evaluation of each of the processes as designed at the time.   As noted in designing the intervention in Chapter 12, the conceptual integrity, the meaning/rapport, and the process effectiveness can be assessed as each process intervention is considered at any phase of the transformative experience.   On-the-spot evaluation must become a user friendly mode for every consultant and client alike to be able to count on success in the implementation.

Evaluation is first focused in Chapter 12, however, in reality evaluation is a tool that must be consistently and constantly used in all consulting interactions.   Phase 4 tests the success of the change in the key elements in the structure, processes, and functional output of the organization as a whole.   Figure 41. The Consulting Systems Worldview: Implementation & Evaluation together frame the success level in the results of implementing and evaluating the action plan interventions. The purpose of this phase is to reinforce the value to the consultant and to the client of evaluative design, mainly recognizing the importance of Phase 4 in "refreezing" and stabilizing the change in the organization. The refrozen change in the organization then becomes the basis of recycling through the phases of the consulting systems worldview on a new problem to refocus the current problem when it has been unsuccessfully addressed.

Transformation Process

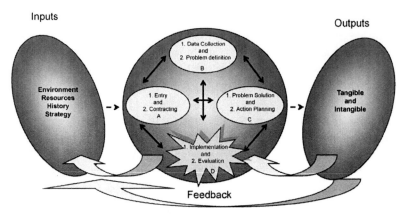

The Consulting Systems Worldview
© Marilyn E Harris, 1996

**Figure 41: The Consulting Systems Worldview – Focusing Phase 4:
Implementation and Evaluation © Marilyn E Harris 1996**

Implementation is DOING The heart of Learning to DO is in "doing" the implementation and evaluation phase, for this is where the "proof of the pudding" is evident.   Learning to DO is learning to manage the interactions in application.   It is learning to manage complexity in the application of knowledge and skills in implementation and evaluation.

In many cases, this may mean managing new learning or relearning for application -- or it may be helping the client unlearn what is not working. This often means identifying the behaviors that fit the learning and provide an opportunity to practice it, actually linking to experience. Remember that adults learn best through experience, which often means creating a practice field for them to try out the new learning, relearning, or unlearning.   Often, when starting on the implementation of a new action plan, some time should be taken to review it in its entirety, looking at how it fits into the whole change process and getting comfortable articulating the relevant concepts. Recall that presenting concepts and ideas serves another purpose – to help others to understand and to transfer the learning to a larger context.

Theoretically and practically all of the stakeholders should participate in all of the phases to be able to fully understand what is expected in implementation. However, when full participation is true, it does not guarantee understanding in implementation. Learning to DO requires articulation by the user to learn and begin to identify what is needed. It may take several iterations before the steps begin to emerge. This is not wasted time; this "learning time" increases the potential for success on the first administration. However, today many of our planned activities involve numerous complexities and may require several iterations before success is achieved.

Making Action Plans and evaluation Public Most often when people get to Implementation they relax and think that all the hard work is done. Actually it is just when the hard work begins. The hard work that results from taking plans from the paper to practice – translating, interpreting, and transferring the learning to the context for which it was designed is often a big jump. Communicating action plans throughout the organization and requesting feedback can be helpful and may actually improve support for implementation, identify potential resistance to change, and highlight unanticipated problems or "glitches". There is learning for the presenter by articulating the plan and discussing relevant actions and requirements. There is additional learning from managing the interactions in the presentation which yield high payoff value.

A factor that is often overlooked in communicating action plans throughout the organization is that the audience is in a position to support and to aid implementation even if not actively involved in it. The more people that know about the plan to be implemented, the more that can assist in easing its implementation

In subtle ways learning and implementation become linked. As the implementation develops, one receives feedback from the system in the form of consequences from the actions taken, which provide a valuable opportunity to learn about the system. It has often been said that those that do not learn from history are doomed to repeat it. This statement applies to organizations as well as people – in the short term as well as the long term. Too many fail to take the opportunity to reflect on implementation and as a result relive history again and again – whether in times of boom and bust, growth and decline, or overproduction and down times. Experience is inevitable, but learning is not.

If an organization is to profit fully from its implementation efforts, it must "mine" its mistakes for all the insight it may provide.

Implementations are imperfect, regardless of how good the solution may have been designed, or the quality of the planning. Consultants and clients alike must learn to capitalize on mistakes as they happen. Remember, learning takes place while designing interventions and working with specific tools – not only during the implementation phase. Maintain the flexibility to move back and forth between phases – often intentionally reiterating steps and continually communicating throughout the organization the learning captured as one goes along. Analysis, synthesis, evaluation, implementation, and learning must happen together.

Revisiting success As noted earlier, success is an emergent property and the product of interaction among several elements or processes. These processes have to be reproduced continuously – for if the processes that generate them come to an end, the phenomenon ceases to exist. Success in phase 4, in handling the challenge of implementation transforms the nature of the problem. Just as in the case of Henry Ford creating the mass production machine effectively dissolved the production problem -- a familiar concern for production was replaced with an unfamiliar concern for markets. Success in the fully evaluated implementation acts the same way. Once the problem is dissolved in the implementation it is replaced with a new problem to work on, thus the cycle of transformative action continues.

To take advantage of this phenomenon in phase 4, the management consultant heightens the awareness of success in the implementation of action plans, by focusing on celebrating success on the specific action plan and thereby stabilizing the change. The stabilization of the change is very important in arriving at the point of success in the full implementation where recognizing the effective dissolution of the problem is accomplished. Often times, management consultants hurry the implementation trying to get to the end of the phase in a shorter time for various reasons. Short circuiting the stabilization may cause problems in the learning about the change that is put into practice in phase 4. Hurrying along causes the client to have an incomplete experience and not properly lock in the learning.

In complex settings, it is difficult to keep abreast of the successful completion of different action plans in assessing problem dissolution. A large wall chart is an excellent way of tracking progress and completion and in noting successful dissolution of the problem. This is a "must" place for celebration, before going on to the next problem. .

Effectiveness in Learning to DO is in Role Shift for both consultant and client. For the management consultant and the client alike there is a gradual shift in responsibility and leadership in the different activities. In the first three phases the consultant has more responsibility to be sure -- responsibility for client exposure to learning, and assurance to the client that they are learning what is appropriate in the specific phase. While in phase 4 the client takes full responsibility for implementing the learning of the earlier phases and adding the learning of phase 4 in Learning to DO. Actually, there is a gradual decline in time spent and in responsibility taking in the earlier phases – this is not an abrupt change.

In phase 4, the management consultant is observing and caring about implementation -- but at a distance. All of the work up to this time should have prepared the client to implement. There is always a risk in doing something for the first time and the client must be encouraged to take this risk to implement and then evaluate. When the client finds problems after evaluation and cannot figure out what the problem is "in being off course" then it is important to check with the consultant. The client should have transferred earlier learning to the context and can begin to figure out what didn't work right in the setting. It is important that the client grow to a position where she can own "effectiveness" based on their earlier learning and action in implementation. In many settings, there is still an apparent sense of the client system that contributes to actions of a flight from "success" or "competence." This is left over from traditional learning situations where success and competence have not been universally valued or celebrated – allowing the individual to get comfortable with the new found result.

The client responsibility-taking aids the shift to a much healthier interdependent relationship with the consultant, and in using the consultant only when necessary. The value for the consultant is in enabling the leveraging of their time and expertise in a more productive fashion within the context.

Critical Tasks of IMPLEMENTATION

Making it happen remains the primary challenge of implementation. However, there are several aspects that contribute to making it happen successfully. The critical tasks of implementation are in presenting action plans throughout the organization in advance, using evaluation to reward and to energize change, and in communicating implementation success(es) publicly. All three of these tasks are counter to the way the organizations effected change in the 20th century. Many organizations never wanted to make action plans public in advance for several reasons. The plan may not be complete before starting – many organizations went off "half cocked." If communicated too early, they couldn't change as they went along without many questions from employees. They used the employee's action as a test of their support. In the 21st century, management consultants and management alike know that by communicating action plans throughout the organization in advance, they not only gain support, but trust of employees in their willingness to question, and many times correct on line errors not known to management. In many cases they have gained a partner in implementation.

In many cases in the past, evaluation was used to punish, making employee errors public, and ultimately detracting from their successful completion of a task. Currently, managers and consultants know that they can capitalize on evaluation, not only rewarding the employee, but providing new knowledge and means to accomplish the task by sharing the results of evaluation at different points in the implementation. These actions are energizing to the implementation and often speed up the process.

Continually communicating success(es) during implementation allows the sharing of the success(es) with others, and in so doing valuing the implementation action itself. Often, the implementation phase has been long and tedious resulting in a potential of lost focus; the challenge is regaining that potentially lost focus on the implementation. This is an easy, positive way to do it, and at the same time reward the people that have been actively involved.

Presenting action plans publicly   The value of communicating action plans throughout the organization is the unspoken invitation for organization members to participate in the implementation. Recall Kent and Anderson's (2002) statement "that the *people* in the organization take them all the way to success (italics added)." Involving the people, the organization members add value. There are many new eyes, ears, and energy on the project. These people can search out things that were missed earlier, work at a better "fit, " since they are closer to the action in many cases, and energize others to cooperate for success in the implementation. Once, the action plans are presented publicly, action and implementation are not surprises – it is no longer a secret. The power of sharing new knowledge by publicizing the action plans capitalizes on involving others allowing them to anticipate the coming change.

The timing of communicating action plans throughout the organization should be carefully worked out, giving listeners the big picture, and just enough of the specifics that are relevant in their current time line. Making the action plans public does not have to be done all at one time. Several presentations may be worked out organization-wide and specifically in areas where the change is actually being implemented. Presenting action plans publicly is an opportunity that should be embraced and not overlooked.

Using evaluation to reward and energize change   Many people believe that the design of the intervention addresses the evaluation of the intervention. In the last chapter, frameworks for designing and evaluating an intervention were presented (see Figures 2 and 3). Capitalizing on this framework in the Implementation provides hindsight for action planners and   implementers for use in replanning or redesigning the intervention.

Creating an explicit design theory helps frame and leverage an intervention for learning from the project. In addition, there are some clear recommendations that Kreutzer and Wiley (1996) make:

- Link learning and implementation
- Set appropriate project boundaries
- Develop high performance teams
- Design an appropriate practice field
- Reach completion

The developing management consultant needs to insure the completion of several cycles of learning, action and communication initiated within the planning and implementation teams. Nothing can discredit a good idea or destroy the chance for significant change as much as poor implementation. The very best ideas or approaches can backfire if careful thought is not given to how they should be introduced for maximum effectiveness. Even worse, a poorly executed implementation plan can not only create organization-wide resistance to the particular methodology currently used, but increase resistance to change in the future. But by following an explicit design and evaluation process, one can better ensure that all projects – whether successful or not – contribute to an organization's overall learning objective.

Evaluation is an integral part of achieving success during implementation. Evaluation is instrumental in Learning to DO. Recognizing the value of evaluation in designing and evaluating interventions in implementation appears to be cumbersome for many consultants and clients alike. Often, It may appear that evaluation has not proved to be a "friend." Evaluation has often pointed a finger to some wrong. Changing the image and value of evaluation depends heavily on a cultural change.

To change the culture and cultural thinking one must confront past experience, and reward evaluators on the spot, and at the time, for their contribution to success. In addition, consultants need to point out how evaluation has helped direct the change and cost out the savings in human energy and time. Showing how mistakes when corrected earlier, not only save time and resources, but expedites the movement of the organization in the right direction. Publicly recognizing the values of evaluation helps change the culture and the thinking that may be blocking evaluation and success. The consultant and the client need to be constantly vigilant for opportunities to value evaluation and to develop new knowledge while using it during implementation and rapidly addressing the problem.

A new perspective on Implementation and Evaluation

Implementation is the ultimate challenge for both the management consultant and client. This is the time where all of the previous efforts and learning must suddenly become practicable – it is moving from head work and talking about the "problem" to acting successfully in the real setting to dissolve the problem. This has been referred to as "walking the talk". The management consultant must be aware and prepared to deal with the discomfort and dis-ease that exists at this moment of truth. The discomfort and dis-ease in each new situation is normal, natural and should be expected. However, the tendency is to forget this knowledge and past experience at the time, trying to deny its existence in the present. Management consultants and clients alike must recognize the discomfort as normal and natural and move beyond it as quickly as possible – energizing action for a long awaited change. Energy to change in the situation and implement the truest form of the action plan is at the heart of the challenge. At the beginning of any implementation effort the consultant must encourage, recognize, and reward even the smallest steps in the right direction. There will be many opportunities for the developing management consultant to reward the different actors, as each approaches the challenge of implementing the plan.

The management consultant becomes a cheerleader at this point, cheering the client on to a fuller implementation all of the time. The consultant must be intimately involved in phase 4 as a partner to the change, but only from the sidelines "cheering" the client in testing the plan in action.

Providing the psychic energy to change through supportive behavior during the initial implementation efforts throughout the organization is critical to success in the engagement. It is difficult for the consultant to be everywhere "at the right time" – therefore it is important to prepare the client for implementation before it begins, by talking about the first uncomfortable experience that accompanies any change effort whether planned or unplanned change. This knowledge may be very reassuring to the client. It may also make it possible for the client to articulate or talk about his discomfort to others – thereby "legitimizing" the experience of discomfort for others, and decreasing the anxiety around the experience, simply by making the experience of discomfort public knowledge. On the surface, recognizing these small experiences of discomfort and equating them with natural and expected anxiety may seem miniscule in the whole approach of the management consultant during implementation. However, self-trial in recognizing the discomfort will demonstrate a large reward, contributing to overall success and positive affect in the implementation phase.

In addition, it is necessary to energize the beginning in implementation and to provide a higher level of satisfaction in the client's experience thereby providing the psychological strength to evaluate the implementation.   One must stay the course during Evaluation in Implementation to make the necessary corrections in the path to reach success. No implementation plan is perfect or all seeing of the future. It is necessary to make adjustments – but it is also necessary to make the right adjustments. Adjustments should not be made just to ease the pain or discomfort in doing something new. This is a potential trap that will backfire on the developing management consultant.

Many people fail in implementation because they misunderstand the pain or discomfort associated with any change caused by taking the plan to action. Likewise, it is important for the consultant not to overuse the understanding of discomfort around change, but to work with the client in planning or replanning to get just enough discomfort to nudge the implementers into changing, and not returning to the old ways of doing things. Supporting and aiding the use of evaluation may be just the step to take clients to a new level – giving them the needed feedback on their change efforts to continue to move toward the goal.

Using evaluative tools that have been designed earlier is key to addressing the challenge of successful implementation. Similar to the implementation of the action plan, the challenge in evaluation is in making it routine practice, making it pay off for the client. For many consultants and clients, the implementation of evaluation tools is too "researchy" a task.   To confront this image, the consultant must take a strong leadership role -- rewarding the client in the use of evaluative tools and citing value in evaluation.

The new perspective for the developing management consultant may be summed up in sticking close to the client during implementation, that is, being present and fully available to help, helping or assisting in some different ways than previously considered. It is important to put oneself at ease with the initial discomfort experienced in any implementation – and then to assist the client in "becoming comfortable being uncomfortable." The consultant may be supportive by simply supplying the psychic energy and excitement to change – to do something different in implementing the plan than has been done in the past. The consultant can aid understanding that much good work has gone into the problem definition, the solution design, and the action planning and evaluation design; noting the real challenge is in moving beyond the conceptualized work plan into live action to change.   To have the client address this challenge, an effective "supporting effectual nudge" may be necessary, based in a partnership approach that briefly exercises strong leadership. The emphasis in this phase is on "making it happen."   In perspective, the consultant is working through the four transformative phases supporting the necessary client development experiences with many new and different behaviors required to succeed.   Change becomes an integral part of the process of "breathing in and breathing out" in existence.

Fourth Phase Process Summary Chart

The key tasks identified in the process summary for the fourth phase in Figure 41.   The Management Consulting Process -- Phase 4: IMPLEMENTATION & EVALUATION

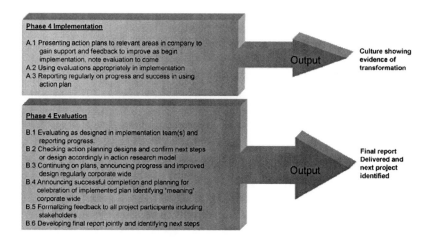

Figure 41: The Management Consulting Process – Phase 4:
IMPLEMENTATION & EVALUATION
© Marilyn 1996

are comprehensive, iterative, and overlapping due to the complexity involved acting in the real situation while bringing a plan to life, and evaluating success as implementation unfolds.

As in the three previous phases, the key tasks are interdependent and, if singularly addressed, do not produce success. Likewise the fourth phase is interdependent and intricately involved with the other three – in fact, phase 4 is completely dependent on the other three phases, but most specifically on phase 3 in the design of the action plan and evaluation. In mastering Learning to DO   success during implementation and evaluation phases, it is important to fully understand a practice, of publicly recognizing the values of interdependence.

The fourth phase process summary chart that is graphically displayed may be used both before and after the phase to reinforce Learning to DO that is phase-relevant.   The developing management consultant is encouraged to reflect on the findings from evaluating performance in the fourth phase – according to the Summary Chart – identifying the exact positions and means to continuously improve in this phase, and thereby in the overall four phased intervention in the transformative change process.

Gaining Perspective from Applications

The Columbus Medical Association (CMA) With feedback from the first phase clearly documented and understood and pervasive demonstration of leadership throughout the organization, CMA is well positioned to continue its learning and development. This year when the CEO, employees, boards of directors, and selected community stakeholders convene at the annual strategic retreat, the foundation for past achievements will provide greater confidence and creativity regarding future goals. Sustainability has been identified as a primary objective – not as a desire to maintain the status quo, but to continually challenge status quo and further develop the organization.

The value of Systems Thinking at CMA is evidenced in tangible results at the community project level and in the higher level dialogue practices within the organization. Functional departments are actively seeking a systems perspective with each other and their respective external constituencies. Leaders have emerged from all levels of the organization to express creative ideas for change. The employees have become more comfortable with change and look for opportunities to better serve the stakeholders. Sustainability is not a question of if, but how. This is the frontier of new thinking and *Presencing* at the CMA as they seek to develop strategies that drive the organization forward into the future.

Application in The Long Island Company (LIC)   Implementation and evaluation is where the proverbial rubber meets the road in sustainable change for organizations. In the LIC case, the implementation and evaluation were transitioned to the new leader of the organization in its fourth and current evolutionary phase. The new leader at LIC was required to complete the actionable steps and properly empower individuals within the organization prior to commencing implementation. The evaluation remains to be seen as the implementation is just commencing.

The new leader of LIC was hired based on his knowledge of the organization (he was actually the management consultant who began the CSW approach with LIC), knowledge of the industry, and most importantly, his ability to create an actionable and implementable plan. Establishing clear roles and empowering individuals as part of their functional responsibilities provided a clear path towards realizable objectives for positive and sustained change and growth. As described by the fourth phase of the CSW framework, implementation is doing, and LIC has begun to see tangible results which foster momentum for continuous change. Most notably has been the new leader's support in making the actionable plans public throughout LIC resulting in true accountability for results through empowerment.

Evaluation remains to be addressed and was not evident across LIC. In certain functional units, evaluation began through the analysis and posting of tangible (and sometimes quantitative) results in specific functions. The ability to display consistent and harmonious results across functional units has yet to be realized. It would be at this phase in the CSW framework that LIC may enjoy some of the most notable results, especially as they pertain to the creation of a learning environment. LIC will need to learn from its "doing" and this will be a significant shift in thinking for those involved.

Emerging Opportunities

In summary, the value of the implementation and evaluation is that it is the "proof of the pudding." The question that this phase addresses is this: can the problem solution design and action plan actually be put into practice and even more importantly – will it work, will it actually dissolve the problem in a way that is not resolving the same problem over and over again? The successful implementation and the evaluation of practice clearly demonstrate the value of the carefully orchestrated previous phases – focusing the important role that the action planning groups play in "making it happen."

One of the most important aspects of evaluation is that it provides specific feedback on what worked and what didn't work relative to what was planned. Usually there are some indications of what additional factors need to be taken into account – providing direction for emerging opportunities and change. Taking advantage of the evaluative aspect in this fashion makes the implemented "opportunity" have an even higher payoff. In many cases, relatively small adjustments at the time, e.g. redoing or replaying a micro action step makes a great deal of difference. It makes it possible to move ahead on the superordinate goal of the intervention, rather than going back to ground zero or in some cases beginning the problem definition component all over again. The more robust use of evaluation, both in designing in phase 3 and the actual evaluation in phase 4 implementation, increases attaining a better perspective of the whole while valuing each of the components to the transformation process. In simpler language, it helps fill in the blanks or openings in the whole process, and actually stretches the perspective of both consultant and client.

Implementation and Evaluation as a phase to "make it happen" are very stressful for everyone involved, especially the consultant – for it is like being "on stage" all the time. The developing consultant must learn to deal with this stress, particularly in the early stages of implementation before the client has gained much confidence in their new found capabilities to implement an action plan that achieves problem dissolution.

There are thousands of questions that the consultant must answer and it is important to treat each one as though it were the only one evident – not allowing the client to experience any problems with your responding in a familiar way to the question. Recall again, that it is important to *"go slow to go fast."* Balancing the answer with a straightforward positive demeanor is a skill that the developing consultant should continually evolve, even in very stressful situations. The consultant's calm response will be a model for the client and soon the atmosphere will not be so tingly and tight.

The consultant's strong leadership through modeling understanding and control in addressing the problematic issues of implementation and evaluation is needed in the beginning. The consultant's role slowly diminishes until they are literally not needed during the final stages of implementation – except to reward the client for their successful contribution and emerging leadership during the consultation. Recall for a moment the importance for the stabilization of change for the client in these final stages. Rewarding the appropriate interventions and success is a healthy way to support and thereby stabilize the change. Further, it may open the door to additional consultations in different areas.

Finally, in terms of emerging opportunities the consultant has the responsibility in this phase to produce some kind of report of the system intervention and resulting change. This may take many forms, but the consultant must focus in their articulation of the four phased process of the legitimate transformative efforts; they are at the core of success in the organization. Often there are problems in expression – ranging from the right language to use, -- should this be a research report, should this only be a glaring summary of successes – no learning from failures, or simply filling in the blanks in pre-written format. When the consultant treats this as a learning instrument both for them self and the client, the most will be gained. Thus, the focus may shift to what has been understood and mastered in Learning to DO.

Part 5 Learning TO LEARN from the FUTURE
Chapter 14 Learning TO LEARN from the FUTURE

"the future is not completely contained in the past, much of it is yet to be
written"

> Russell Ackoff, in Redesigning the Future *(1974)*

<u>**Why is new understanding necessary**</u> The understanding needed for
consultants to learn from the future requires a new and different goal.
Developing management consultants requires a goal that does not
speculate on what might
happen, but focuses on what
may be made to happen. For
acting on what may be made
to happen frees individuals
and collectivities to *create*
and *design* the future.

**Learning TO LEARN
from the
FUTURE**

Ackoff (1974) wrote in
Redesigning the Future that
Systems Thinking does not
regard the past as the sole
determinant, but only as a
co-producer of the future. Initially, the future influences the present, and
secondly, that man is a *purposeful system* in the present, capable of
influencing change. Understanding these realities makes learning from
the future possible, for it incorporates the means to focus on what *may be
made to happen.* This understanding places the developing management
consultant in a very different, but exciting position. The current task is
summarizing the key concepts and skills required to *enact the future*
innovatingly, using our pasts, present and future. This review then acts as
a springboard to create a new and expanding universe of possibility.

Man is at the center of the universe of possibility. Activating the
universe of possibility, man is seen as a powerful actor and inter-actor,
where his/her behavior is that of a purposeful individual *responding* to the
environment and not merely reacting. Response and reaction are not
equivalent. There is a difference that makes a real difference; for response
deepens *purpose*. The recognition of the element of choice in the behavior
of social systems leads to the belief that these systems have the capability
to select their own future and can successively approximate it by
choosing the appropriate means. The task of the developing consultant is

to recognize the power of a purposeful individual, and to assist in responding to the environment focusing interdependence in relationships, self-organization and choice.

The structure of a system defines its components and their relationships. These relationships, in turn, depend on the nature of the bonds that link and hold the components together. Presently, social systems are information-bonded and the knowledge levels determine the mode of organization in social systems. Unlike energy, knowledge is not subject to the "law of conservation"; nor is it subject to the law of diminishing returns. It is critical to understand that the ability to learn and create knowledge enables social systems to constantly recreate their structures – evident in *self-organization*. The knowledge level of a social system is not the sum of the knowledge of its individual members. The knowledge level is the shared knowledge, or shared image, as manifest in the culture and defines the knowledge level of a social system – evidenced in the *interdependence* among members. Recall how powerful a shared image of a desired future can be. In many cases, it is the mobilizing factor transforming organizational cultures. Cultural change is ignited by a powerful shared image of a desired future occurring in the present. The future may be manifest in the actions of the present – evidenced by man's *choice*.

In this text a learning system is developed: Learning "TO BE," "TO LEARN," and "TO DO," emphasizing the value of the systems approach to *idealization*. Basically, it is to design an *ideal-seeking system,* not an ideal state. This is designing ideal-seeking systems of innovation over and over, each time anew. The design of an ideal-seeking system is in fact at the core of any effective means for dealing with social problems apparent today, and in realizing the full potential of purposeful individuals as a part of purposeful organization through developing:

- A participative process which enables the members of a social system to collectively define and redefine their desired futures and relate their roles to the totality of the system of which they are a part
- A learning and adaptive system that is able and willing to alter its course at any time in recognition of emerging values and new realities
- A pluralistic social setting which will encourage and facilitate questioning of sacred assumptions and challenging the implicit default values of the culture

In short, management consultants may bring the future into the present most easily by creating ideal-seeking systems. These systems are at first purposeful, integrative, and differentiating, and at the same time adaptive when in a learning mode. It is still necessary to encourage and to facilitate questioning of the sacred assumptions and to challenge implicit default values of the culture-in-development. To accomplish this requires starting with a different goal, from a different position. Starting from a universe of possibility, believing it is worth the risks to innovate to achieve. Innovation is the journey, not the destination. Starting from a different perspective: enacting the future is necessary because it makes possible purposeful management consultants' focus on *mastering*.

Mastering the challenge of enacting the future   Today, enacting the future is confounded by a set of challenges in emerging new business environments that can rarely be addressed successfully with the traditional methods and concepts of organizational learning. Currently, management consultants may not approach the significant leadership challenges successfully because the experience base of the client often is not relevant for the issue at hand. For developing management consultants to do well in the new emerging business environments, they may need to take the lead with organizations and their leaders to develop a new cognitive capability – *Presencing*. *Presencing* is the capacity for *sensing, embodying, and enacting emerging futures.*

Scharmer (2000) sharpens the challenge to master *Presencing* by identifying three issues to be directly addressed by the developing management consultant.   They are: 1) Tapping a second source of learning (*Presencing*), 2) Managing the complexity of large-scale change, and 3) Assessing the deep levels of knowing.

Briefly, to master the challenges framed by these issues Scharmer focuses on some leading questions to be addressed as consultants explore learning in the emerging business environments. On the first issue – using another learning cycle (seeing, sensing, *Presencing*, enacting) focuses how to compete and cooperate under the conditions of the new economy – that is, how to learn from a reality that is not yet embodied in manifest experience?

On the second issue: managing the complexity of large-scale change means recognizing that transformational change plays out on several levels.   For example, using Scharmer's construct:: *reacting* is level 0, *restructuring* is level 1, *redesigning* is level 2, *reframing* is level 3, and *regenerating* is level 4.   Until recently, most approaches to managing change have followed the basic Lewinian sequence: *unfreezing, moving, and refreezing*. Scharmer suggests taking advantage of this Lewinian model of change, but expanding the unfreezing, where the highest leverage point to change exists. At this point, deepening knowledge to *uncover common will (purpose)*, before regenerating (*redefinition*), and enacting/incorporating (refreezing). The key challenge for developing management consultants at this stage of the change cycle is how to enable teams and organizations to uncover the layers of organizational reality that will move them from level 3 to level 4. (Level 3 is reframing new mental models and cultural assumptions, and level 4 is deep purpose and common will.) This involves a shift from reflective learning (learning from the past) to generative learning (learning from emerging futures). The primary issue for the consultant is identifying a sound methodology that takes the client from the reflective space in level 3, to the space of deep intention of will in level 4.

The third issue concerns competing in the new economy. To do well in the new economy management consultants must deepen their ways of knowledge creation and knowing. Essentially, this is the same issue as faced above: What theories, methods, and tools will help developing management consultants switch from the surface levels of cognition to the deeper sources of knowing (sensing and *Presencing*)? In conclusion, Scharmer (2000) offers three tools: Listening, Languaging and Leadership Practice available to consultant and client alike(described earlier in the text). Mastering the three emergent properties (tools) is at the base of successfully addressing the challenge to presence. The bottom line question is to how does the management consultant get himself and the client to think and act generatively?

Seeing innovation as purposeful The developing management consultant is in an exciting position to learn from the future. Now consultants, both individually and collectively, may create opportunities capitalizing on a full cycle of experience using knowledge and experience of the past, present, and future.

First is letting go of the past as the only producer of the future. For in the past, there have been many futile attempts to see or to know the future. From the time of Nostradamus to Alvin Toffler, people have been trying to see the future before it arrives. Many have tried to predict the future to aid business preparedness in a new era. However, when it comes to predicting the future there has been little success. For example, forecasting does attempt to predict what will happen, and is largely futile.   Strategic flexibility (being agile in the present as a way of being ready to better react to the future when it arrives) has been ineffective for it does not respond to the environment.   Scenario planning speculates on what might happen.   The goal in scenario planning is to develop a number of alternate scenarios as a way of sensitizing oneself to the possibility that the future may be quite unlike the present.   By focusing in on a few big uncertainties, scenario planning lets a company rehearse a range of possible futures.   Scenario planning has many strengths, but it is not, by nature, proactive.   Scenario planning tends to be defensive about the future, not offensive. It is literally learning in the present about what scenario to seek in order to make a good future happen.   In contrast, *Presencing* moves to enact the future in the present.   Quite a difference in outcome and time expended.   Management consultants are encouraged to let go, to unlearn these past methodologies that do not *enact the future*, relearning new ways to learn from the future.

Successfully mastering *Presencing* requires developing management consultants to make two major changes:

- To know that wealth flows directly from *innovation*; and that wealth is gained by *imperfectly seizing the unknown* (Kelly, 1998) emphasis added
- To shift from learning by reflection (Type 1) to learning by *Presencing* (Type 2), which involves a profound aesthetic experience – a spheric expansion and enhancement of one's own experience of self in the surrounding larger whole (Scharmer, 2000)

The first affects the starting goal, which is what may be *made to happen is innovation*.   In fact, in this text, the larger goal is to *institutionalize innovation*. The second involves lighting the fires of imagination, going deeper into knowing, becoming purposeful in developing a "common will" to direct embodying and enacting in the present.   Certainly, Scharmer's tools aid the shift enacting the future in the present. Developing management consultants are encouraged to go to practicing the "C–C 2 Step" Learning process defined earlier, carefully working through the whole process, first for self in each area, and then with the client. One must "desire" to innovate, one must be willing to learn from the future, and one must be willing to put into practice by doing what is innovative.   This may mean unlearning the rhetoric and cynicism immobilizing each of us individually and collectively before we can freely imagine and innovate.

Gareth Morgan (1997) says that imagination is needed to innovate. Hamel finds imagination key to innovation, key in creating curiosity, and key in creating innovators. Imagination creates new mindsets, new mental models for seeing, organizing and managing innovation. Imagination taps new brainpower and experiences to innovate.

The Learning to LEARN section identifies several ways to stimulate new learning, and most importantly by becoming a self-educator. Becoming a self-educator frees one to create and design his future, first by creating new mental models. Beginning very simply in questioning the present ones, searching for disconfirming evidence, things that don't fit, and never stop asking why? The why question leads to new understanding and to awakening curiosity. In support, Hamel (2000) says, "You can, and must, regain your lost curiosity. Learn to see again with eyes undimmed by precedent." Hamel notes that all that matters is that you care enough to start from where you are. He talks often of gray haired revolutionaries – thus at any age one may choose curiosity to imagine to innovate in the present to make the future happen in the present. Thus, learning from the future requires regaining imagination to innovate and to institutionalize innovation.

Hope is required to create the universe of possibility Hope arouses, as nothing else can arouse, a *passion* for the possible. Søren Kierkegaard enlightens our passionate sense with this quote:

> "If I were to wish for anything I should not wish for wealth and power, but for a passionate sense of what can be, for the eye, which ever young and ardent, sees the possible. Pleasure disappoints, possibility never. And what wine is so sparking, what so fragrant, what so intoxicating as Possibility?

> **Søren Kierkegaard, *Either/Or* quoted in Zander & Zander (2000) The Art of Possibility**

Passion is the conduit to vitality. It is the connection to vibrancy and energy, where the universe is sparking with generative power. Giving way to passion, has two steps (Zander & Zander, 2000).

- The first step is to notice where we are holding back, and let go. Release those barriers of self that keep you separate and in control, and let the vital energy of passion surge through you, connecting you to all beyond
- The second step is to participate wholly, allow yourself to be a channel to shape the stream of passion into a new expression for the world

Respecting these two steps, in the world in which we are striving, that tends to keep us as persons in a state of separateness, may take an act of surrender to let the gates give way between ourselves and nature to fully experience passion.

Revolutionary shifts in the operational structures of our world seem to call for new definitions of who we are and why we are here. For example, "That a vote taken in Europe, a financial decision made in Tokyo, or an unusually warm flow in the South Pacific can directly affect lives a world apart calls into question our assumption that we are self-activated and self-managed (Zander & Zander, 2000)." Our customary mindset about who we are may even undermine our ability to have a say in the way things go from here. So this is a book with suggestions for novel ways of defining ourselves, others, and the world we live in – ways that may be more apt for the challenges of our time. It uses the metaphor of a new learning system: Learning "TO BE," Learning "TO LEARN," and Learning "TO DO," as the gate to Learning from the Future. Learning, after all is about rearranging us, creating surprising juxtapositions, emotional openings, startling presences, flight paths to the eternal.

Appendix 1   Introduction of the Cases Used to Learn to DO
In the Consulting Systems Worldview

Case Study A: THE LONG ISLAND COMPANY (LIC)

Organizational Overview

The Long Island Company (LIC), an assumed name for a manufacturing company in Long Island, New York, manufactures metal cabinets for information technology equipment collocated in commercial data centers. In addition, to the actual manufacturing of the metal cabinets, LIC has integrated firmware and software which allows for the monitoring of power and cooling within the enclosures to ensure optimal performance of the information technology equipment housed within. LIC also performs contract manufacturing required for many sheet metal products.

Manufacturing in the United States began to come under global competitive pressure during the late 1960s and early 1970s. It was during this shifting competitive landscape that LIC began operations in 1970 as a sheet metal manufacturer. At that time, manufacturing in the US, and especially on Long Island had many competitive organizations which rapidly eroded over the next two decades. LIC has survived a shrinking industry and a diminishing need for manufacturing in the US. It successfully transitioned through three phases over nearly four decades and has embarked on a fourth phase that commenced in early 2008.

Phase one began in 1970 when the founder launched the firm with two other partners who had a keen focus on listening to customer business problems, and assisting those customers in engineering viable solutions for profit growth.   The second phase occurred when the founder bought out the other partners in the early 1980s and introduced three of his sons to the business continuing on a growth path. In the 1990's a third phase of the business began, where the three sons became sole owners without the founder. Each of the sons assumed functional leadership responsibilities within the business. One was a visionary and took the role of chief executive officer; another managed the operational aspects of manufacturing; and, the third managed the engineering function.

It was during the third phase where LIC began to manufacture its own product line focused on the metal cabinets for information technology equipment that revenues and profits began to soar. By 2004 growth at LIC slowed and began to stagnate; however maintaining relatively stable revenue and profitability. It was in early 2008 the owners recruited a new president to stimulate a vision for development commencing the fourth and current phase.

Change Dynamics at LIC

During its initial formation, the founder of LIC focused on listening to customer business problems and trying to help satisfy their needs. He strongly believed that his company would differentiate itself through this total focus on their customers. Although he had less than a high school education, he exhibited a keen sense for cost management, profitable pricing, and a straightforward approach of treating each customer with the utmost care and respect. As the business began to grow and expand, the founder demonstrated a unique skill in keeping all of his employees focused on creating a quality product in a cost conscious environment.

As the original partners began to tire of the business, the founder decided to buy them out and maintain the original focus on his customers' needs. During the second phase of LIC the sons of the founder were introduced to the business and worked on weekends, school holidays and summer vacations. Each of the sons learned all aspects of the sheet metal manufacturing business, as well as the principles religiously practiced by their father. Eventually, they each joined the company in a full time capacity and began to assume the leadership of the organization.

During the third phase of LIC's evolution, one of the sons, who eventually became the chief executive and visionary; created the product line of metal cabinets for information technology equipment. This development and eventual execution resulted in exponential revenue and profit growth over the subsequent ten plus years. The exponential growth required additional manufacturing capabilities, as well as an expanded employee base. LIC began to experience levels of complexity in managing more employees, servicing an expanded customer base, and managing its business in general.

During the latter stages of phase three, the vision became distorted; certain roles within the organization were not clearly defined nor fulfilled,; and an emerging need for more sophisticated business processes became evident. LIC's growth slowed significantly. A Consultant was engaged to define LIC's current state, its desired state and the potential obstacles to reaching its desired state. The LIC consultant reported his findings to the owners. Upon completion of the consulting engagement, the owners decided that new leadership was required. In early 2008, the owners engaged a new President to envision the future at LIC, instill appropriate processes to support development at the organization.

Management Consulting Challenges

LIC demonstrated staying power through four decades. It transcended a shrinking manufacturing base in the US; it evolved from a pure contract sheet metal manufacturer to one that provided its own product line; and, it maintained a focus on listening to customers, which was originally instilled by its founder. Several challenges exist at LIC for sustaining change of the past in its exponential revenue and profitability growth while maintaining the values instilled by its founder in terms of development. The owners of LIC summarize the existing challenges to include re-establishing a clear and communicated vision for its next phase; defining and instilling processes to support development; appropriately organizing LIC with clear roles and responsibilities; and, developing a way to continually review each of these for change as needed.

Management Consulting Questions

From a management consulting perspective, LIC's challenges are briefly summarized herein, but formative action remains. As a management consultant, several questions need to be addressed:

1. How might the new President interact with LIC to help drive required change
2. What kind of data collection plan assists LIC in understanding its current challenges
3. Describe approaches which might be beneficial in executing a successful output
4. Describe the kinds of changes that LIC experienced during its evolution. Were these changes incremental or transformative
5. What kind of processes would assist in changes at LIC; and describe how they might contribute to sustainability

Additional Details

Further details pertaining to the LIC Case Study can be found in research conducted by Becker (2007).

Case Study B: THE COLUMBUS MEDICAL ASSOCIATION (CMA)

Organizational Overview

Throughout the United States support for physicians and community healthcare is made possible by state and county medical associations or societies; these organizations are affiliated with the American Medical Association. Medical associations typically operate as not-for-profit organizations to provide advocacy for physicians' interests, ongoing education and training, and citizen assistance in locating an appropriate medical professional. Physician membership is voluntary.

The Columbus Medical Association (CMA) began in 1869 as a professional association for physicians in Franklin County, Ohio. In the period 1869-1958 the organization had a singular focus—professional support and advocacy for local physicians. In 1958 the Columbus Medical Association Foundation (CMAF) was created to provide medical education. In the 1990s the Central Ohio Trauma System and the Physicians Free Clinic were added, expanding the service offering to state and local stakeholders outside the medical community. Today these four affiliates operate as separate entities with unique missions and separate governing boards, but share a common chief executive officer and office space. Between 1869 and 1999 the organization was led by a series of executive directors with traditional hierarchical management skills.

Over the years, CMA enhanced its original physician-oriented goals with a community focus and contributions for improvements in community health care. By 1999 the organization began to see a need to support continued growth and initiated a nationwide search for a chief executive officer (CEO) to lead the four affiliates. The ideal candidate needed to possess business savvy, trustworthy, and well connected in the community, while simultaneously advocating for physicians, the medical association, and citizens. After a nationwide search, the current CEO was hired from the Columbus, Ohio, professional community.

Change Dynamics at CMA

Upon his arrival, the CEO stated general goals: become a learning organization; increase interaction with the community; and, foster improved focus on individual leadership among the staff. With the new vision the collective organizations began to evolve. Executive and staff interactions increased and the organization moved away from a traditional hierarchy to a flatter structure typified by increased communication. In parallel, staff began interacting with the external stakeholders on a more frequent basis. The CEO introduced learning activities with a book club, new group communication techniques, and guest speakers, and made these opportunities available to every person in the organization. Rather than mandate change or delegate learning to others, the CEO participated as a contributor and became an integrated partner in the changes. For cultures undergoing change discomfort is common and can be unsettling as new ideas challenge existing practices and the established status quo. The CEO's role was to maintain focus on organizational goals while creating a safe environment for learning, exploration, and creative expression among the staff.

As the organizations gained greater access to the community and practiced better communication, they began to think and act differently. Instead of looking to the past to guide incremental change, employees started to focus on the "here and now" for inspiration and ideas. With a new perspective the organization has continued to grow in size, in membership and interaction with the community. Positive change is evidenced by a highly creative staff, hiring practices that foster a learning culture, leaderful behavior by all staff members, and a cooperative partnership with local citizens for improved health care all focusing development of individual competencies. Today the Columbus Medical Association is one of the largest medical associations in the United States demonstrating success.

Management Consulting Challenges

CMA and its affiliate organizations have made tremendous strides in how they interact with each other, and in how they cooperate with stakeholders in the community. In order to perpetuate this pattern of success the organizations will need to recognize when status quo is settling in and impeding continued forward movement. Sustained success amidst the rapid level of change in business practices and stakeholder needs presents the next level of challenge for this collective organization.

Management Consulting Questions:

1. Given the medical association's long term goals, what type of data did the CEO need to collect before he revisited the organizational vision and goals
2. Did the CEO "contract" with the organization to drive change? Describe the tactics and process used
3. Were the resulting changes incremental or transformative? What evidence supports your response
4. What leadership actions will support sustained and progressive cycles of change at CMA

Additional Details
Further details pertaining to the CMA case study can be found in research conducted by Hallcom (2007).

Appendix 2

THE CONSULTING SYSTEMS WORLDVIEW
A Four-Phased Intervention Approach

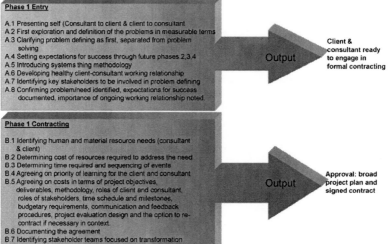

The Consulting Systems **WORLDVIEW**
Keys to Master a **FOUR** phased Intervention Approach
ENTRY and CONTRACTING

Phase 1 Entry

A.1 Presenting self (Consultant to client & client to consultant
A.2 First exploration and definition of the problems in measurable terms
A.3 Clarifying problem defining as first, separated from problem
     solving
A.4 Setting expectations for success through future phases 2,3,4
A.5 Introducing systems thing methodology
A.6 Developing healthy client-consultant working relationship
A.7 Identifying key stakeholders to be involved in problem defining
A.8 Confirming problem/need identified, expectations for success
     documented, importance of ongoing working relationship noted.

Output → Client &
consultant ready
to engage in
formal contracting

Phase 1 Contracting

B.1 Identifying human and material resource needs (consultant
    & client)
B.2 Determining cost of resources required to address the need
B.3 Determining time required and sequencing of events
B.4 Agreeing on priority of learning for the client and consultant
B.5 Agreeing on costs in terms of project objectives,
    deliverables, methodology, roles of client and consultant,
    roles of stakeholders, time schedule and milestones,
    budgetary requirements, communication and feedback
    procedures, project evaluation design and the option to re-
    contract if necessary in context.
B.6 Documenting the agreement
B.7 Identifying stakeholder teams focused on transformation
B.8 communicating the project to whole system

Output → Approval: broad
project plan and
signed contract

Appendix 2   (Continued)
THE CONSULTING SYSTEMS WORLDVIEW
A Four-Phased Intervention Approach

The Consulting Systems **WORLDVIEW**
Keys to Master a FOUR phased Intervention Approach

Phase 2 DATA COLLECTION and PROBLEM DEFINITION

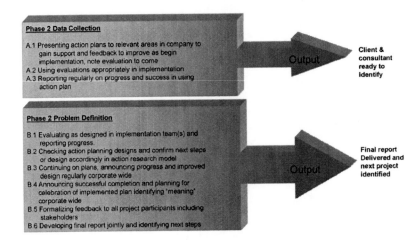

Phase 2 Data Collection

A.1 Presenting action plans to relevant areas in company to
gain support and feedback to improve as begin
implementation, note evaluation to come
A.2 Using evaluations appropriately in implementation
A.3 Reporting regularly on progress and success in using
action plan

Output

Client &
consultant
ready to
Identify

Phase 2 Problem Definition

B.1 Evaluating as designed in implementation team(s) and
reporting progress.
B.2 Checking action planning designs and confirm next steps
or design accordingly in action research model
B.3 Continuing on plans, announcing progress and improved
design regularly corporate wide
B.4 Announcing successful completion and planning for
celebration of implemented plan identifying "meaning"
corporate wide
B.5 Formalizing feedback to all project participants including
stakeholders
B.6 Developing final report jointly and identifying next steps

Output

Final report
Delivered and
next project
identified

Appendix 2 (Continued)
THE CONSULTING SYSTEMS WORLDVIEW
A Four-Phased Intervention Approach

The Consulting Systems **WORLDVIEW**
Keys to Master a **FOUR** phased Intervention Approach

Phase 3 PROBLEM SOLUTION and ACTION PLANNING

Phase 3 Problem Solution

A.1 Defining business purpose, business, strategic intent,
   measures of success, and core values (stakeholder
   problem solving teams)
A.2 Defining vision of future to replace existing order
A.3 Developing idealized design
A.4 Designing iteratively successive approximation of idealized
   design
A.5 Defining action planning teams to work simultaneously
A.6 Preparing presentation of idealized design solution
A.7 Presenting idealized solution

Output

Problem solution
design accepted

Phase 3 Action Planning

B.1 Identifying macro steps in stakeholder action planning
B.2 Identifying micro steps in action planning of B.1 areas
B.3 Designing evaluation (in advance) appropriately for all
   macro areas
B.4 Testing reality of action plans including evaluation
   performance criteria and measures
B.5 Identifying Action Research Team(s)to implement action plans
B.6 Practicing use of evaluation findings to update action plan
B.7 Announcing implementation of action plans company wide

Output

Implementation
announced,
timeline posted
corporate wide

Appendix 2 (Continued)
THE CONSULTING SYSTEMS WORLDVIEW
A Four-Phased Intervention Approach

The Consulting Systems **WORLDVIEW**
Keys to Master a **FOUR** phased Intervention Approach

Phase 4 IMPLEMENTATION & EVALUATION

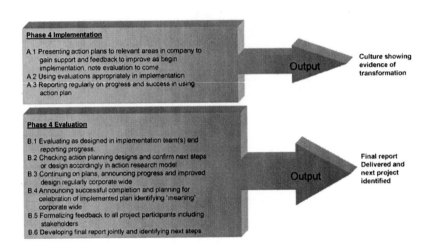

Phase 4 Implementation

A.1 Presenting action plans to relevant areas in company to
gain support and feedback to improve as begin
implementation, note evaluation to come
A.2 Using evaluations appropriately in implementation
A.3 Reporting regularly on progress and success in using
action plan

Output

Culture showing
evidence of
transformation

Phase 4 Evaluation

B.1 Evaluating as designed in implementation team(s) and
reporting progress.
B.2 Checking action planning designs and confirm next steps
or design accordingly in action research model
B.3 Continuing on plans, announcing progress and improved
design regularly corporate wide
B.4 Announcing successful completion and planning for
celebration of implemented plan identifying 'meaning'
corporate wide
B.5 Formalizing feedback to all project participants including
stakeholders
B.6 Developing final report jointly and identifying next steps

Output

Final report
Delivered and
next project
identified

Acknowledgements for the Second Edition

Obviously, the material for the second edition would never have been developed and integrated in an outstanding publication without the inspiration and cooperation of the co-authors facilitating transformative change in the production of new cases, developed new understanding relative to learning, demonstrated through extraordinary digital capability. The second edition is a new undertaking.

For active leaders in change, the co-author group of four soon formed a functional team identifying tasks, meeting deadlines, and performing writing tasks grounded in their doctoral learning experience at Capella University. It is through the cooperative relationships established early that the team capitalized to produce a viable product.

When one is charged with developing a second edition, there are many decisions to be made. In this case, the decision to incorporate multiple authors was expeditious in terms of developing new working relationships in consulting, and generating deep interest in application. Thanks to a common academic background and leadership learning experience at Capella University, development of the second edition was aided by early communication along with a desire to work together on application beyond achieving the degree. The Capella University experience became the melting pot stimulating development of new competencies needed in new applications.

Thanks to the common need to apply learning in the real world, along with the capability to communicate, work began while at an International Academy of Business and Economics meeting last Fall. The group shifted in one short meeting into high gear on the revision, all leaving with specific tasks. A new energy emerged from the meeting in Las Vegas driving co-authors to higher and higher levels of performance taking risks to develop deep trust in each other and the product being born.

Only as incidental observer on-the-side of the developing group, and the driver for cooperative work, Don Harris was able to support work on the second edition, constantly chanting: Keep Going! It was only after his untimely death in Fall 2007 that the co-authors decided to dedicate their work to him in his drive to Keep (them) Going!

Progress continued with the development of new cases, sophisticating charts and diagrams, and editing to meet the requirements of production by early summer. Our gratitude to all will remain a debt that can never be repaid, but only experienced anew as we all lead from the future as it emerges.

Marilyn E Harris
With: Gerard F. Becker, Anne Hallcom
Richard L. Ponschock
Spring, 2008

REFERENCES

Ackoff, R.L. (1974). *Redesigning the Future*. New York: John Wiley & Sons.

Ackoff, Russell L. (1997). *Transformational Consulting – Changing Thought Patterns, Not Just Processes*, presented at the 1997 Institute of Management Consultants Meeting in Chicago, IL.

Adams, S.M., and Zanzi, A. (2001). *The role of academia in developing management consultants: A study of U.S. business schools course offerings*. Presented at the Knowledge and Value Development in Management Consulting Conference, (March) Lyon, France.

Allee, Verna. (1997) *The Knowledge Evolution: Expanding Organizational Intelligence.* Boston: Butterworth-Heinemann.

Allee, Verna. (2003) *The Future of Knowledge, Increasing Prosperity through Value Networks.* Boston: Butterworth-Heinemann.

Argyris, C. (1970*). Intervention Theory and Method.* Oxford, UK: Oxford University Press.

Argyris, C. (2000) *Flawed Advice and the Management Trap.* Oxford, UK: Oxford University Press. Arthur, W.B. (2000). Sense Making in the New Economy. Conversation with W. Brian Arthur. Xerox Parc, Palo Alto, April 16, 1999, in: Scharmer, C.O. et al (eds.), *Accessing Experience, Awareness and Will.* 25 Dialogue-Interviews on the foundation of knowledge, awareness and leadership. Unpublished project report, Cambridge, MA, August 2000, Vol. IV: 541-576.

Becker, G.F. (2007). *The alignment between leadership, organizational culture and functional maturity: An ethnographic case study for transformational change in the small business environment.* (Doctoral dissertation, Capella University, 2007). Retrieved from ProQuest, AAT 3274975.

Berger, P., and Luckmann, T. (1967). *The Social Construction of Reality.* New York: Penguin.

Buckley, W. (ed.)(1968). *Systems Research for the Behavioral Scientist: A Sourcebook.* Chicago: Aldine.

Burke, W. W. (1992). Organization development: A process of learning and changing (2nd ed.). Reading, MA: Addison Wesley.

Covey, S.M.R., Covey, S.R., and Merrill, R.R. (2007). The speed of trust: The one thing that changes everything. New York: Free Press.

Davenport, T.H., and Beck, J.C. (2001) *The Attention Economy: Understanding the New Currency of Business.* Cambridge: Harvard Business School Press.

Deming, W. E. (1975). On some statistical aids toward economic production. *Interfaces,* 5(4), 1-15.

Eagly, A.H., and Chaiken, S. (1993) *The psychology of attitudes.* New York: Harcourt Brace.

Fast Company (2000). Issue 40.

Gergen, K. J. (1994). Realities and relationships: Soundings in social construction. Cambridge, MA: Harvard University Press.

Gharajedaghi, J., and Ackoff, R.L. (1984). Mechanisms, organisms and social systems. *Strategic Management Journal,* 5(3), 289-300.

Gharajedaghi, J. (1985). *Toward a systems theory of organizations.* Seaside, CA: Intersystems Publications.

Gharajedaghi, J. (2006). *Systems Thinking: Managing chaos and complexity. A platform for designing business architecture* (2nd ed.). Boston: Butterworth-Heinemann.

Goethe, J. W. von (1985). *Goethe's Scientific Studies.* Translated by D. Miller, Edited by Al.P. Cottrell and D. Miller. Boston: Suhrkamp Inset.

Goleman, D. (1998). *Working with emotional intelligence.* New York: Bantam Books.

Hallcom, A.S. (2007). *Exploring intentional learning in mature organizations: A phenomenological case study.* (Doctoral dissertation, Capella University, 2007). Retrieved from ProQuest, AAT 3277691.

Hamel, G. (2000). Leading the revolution. Boston: Harvard Business School Press.

Harris, M.E. (1996). *Developing a consulting approach worldview.* An unpublished paper prepared for class use in International Management at Central Michigan University.

Harris, M.E., and Wang, G. (2001). Dual challenges in management consulting: Learning and leadership in learning from an international perspective. Paper presented at the Knowledge and Value Development in Management Consulting Conference, (March), Lyon, France.

Isaacs, W. (1999). *Dialogue: The art of thinking together.* New York: Doubleday.

Isgar, T. (1993) *The ten minute team, 10 Steps to building high performing teams* (2nd ed.). Boulder, CO: Seleura Press.

Jaworski, J., and Scharmer, C.O. (2000). " Leadership in the New Economy: Sensing and Actualizing Emerging Futures." Working Paper: Society for Organizational Learning, Cambridge, MA and Generon, Beverly, MA.

Kelly, K. (1998). *New rules for the new economy.* New York: Viking.

Kent, C.A., and Anderson, L.P. (2001). Old values for a new economy. *Mid-American Journal of Business, 16*(2), p.3.

Kolb, D. (1984*). Experiential learning.* New York: Prentice Hall.

Kotter, John P. (1990). What leaders really do. *Harvard Business Review, 68*(3), 103-111.

Kotter, John P. (1995). Leading change: Why transformation efforts fail. *Harvard Business Review, 73*(2), 59-67.

Kubr, M. (1993). How to select and use consultants: A client's guide. London: International Labour Office.

Laszlo, E. (1972). *The system view of the world.* New York: George Braziller.

Levering, R., Moskowitz, M., Munoz, L., Hjelt, P., and Wheat, A. (2002). The 100 best companies to work for. *Fortune,* 145(3). 72-90.

Levesque, Lynne. (2001). *Breakthrough creativity*: Achieving top performance using the eight creative talents. Mountain View, CA: Davies-Black.

Lewin, K. (1946). *Field theory in social science*. New York: Harper.

Lewin, K. (1952). Group decisions and social change. In: G.E. Swanson, T.N. Newcomb, and E.L. Hartley (Eds.) *Readings in social psychology, revised edition*. New York: Holt.

Kreutzer, D.P., and Wiley, V. (1996). Making it happen: The implementation challenge. *The Systems Thinker*, (7)3.

Maister, D.H. (1997). *True professionalism*. New York: Free Press.

Manz, C.C. (2002). *The power of failure: 27 ways to turn life's setbacks into success*. San Francisco: Berrett-Koehler.

Morgan, G. (1997). *Imaginization*. San Francisco: Berrett-Koehler.

Pfeffer, J. (1992*). Managing with power: Politics and influence in organizations*. Boston: Harvard Business School Press.

Ponschock, R. L. (2007). Computer technology, digital transactions, and legal discovery: A phenomenological study of possible paradoxes (Doctoral dissertation, Capella University, 2007) (UMI No. 3246872).

Prahalad, C.K., and Krishnan, M.S. (2008). *The new age of innovation: Driving cocreated value through global networks*. New York: McGraw-Hill.

Proust, M. (1993) *Reinventing Government* (in preface, p xxii) New York: Plume.

Rasiel, E.M. (1999*). The McKinsey way*. New York: McGraw-Hill

Rasiel, E.M.,and Friga, P.N. (2000). *The McKinsey mind: Understanding and implementing the problem- solving tools and management techniques of the world's top strategic consulting firm*. New York: McGraw-Hill.

Rosch, E. (1999). When the Knowing of the Field Turns into Action. Conversation with Professor Eleanor Rosch, University of California, Berkeley, Dept. of Psychology, October 15, 1999 in: C.O. Scharmer et al (eds), *Entering the meditative space of leadership: 25 dialogue-interviews on the foundation of knowledge, awareness and leadership.* Unpublished Project Report, Vol. III, August 1999, Cambridge, MA: 371-404.

Scharmer, C.O. (2000). *Presencing: Learning from the future as it emerges.* Paper presented at Conference on Knowledge and Innovation, May 2000, Helsinki School of Economics, Finland.

Schein, E. (1987). *Process Consultation.* Volume II. Reading: MA: Addison-Wesley.

Searle, J. R. (1969). *Speech acts.* Cambridge, England: Cambridge University Press

Senge, P. M. (1990). *The fifth discipline, the art and practice of the learning organization.* New York: Doubleday.

Vaill, P.B. (1996). *Learning as a way of being.* San Francisco: Jossey-Bass.

Von Krogh, G., Ichijo, K., and Nonaka, I. (2000). *Enabling knowledge creation: How to unlock the mystery of tacit knowledge and release the power of innovation.* New York: Oxford University Press.

Wardman, K.T. (1994). From mechanistic to social systemic thinking: A digest of a talk by Russell L. Ackoff. *The Systems Thinker, 5(1).*

Weick, K.E. (1995). *Sensemaking in organizations.* Thousand Oaks. CA. Sage.

Weick, K.E. (1999) The collapse of sensemaking in organizations: The Mann Gulch disaster. *Administrative Science Quarterly, 38, 628-652.*

Womack, J.P., Jones, D.T., and Ross, D. (1990). *The machine that changed the world.* New York: Macmillan.

Zander, R.S., and Zander, B. (2000). *The art of possibility: Transforming professional and personal life.* Boston, MA: Harvard Business School Press.

About the Authors

In the early dawning of the new age of innovation the second edition of *Mastering A New Paradigm in Management Consulting* is particularly useful based on the authors experience in the transformation of business focusing *collaboration, computing,* and *connectivity*. Each has contributed in specific ways to the revision co-creating unique value with individual customers and clients in global networks. In this way, each has identified BIG ROCKS in the learning paradigm: Learning to BE, Learning to LEARN, and Learning to DO.

Marilyn E Harris earned her PhD at the University of Michigan where she spent a decade in applied action research at the Institute for Social Research, and consulting to management in business and industry. She has balanced her professional life between academia and management consulting; heading her own consulting firm and holding adjunct appointments at several universities and business schools, both online, and in residential settings, as well as Visiting Professorships abroad driving co-created value through global networks. She has had extensive involvement in the Management Consulting Division of the Academy of Management ranging from Chair to Consultant in Residence.

Gerard F. Becker earned his PhD. in Organization and Management and teaches at New York University and Central Michigan University. He has been instrumental in major business process initiatives as an enabler of innovation (in many cases he was an organizational change agent) for small to large organizations; mentoring and evolving emerging senior leaders in various organizations; as well as leading major initiatives in the financial services industry (European monetary conversion; establishment of global technology risk programs; major data center builds and relocations). He is currently President and COO of a mid sized information technology company.

Anne Hallcom earned her PhD. in Organization and Management with a Leadership Specialization. She has senior leadership experience in operations, development, marketing, quality, regulatory compliance for the regulated healthcare industry. Dr. Hallcom's primary research is in transformative learning, organizational change, and the leadership practices that support sustainable cycles of transformation in a dynamic, global workplace. Her experience with Lean and the ongoing re engineering of business processes to promote innovation are supportive of the granularity, transparency, and flexibility that challenge today's business environment. Dr. Hallcom's work has been presented as papers and workshops in professional societies including the Academy of Management and the International Academy of Business and Economics.

Dr. Richard L. Ponschock earned his PhD. in Organization and Management with an Information Technology specialty. He is currently the General Manager of a 3rd Party Logistics operation, and Director of Information Technology for a private multi-national organization. Dr. Ponschock's career focuses on the alignment and application of technology to achieve strategic organizational initiatives and growth. Dr. Ponschock has written papers on technology architecture, applied technology, and the future impact of today's virtualization and social networks on future generations. Presentations included industry and academic conferences including International Academy of Business and Economics.

DATE DUE

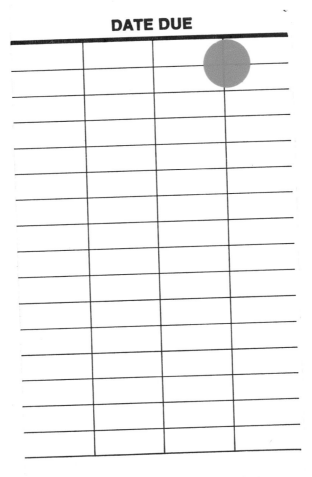

Made in the USA